"When a technica
Banks is probably w
—Lawrence Blasko, Associated Press

"Banks is rapidly attaining in telecommunications the same status as Peter Norton has in hardware—a clear, no-nonsense expert whose works are indispensable."
—Paul Gilster, *Computer Focus*

"Banks has put together just about everything you need to know about communications."
—Jerry Pournelle, *InfoWorld*

"Michael Banks is not your average computer-hacker-become-writer. He is a seasoned professional who has to his credit many non-fiction books and monthly telecommunications columns in several magazines."
—Clayton Walnum, Editor, *ANALOG Computing*

Also by Michael A. Banks

DELPHI: THE OFFICIAL GUIDE
GETTING THE MOST OUT OF DESKMATE 3, 2nd Edition
THE MODEM REFERENCE, 2nd Edition
THE ROCKET BOOK (with Robert L. Cannon)
THE ODYSSEUS SOLUTION (with Dean R. Lambe)

Portable Communications

The Traveling Executive's Survival Guide

Michael A. Banks

BRADY

New York   London   Toronto   Sydney   Tokyo   Singapore

Copyright © 1992 by Michael A. Banks
All rights reserved,
including the right of reproduction
in whole or in part in any form.

 Brady Publishing

Published by Brady Publishing
A division of Prentice-Hall Computer Publishing
15 Columbus Circle
New York, New York 10023

Manufactured in the United States of America

1 2 3 4 5 6 7 8 9 10

Every effort has been made to make this handbook as complete and factual as possible. However, information contained herein is subject to change without notice and should not be construed as a commitment by the author, the service providers, publishers, and manufacturers named herein, or Brady Books, who assume no responsibilities for any errors that may appear.

Library of Congress Cataloging-in-Publication Data
Banks, Michael A.
    Portable communications : the traveling executive's
    survival guide / Michael A. Banks.
        p.   cm.
    Includes index.
    ISBN 0-13-524364-5
    1. Computer networks.   2. Portable computers.
    3. Modems.   4. Communications software.
I. Title.
TK5105.5.B345 1992
  004.6—dc20   92-4692
                                                             CIP

For Martin von Strasser Caidin and Earl Dilbeck, Sr., ultimate travelers.

Acknowledgments

As with any human endeavor, artistic or otherwise, writing a book is never a solo effort. The author benefits from the material, technical, and even the psychological support of many people during the course of creating a book. Thus, I wish to express my sincere gratitude for the support provided by the following individuals in the preparation of this book:

Rosa L. Banks, BBS sysops Rick Schradin and Mark Hoemmelmeyer, Burton Gabriel, Tony Lockwood, Akira Shinjo, Sharon Baker Magee, Chuck Berndt, Mike Getz, Jack Smith, Jack Cunkelman, Roger Krueger, Jennifer Jumper, Arthur Bozlee, Dr. Dean R. Lambe, Bill Brohaugh, Jerry Pournelle, Fred Langa, Betty & JD Gallivan, James C. Dunaway, Larry Judy, Jim Reed, Allen Davidson, Jack Nimershiem and his Zenith laptop, and Robert J. Banks.

Trademarks, Registered Trademarks, Service Marks, and Copyrights

1-2-3, Lotus, and Lotus Express are registered trademarks of Lotus Development Corporation.

AAdvantage and Eaasy Sabre are registered service marks of American Airlines, Inc.

Above, Connection CoProcessor, FaxBack, i386, i486, Intel, Intel 386, Intel 386SX, Intel 486, the Intel Inside logo, and SatisFAXtion are trademarks or registered trademarks of Intel Corporation.

Academic American Encyclopedia is a service mark of Grolier Electronic Publishing, Inc.

Accu-Weather is a trademark of Accu-Weather.

America Online, AppleLink, PC-Link, Promenade, and DemoWare are registered trademarks or registered service marks of Quantum Computer Services, Inc./America Online, Inc.

Amiga, Commodore, Commodore-64, and Commodore-128 are trademarks of Commodore Business Machines, Inc.

AP is a trademark of The Associated Press.

Apple, Apple II, Mac, Macintosh, and PowerBook are trademarks or registered trademarks of Apple Computer, Inc.

ARC is a trademark of Systems Enhancement Associates, Inc.

AT&T, Digital Data Service, DDS, Mail Talk, Touch-Tone, Trimline, and UNIX are trademarks or registered trademarks of, and EasyLink is a service mark of, American Telephone & Telegraph.

Atari and ST are registered trademarks of, and Portfolio is a trademark of, Atari Corp.

Attaché is a trademark of Forefront Technology Corporation.

BillPay USA is a registered service mark of Prodigy Services Company and Manufacturer's Hanover Trust Company.

BIX and Byte Information Exchange are trademarks of General Videotex Corp.

Broderbund is a registered trademark of, and *Where in the World is Carmen Sandiego?* is a trademark of, Broderbund Software.

Canon is a registered trademark of, and Bubble Jet and BJ-130e are trademarks of Canon, Inc.

CHECKFREE is a trademark of Checkfree Systems.

Compaq and Compaq SLT/286 are trademarks of Compaq Computer Corporation.

CB Simulator, CompuServe, CompuServe Information Manager, CompuServe Interchange, CompuServe Mail, *CompuServe Magazine*, CIS B+ Protocol, The Electronic Mall, E-Mail, IntroPak, EasyPlex, FAX-EasyPlex, MicroNet, and VIDTEX are trademarks, registered trademarks, and/or service marks of, and GIF is a service mark of, CompuServe Incorporated, an H&R Block Company.

Comp-u-Store Online and Comp-u-Card are trademarks of Compu-Card of America, Inc./CUC International.

ConnNet is a trademark of Southern New England Telephone Company.

CoSy is a trademark of the University of Guelph.
CP/M, DRI DOS, and GEM are trademarks of, and Digital Research is a trademark of, Digital Research, Incorporated.
CASL, COMMUNICATIONS, Crosstalk, Crosstalk XVI, CrossTalk Mark 4, Mk.4, and DCA are trademarks or registered trademarks of Digital Communications Associates/Crosstalk, Inc.
DASnet is a trademark of DA Systems, Inc.
DataPac is a trademark of Bell of Canada.
DEC, VAX, VMS, VT52, and VT100 are trademarks of Digital Equipment Corp.
DELL SYSTEM is a registered trademark of, and Dell is a trademark of, Dell Computer Corporation.
DELPHI is a trademark of General Videotex Corporation.
DESQview and Quarterdeck Expanded Memory Manager are registered trademarks of Quarterdeck Office Systems.
DIALCOM is a registered trademark and a registered service mark of British Telecommunications, plc.
DIALOG and DIALOGLINK are registered trademarks of, and DIALOG CLASSMATE, DIALOGLINK, DIALMAIL, DIALNET, and Knowledge Index are registered service marks of, Dialog Information Services, Inc., a Knight-Ridder Company.
Discover is a service mark of Sears Financial Services.
Dow Jones, Dow Jones News/Retrieval Sports Report, Dow Jones News/Retrieval Weather Report, Dow Jones News/Retrieval World Report, Historical Dow Jones Averages, and Text Search Services are registered service marks of, and Dow Jones News/Retrieval, Dow Jones News Service, *The Wall Street Journal*, *The Wall Street Journal Highlights*, and "Wall Street Week" are registered trademarks of Dow Jones & Company, Inc.
Epson is a trademark of Epson America, Inc.
Eye Relief and No-Squint are trademarks of SkiSoft Publishing Corporation.
Federal Express and FEDEX are registered trademarks of Federal Express Corp.
Franzus is a registered trademark of Franzus International.
GE Mail, GE Mall, GEnie, GEnie Quik-Gram, LiveWire, and UIK-GRAM are trademarks of, and GEnie is a service mark of, the General Electric Company, U.S.A.
GeoWorks, GeoWorks Ensemble, Ensemble, and GeoComm are trademarks of, and GEOS is a registered trademark of, GeoWorks.
Hayes and Micromodem are registered trademarks of, and OPTIMA, Hayes Smartmodem, Smartmodem 300, Smartmodem 1200, Smartmodem 1200B, SmartCom, SmartCom II, and ULTRA 96 are trademarks of, Hayes Microcomputer Products Inc.
Hercules is a trademark of Hercules Computer Technology.
HyperACCESS and HyperACCESS/5 are trademarks of Hilgraeve, Inc.
IBM, IBM PC, AT, CGA, EGA, MDA, OS/2, Personal System/1, Portable PC, ProPrinter, PS/1, PS/2, System/2, VGA, and XT are registered

trademarks of, and PC/XT and IBM Personal Computer AT are trademarks of, International Business Machines Corporation.
Infomaster, Mailgram, and RediList are registered trademarks of The Western Union Telegraph Company.
Kermit is a trademark of Henson Associates.
Kodak is a registered trademark of Eastman Kodak Company.
LapLink, Battery Watch, DeskLink, Traveling Software, and the Traveling Software suitcase logo are registered trademarks of, and Smart Tracker, TraveLite, and WinConnect are trademarks of, Traveling Software, Inc.
Magazine Index and Newsearch are registered trademarks of, National Newspaper Index is a trademark of, and Magazine Database Plus is a service mark of, Information Access Corporation.
MasterCard is a trademark of MasterCard International.
MCI and MCI Mail are registered trademarks of, and the MCI logo, MCI Mail, MCI Mail Link, MCI Bulletin Board, and MCI Shared Lists are service marks of MCI Communications Corporation.
MNP is a registered trademark of, and Microcom Network Protocol, MicroPorte, and Carbon Copy Plus are trademarks of, Microcom, Inc.
Mirror, Mirror II, Mirror III, and Takeover are registered trademarks of, and SoftKlone is a trademark of, SoftKlone Distributing Corporation.
MITE is a trademark of Mycroft Labs, Inc.
Microsoft, MS, MS-DOS, MS-WINDOWS, XENIX, WORD, GW-BASIC, and the Microsoft logos are registered trademarks of, and BallPoint, QuickBasic, QBasic, Visual Basic, Windows, and Windows/386 are trademarks of, Microsoft Corporation.
NEC is a registered trademark of NEC Corporation.
NewsGrid is a service mark of Comtex Scientific Corp.
NewsNet and NewsFlash are registered trademarks of NewsNet, Inc.
Northgate is a registered trademark of, and Slim*Lite* a trademark of, Northgate Computer Systems, Inc.
Calibrate, Commander Link, Commander Mail, Norton Backup, Norton Disk Doctor, and Symantec are trademarks of, and The Norton Commander, The Norton Utilities, and UnErase are registered trademarks of, Symantec Corporation.
OAG and Official Airline Guide are registered trademarks of Official Airline Guides, Inc.
OS-9 is a trademark of Microware Systems Corporation and Motorola, Inc.
Panasonic is a registered trademark of Panasonic Corporation.
PARS is a trademark of Northwest Airlines.
PC Magazine and ZiffNet are registered trademarks, and Computer Library is a trademark of, Ziff Communications Company.
PC Paintbrush and Paintbrush are trademarks of ZSoft Corporation.
Peterson's College Selection Service is a service mark of Peterson's Guides, Inc.
Poqet is a registered trademark of, and PoqetTools and The Poqet PC are trademarks of, Poqet Computer Corp.
Princeton is a registered trademark of Princeton Graphic Systems, Inc.
PKLITE, PKZIP, PKUNZIP, and ZIP are trademarks of, and PKWARE is a registered trademark of, PKWARE, Inc.

Practical Peripherals is a registered trademark of Practical Peripherals.
ProComm is a trademark of, and DATASTORM and PROCOMM PLUS are registered trademarks of, DATASTORM TECHNOLOGIES, INC.
PRODIGY is a registered service mark and trademark of Prodigy Services Company, a partnership of IBM and Sears. The following are also service marks or trademarks of Prodigy Services Company: ACTION, Baseball Manager, Custom Choice, FIND, FINDword, FunHouse, GUIDE, HELP, Homelife, HUB, JUMP, JUMPwindow, JUMPword, LOOK, MadMaze, PATH, PATHlist, QUOTE CHECK, QUOTE TRACK, SmartKids, VIEWPATH, and ZIP.
Qmodem is a trademark of The Forbin Project Inc.
Radio Shack, Tandy, Tandy 1000, 1100 FD and HD, 1000 RL, Tandy 2500 XL, Tandy 1400 LT and HD, Tandy 1800 HD, Tandy 2810 HD, Tandy 3810 HD, TRS-80, Color Computer, DeskMate, and MicroExecutive Workstation, are trademarks or registered trademarks of Tandy Corporation.
REDline is a trademark of DynaCorp Incorporated.
Red Ryder is a trademark of FreeSoft/Scott Watson.
Reflex is a trademark of, and C++, SideKick, Turbo Lightning, and Turbo Pascal are registered trademarks of, Borland International, Inc.
Road Warrior Toolkits, Telecoupler, Tele-Toolkit, The Traveler, PLUSdrive, CP+, CP+ Connection, CP+ Connection II, and the CP+ logo are trademarks or registered trademarks of Computer Products Plus, Inc.
Samsonite is a registered trademark of Samsonite Corporation.
ScanMan and TrackMan are registered trademarks of, and Logitech is a trademark of, Logitech.
Sharp and Wizard are registered trademarks of Sharp Electronics Corporation.
Sony is a registered trademark of Sony Corporation.
SpeedModem and Champ are trademarks of CompuCom Corporation.
Sprint is a trademark of US Sprint.
Sprintnet and SprintMail are trademarks of, and PC SprintMail is a registered service mark of, GTE/Telenet Services, Inc.
Standard & Poor's Online and S&P Online are registered trademarks of Standard & Poor's Corporation.
TAPCIS is a trademark of Support Group, Incorporated.
Targus is a registered trademark of Targus.
Telebit is a registered trademark of, and QBlazer is a trademark of, Telebit Corporation.
Teletype is a registered trademark of Western Electric Corporation.
Teletypewriter is a trademark of Teletypewriter Corporation.
The Brick is a trademark of Ergo Computing, Inc.
Texas Instruments and TI are registered trademarks of, and BatteryPro, TravelMate, and WinSX are trademarks of, Texas Instruments, Inc.
Toshiba is a registered trademark of Toshiba Corporation.
TRAVELSHOPPER is a trademark of Travelshopper, Inc.
TRW Credit Profiles is a service mark of TRW.
TYMNET is a registered trademark of, BT and the BT Tymnet logo are trademarks of, and TYMNET is a registered service mark of, British Telecommunications, plc.

UL is a registered trademark of Underwriters' Laboratories.
UltraLite is a registered trademark of NEC Corporation.
UPI is a trademark of United Press International.
USA TODAY and USA TODAY Decisionline are registered trademarks of Gannett Co., Inc.
USRobotics, the USRobotics logo, and HST are registered trademarks of, and Courier, Courier 2400e, Courier HST, Courier HST Dual Standard, Courier V.32*bis*, and Adaptive Speed Leveling, ASL, and Total Control are trademarks of, USRobotics, Inc.
VESTOR is a trademark of Investment Technologies, Inc.
Visa is a trademark of Visa.
Waldenbooks is a registered trademark, and Waldensoftware is a trademark of, Waldenbooks.
WordPerfect is a registered trademark of WordPerfect Corporation.
WordStar and WordStar 2000 are trademarks of WordStar Corporation.
WorldPort is a registered trademark of, and WorldPort 2496 is a trademark of, Touchbase Systems, Inc./USRobotics.
Xerox is a registered trademark of Xerox Corporation.
XyWrite is a registered trademark of XYQUEST, Inc.
Zenith is a registered trademark of Zenith Radio Corporation, and MasterSport and SuperSport are trademarks of Zenith Data Systems Corporation, a Groupe Bull company.
ZEOS is a registered trademark of ZEOS International, Ltd.
Zortech is a trademark of Zortech Corporation.

■ ■ ■

All terms or product names mentioned in this book that are known or suspected to be trademarks or service marks have been appropriately capitalized. Neither the author nor the publisher can attest to the accuracy of this information, nor can the author or the publisher confirm, guarantee, or assume responsibility for the recognition of trademarks or service marks unknown as such, erroneously attributed, or inadvertently not recognized. In sum, the use of a term or product name in this book should not be regarded as affecting the validity of any trademark or service mark, and trademarks or service marks not so-designated in this book remain the property of their respective owners.

■ ■ ■

All photographs and the screens and data reproduced in figures and tables in this book are copyrighted in content and/or format by their respective providers and are reproduced by permission. Original data and graphics on some screens and all uncredited artwork are copyright © 1992, Michael A. Banks.

Table of Contents

Preface	*Getting the Show On the Road*	xvii
Introduction	*Portable Communications Today*	xxii
Why PC Communications?		xxii
Connect with the World		xxii
Who Can Use This Book?		xxiii
How to Use This Book		xxiv
What You Will Need		xxv
Conventions		xxvi
Organization		xxix

Part One
THE BASICS

Chapter 1	*Defining the Field*	3
In the Beginning: Homemade Hardware Hacks		3
Portable, Luggable, Laptop, or Notebook?		4
Palmtop Computers: Is Smallest Best?		11
Telecomputing: An Introduction		12
Messaging		13
Real-Time Conferencing		16
File Transfer		17
Online Research		18
Online Transactions		19
Channels of Telecomputing		19
Chapter 2	*Laptop Basics for Telecomputing*	25
Operating Systems and CPUs		25
Memory		28
Displays		29
Hard and Floppy Disks		37
Power Supplies		38
Chapter 3	*Portable Communications Hardware*	43
Modems: An Introduction		43

Modems for Laptops	47
What You Need: Cables, Phone Hookups, and More	55
Portable FAX	58
Cellular Links	62

Chapter 4 Portable Communications Software — 65

Communications Software: An Introduction	65
Automating Text-Based Online Services with Front-End Software	71
Dedicated Front-End Programs	79
Graphical User Interfaces and Telecommunications	80
Making Your Communications Software More Efficient: Do-It-Yourself Online Front Ends	81
Laptop-to-Desktop Communication: Null-Modeming	85
Portable Communications Support Software	87
Communications Software: Making It Fit	92

Part Two
MAKING THE CONNECTION

Chapter 5 Making Connections: Getting Online, and How to Tap into Hotel Phones, Pay Phones, and Other User-Belligerent Phone Systems — 97

Dialing Up Another System: An Overview	98
Getting Ready	99
Dialing Up and Making Connection	107
Telephone Line Basics	111
Working Around Connection Problems with Support Hardware	115
Cellular Connection Problems and How to Deal with Them	120
Working Around Connection Problems with Direct Phone-Line Connection	122
Dialup Problems	126
Tools and Supplies for Portable Telecomputing	129

Chapter 6 Desktop-to-Laptop Communication: Null-Modeming and Remote Control — 131

Basic File-Transfer Tips, and Some Applications	131
Side-by-Side Communication: Null-Modeming	133

Dialing Up and Controlling Your
    Desktop Computer Via Modem   138

Part Three
APPLICATIONS

Chapter 7   *FAXing on the Road*   **147**
    How FAX Works   147
    Making the FAX Connection   148
    Sending and Receiving FAXes   152
    Viewing and Printing Incoming FAXes   153
    Storing FAXes   155
    Cellular FAX   155
    The Modem Alternative to PC FAX:
       FAX via Online Services   155

Chapter 8   *Online Services for Traveling Modems*   **161**
    Online Service Categories   161
    E-mail Specialty Services   162
    Database and Information-Retrieval Services   165
    Consumer Online Services   166
    Spotlight: Online Resources for Laptop Users   186
    Which Service?   189

Chapter 9   *Portable Telecomputing*
                 Tips, Tricks, and Traps   **191**
    Connection and Communications Problems   191
    Online Service Shortcuts and Time Savers   193
    The Complete Traveling Computer:
       Packing for Portable PC Communications   199
    The Executive Lounge:
       Using Someone Else's Computer System   202
    Making International Connections   204

Chapter 10   *What's Ahead in Portable*
                  PC Communications   **209**
    Hardware   209
    Software   212
    Online Services   213

Part Four
REFERENCE

Appendix A *Manufacturers* — 217
- Laptop and Notebook Computer Manufacturers and Vendors — 217
- Modem Manufacturers and Vendors — 219
- PC FAX and FAX/Modem Manufacturers and Vendors — 221
- Laptop and Communications Peripherals Manufacturers and Vendors — 221

Appendix B *Software and Books* — 225
- Communications Programs — 225
- Online Service Front Ends — 226
- Utilities and Operating Systems — 228
- Reference Books — 229

Appendix C *Online Services* — 231
- Online Services: Overview and Contacts — 231
- Packet-Switching Network Customer Service Numbers — 234
- Getting Online Information from the Networks — 235
- Online Service Network "Addresses" and Direct-Dial Access Numbers — 236

Appendix D *Troubleshooting and Tips* — 239
- How to Avoid Online Problems and What to Do if You Have a Problem — 239
- Common Problems and Solutions — 240

Appendix E *How to Make Modem and Null-Modem Cables* — 245
- RS-232 Cable Components — 246
- Making a Standard RS-232 Cable — 248
- Making a Null-Modem Cable — 249
- Cross-Connecting a DB-9 and DB-25 Connector — 251
- Special Notes on Variations in Pin Assignments — 254
- Notes on Null-Modem Transfers — 257

About the Author — 259

Shopper's Guide — 261

Index — 271

Preface
∎∎∎
Getting the Show on the Road

As a science fiction author, I think about the future quite a bit. As a modem user, I find myself *living* in the future—at least, the future as it was portrayed in the 1950s, '60s, and '70s. The same may be true for you, if you're over 30.

During most of my life, personal computers were science fiction. They were occasionally subjects of speculation in popular journals, but their existence was placed in the far future—say, the year 2051. I've always been the optimistic type, though, and I figured personal computers and even portable computers would show up a little sooner.

I first encountered portable computers in science fiction; the year was 1959, and the source was a science fiction novel published in 1951 (the year I was born). At the time, powerful computers were standard science fiction fare. But computers you could carry around with you were a bit much even for science fiction. (Science fiction authors base their speculations on the leading edges of science and technology, and the leading edge of 1950 computing was the transistor-based mainframe computer. Few writers visualized anything like microprocessors.) But I was a true believer in progress and told myself that I would one day carry a computer in my pocket. I'm happy to say I had to wait only 25 years for fiction to become reality. And the computer I slipped into my shirt pocket was more powerful than the average 1959 mainframe computer.

Similarly, the things we do with modems today were far-away dreams, 30-odd years ago. The concepts were science fiction or, at best, speculative non-fiction. Conventional wisdom held that accessing online databases, collecting E-mail and news updates online, and similar activities were strictly 21st century stuff, probably not to be achieved in our lifetimes. (They said the same thing about Moon landings and robots on Mars; so much for conventional wisdom.) Here again, I kept the faith, knowing that I would one day be able to tap into vast information resources and communicate with people around the world. Which I do daily—and have been doing for a decade.

Given this background, I can't help but marvel at modems and portable computers—even though I use them as often as most people use a telephone. The eight-year-old who marveled at the future of computers and telecomputing looks over my shoulder every time I log on to an online service or BBS. It's probably the same way a lot of people felt when broadcast television took off in the early 1940s—something I take for granted, just as you may take portable computers and telecomputing for granted.

That's my subjective viewpoint. But I think the objective viewpoint is almost as amazing. Consider: Anyone with a portable computer, a modem, and a telephone line can access just about any sort of news or archival information he or she wishes, shop online, exchange E-mail with hundreds of thousands of people, dispatch FAXes and paper mail to any of tens of millions of individuals or companies around the world, and do a number of other equally interesting and useful tasks. This is still science fiction to many people.

In this book, I intend to show you what you can do with a portable computer and modem, and how to do it. If you're already online with your laptop computer, I think I can show you how to do what you're doing more efficiently—and I can probably show you how to do some things you weren't aware existed.

I hope, too, to impart a little of the sense of wonder I feel when I dial up another computer and realize I'm using the technology that I was once told wouldn't be around for decades yet. Or, at least something of the wonder I feel in living in a present that marks the opening of an era in which almost anyone will be able to access vast information resources from anywhere on the planet, and share messages and data with anyone—anywhere, anytime.

If it sounds like science fiction... well, remember what they said about your portable computer.

— Michael A. Banks
Milford, Ohio
March 1992

Introduction

Portable Communications Today

Communication is one of the most popular portable computer activities. It's also among the most confusing. More and more computer users are opting for lightweight portable computers as "on the road" extensions of their desktop machines, or as their primary computers. Switching from a desktop to laptop environment often means learning new work habits, and learning to use new programs.

At the same time, online services are mushrooming in popularity, and everyone wants to get into the game. First-time modem and FAX/modem users are seeking the most efficient means to expand their laptop machines, and encountering an entirely new and often bewildering world.

Learning to use a laptop efficiently (often in "minimalist" fashion), or learning to use modems and computer FAX equipment can be a trial. Put the two together, and you can find yourself dealing with "interesting times," in the sense of the old Chinese curse. While not problematic in itself, portable telecomputing does present some problems and challenges in terms of hardware, software, and making the best use of resources. Hence, this book. In it, I'll guide you through the maze of technical terms, nontechnical procedures, applications, software, and more.

Why PC Communications?

If you haven't already taken the plunge and bought a modem (or didn't get one with your laptop computer), perhaps you're wondering what you might do with one. A more appropriate question might be: Do you know everything you can do with your modem?

You may have heard of the incredible wealth of information and services available online. Near-instant communication across the continent or around the world, with modem users, and even with those who don't have computers. Storehouses of vital business, computer, and personal-interest information waiting to be tapped. All sorts of things you can use to compensate for resources you miss when you're away from your office or home, and to enhance and expand the capabilities of your laptop computers.

In short, there is a host of electronic services online, there to simplify and streamline your business, financial, and personal activities, and keep you in touch with important events. Online, you will find a rich variety of resources to expand your knowledge, put you in instant contact with thousands of other computer users, entertain you, and provide services, knowledge, and learning experiences you didn't know existed.

That's what you can hook up to with your laptop computer and modem, from almost anywhere. With the help of this book, you'll learn what's out there and how to get at it.

Connect with the World

Telecomputing is available to nearly everyone, everywhere. All you need to connect are your computer, communications software, a modem, and a telephone line.

And you don't have to be a computer whiz to "plug in" to the online world. Today's hardware and software packages are a far cry from the user-belligerent systems of the early days of telecomputing. Portable computing and telecomputing have matured. With this maturity has come an awareness of the fact that access to its benefits and services must be extended to those who aren't technically oriented.

It does help to have a little foreknowledge and coaching, though. This applies to the basics of telecomputing, and to using the two major connections to the world of telecomputing—bulletin board systems and online services.

Which, of course, is the reason you should read this book.

Who Can Use This Book

If you find any of the online activities and services alluded to at the beginning of this introduction of interest, telecomputing is for you.

Business and Personal Applications

I've written this book for everyone—personal and business computer users, professionals in every field, and computer hobbyists. I've also kept an eye on the needs of those who have specialized applications—whether they involve sending and receiving FAX messages, or checking E-mail from overseas.

This is a rather broad audience, but no matter whether your telecomputing applications are business or personal in nature, you'll need the same basic equipment and knowledge.

And, just as you'll use the same equipment and knowledge for virtually all telecomputing applications, you'll use some of the same BBSs and online services for both business and personal applications.

The point is this: Virtually everything in this book is potentially useful to you, no matter what your portable telecomputing applications or interests.

Novice and Pro

One of the goals of this book is to make telecomputing easy and interesting for the computer novice as well as the computer pro. So, even if you just unpacked your computer yesterday, you'll be able to get online fast with this book.

But I'm not neglecting you more advanced computer users. Even if you're already online, you'll find that this book has a lot to offer. The hardware and software chapters present vital information, and I guarantee you'll find useful tips throughout the book.

How to Use This Book

As noted, my goal is to get you online as quickly and as easily as possible. I also want this book to serve as a continuing reference to online services and activities, and to accessing online services from remote locations. In these pages you'll find everything you need to know to get started, and to realize the maximum benefit from your portable communications activities. You'll find everything you need to know in this book—from how to buy a modem or FAX/modem, to suggestions for creative telecomputing applications.

Read this book now, and keep it handy when you travel with your laptop. I want you to learn as much as possible before you go online, and then provide a reference you can turn to when you have problems with or questions about using your modem. To that end, I've spent time on every type of BBS and network mentioned in this book, and have experimented with a variety of portable communications hardware and software. You'll find the results in these chapters, presented in a straightforward, easy to understand manner. (And if you want to know more about how and why things work, I've included a little information on those aspects of telecomputing, too.)

Sample screens from software, online services, and BBSs supplement the text, so you can preview exactly what you'll find online. (You don't want to log on to a new service with no idea of what to expect!)

You'll also find step-by-step instructions for a number of important procedures, like network log on, transferring files between your laptop and another computer, and more. These show you exactly what you'll encounter, and how to handle problems that might arise.

By the way, much of this is to help you avoid what I call "online panic"—a feeling of loss of control that eventually drives you to pull the plug on your modem. Obviously, online panic is to be avoided. If you panic, you'll waste time. And, if you're completely frustrated, you may give up on a system and miss just what you were after.

I want to prepare you for what you'll find at the other end of your modem, and I want you to be able to deal with new systems and hardware (like FAX cards) in a civilized manner—to "tame" them to your liking, as it were. So, read this book—it will help keep you in control.

I'll also give you advice on how to avoid costly pitfalls and errors, how to combine telecomputing with other computer applications, such as word processing and gaming, and quite a few other telecomputing topics.

Getting the Most from This Book

The best way to use this book is to take the time to read it completely. Then, dial up a local BBS and practice—especially if you're new to using a modem. If you can't find a BBS in your area, try dialing up SprintNet or Tymnet and using their online information service and directories, as detailed in the chapter titled "Using Commercial Online Services." In fact, you should familiarize yourself with packet-switching networks early on; quite often, they will be your "lifeline" when you're traveling.

I'm suggesting that you experiment with your setup on a local BBS or one of the packet networks, rather than on an online service, for two reasons. First, online services cost money—why pay to learn the basics when you can do it for free? Second, online services are usually more complex than BBSs. If you're new to telecomputing, it's easier to get "lost" and frustrated on a commercial service than on a BBS. BBSs are a good way to test new hardware and software, too.

Before you try out a commercial system, by the way, be sure to read the overview of online services. Take advantage of the previews of online services, as well. These will help you select the service or services best for you, and guide you through your first sessions.

What You Will Need

As indicated at the beginning of this Introduction, you'll need certain specialized hardware and software to telecompute.

Hardware

At the very least, you must have a laptop computer, a modem, and a telephone line. If you're interested in sending and receiving FAX messages while traveling, you will need a FAX card or external FAX/modem. You may also wish to obtain accessory hardware, such as a voice/data switch, an acoustic coupler, or any of several aids to connecting with hotel and pay telephones. These aren't a requirement, but you will probably need one or more of these items eventually. (Note: I recommend the CP+ "Road Warrior" kit for all travelers who want to communicate on the road; with it, you can hook up to any telephone line, anywhere. More on this later.)

Software

The only required software here is communications software (which is sometimes called terminal emulation software, termsoft, comm software, or other names). However, there are any number of accessory programs that enhance telecomputing (such as archiving programs and pop-up notepads). Whether these are necessary depends on your applications. I'll show you how to determine that, as well as how to select communications software.

Conventions

Special Terms of Reference Used in This Book

You'll find several special terms in this book, among them terms that have different meanings in other contexts. These terms are explained here to avoid any confusion.

BBS is an acronym for *"bulletin board system,"* and I use it throughout this book in place of "bulletin board system." (And no, I don't use "BBS" only because it is easier for me to type than "bulletin board system"—though that's a good reason. The reason I use "BBS" is because it is the accepted term for "bulletin board system"—you'll see it used everywhere.)

System refers to your computer and its peripherals and software or to any computer system you may dial up. The latter includes bulletin board systems (BBSs), online services such as DELPHI, GEnie, or CompuServe, communications systems like MCI Mail, etc.

A *menu* is a list of available commands and/or options.

A *command* is anything you type to instruct a computer to take a specific action. Examples of commands are **READ** and **EXIT**. (Certain control characters can be commands, too.) Commands are often used with a modifying word or character called a *qualifier*, which directs a command to operate in a certain manner.

Options and *selections* are choices available on menus. These choices may or may not be commands. If you choose an item from a menu by typing the item's name, you have selected an option or made a selection.

A selection may also be an item upon which a command acts. For example, items on a list of programs in a database are selections, and might be manipulated with any of several commands (such as **LIST**, **READ**, or **DOWNLOAD**) when used as a command qualifier.

A *prompt* is a signal from the computer system to which you are connected—its way of telling you it is waiting for you to do something, like make a selection, enter information, or type a command. Prompts usually consist of a single character, such as ?, !, or >, but sometimes appear in the form of a question or statement, such as "Do you wish to sign off now (y/n)?" or "Press <RETURN> to continue." (Incidentally, most systems will hang up on you if you don't enter anything at a prompt for several minutes—so pay attention to those prompts!)

Menus are normally followed by a prompt. (You may also encounter special prompts that request specific kinds of responses.)

A *response* is your answer to a question or prompt from a computer system, direct or implied. You may, for example, be prompted to enter "Yes" or "No," or to enter a date. Your answer to a direct question is your response. All prompts are in themselves implied questions; thus, commands as well as answers to questions are responses.

Input is normally the text you type to compose a message or description. Input may also be information or directions you type in response to a prompt.

The word *entry* may refer to text entered to compose a message or description, or to a text file or other file on the system to which you're connected.

When I use the word *"current"* with a noun such as *"message,"* *"menu,"* or *"file,"* I mean the item or entry you are now or have just completed reading, downloading, or otherwise accessing. For example, "the current file" would refer to a file you are presently downloading, or have just completed downloading.

Commands and Input: Format and Usage

When referring to commands and your input, this book uses the following conventions:

Commands

Commands are printed in boldface, with all capital letters, so you can distinguish them from surrounding text easily.

Example: To log off, type **OFF**.

The ENTER Key

The key that sends commands or text to your computer or to another system is referred to as the ENTER key, and represented by ENTER. (This key may be marked RETURN, ENTER, or CR, or with a hooked arrow on your laptop's keyboard.)

Type

When you see the word "type," it means you should enter (type on your keyboard) the designated command or text and press ENTER.

Text to be typed literally as shown is enclosed in quotation marks.

Example: Type "Yes" (Type the word "Yes" [without the quote marks] and press ENTER)

Enter

The word "enter" means you should enter the designated text or command, after which you may or may not have to press ENTER. (You normally press ENTER to tell a system you have finished entering a command or text, although some systems may require a different character, or none at all, to signal the end of a text or command entry.)

Text to be entered literally as shown is enclosed in quotation marks.

> Example: Enter your message   (Enter any message you wish)
>
> Enter "A"   (Enter the letter A, and nothing else)

<text>

When you see text enclosed in greater than/lesser than symbols (like this: <text>) it means you should enter the kind of information enclosed by the symbols. For example:

> Type DOWNLOAD <filename>

means enter the command **DOWNLOAD**, followed by a file name, such as DATA.LST or ADVENT.EXE (not the words "file name").

Entering Numbers

A number sign (#) or a lowercase x indicates that a number or numbers should be used or will be displayed with the command or operation under discussion. Sometimes, I'll use several, like this: ### or xxx.

Organization

This book is organized into four convenient sections: The Basics, Making the Connection, Applications, and Reference. The organization is linear, meaning you'll derive the most benefit from reading the book from the beginning, because I move from simple to more complex topics as the book progresses.

The Basics

This section tells you what you need and what's out there, and gives you some background on how all this PC communications magic works. I discuss the basic hardware and software with which you'll be dealing, and help you determine what you need. This section also introduces you to portable PC communications. I cover both modem and FAX communications—but I promise you won't get lost in overly detailed technical explanations. The intent is to give you just enough information to have a good idea of what's going on behind the scenes when you're communicating with your computer.

If you're new to telecomputing, you'll find the answers to many of your questions in this section. If you're already online but looking to upgrade your communications equipment and software, you'll find this section especially useful.

Making the Connection

This section is your personal guide to making physical phone connections and making modem connections with online services. You'll find a step-by-step guide to dialing up another computer system, and look over my shoulder as I go through the preparations for the process of logging on to various systems.

Then, I'll show you how to deal with trickier connections, including cellular phones doing direct file transfers between computers, and more.

Applications

The first chapter of this section opens with the basics of FAX, then moves into hands-on how-to information on sending, receiving, viewing, and printing FAXes. Then, it's on to commercial online services. You'll have a personal tour of several commercial online services, with the emphasis on what each has to offer the traveling PC user.

Use this section to help you decide which online service(s) best suit your needs and interests, as well as how you can put online services to work for you. You'll also find information on international PC communications here.

Then, I provide troubleshooting tips to help you deal with the most common portable telecomputing problems, along with advice on how to prepare for a telecomputing trip, and what's available in terms of rentals and if you forget something. I'll also tell you what you need if you intend to use a rental or someone else's system while away from your home or office. To wind things up, we'll take a quick look at the future of portable computer communications.

Reference

The Reference section leads off with a listing of laptop and .HM 5 communications hardware manufacturers, followed by software publishers (all covered in the book's chapters) and a brief bibliography. Then, a reference and resource listing of the major online services is provided. This is followed by a troubleshooting guide, which shows you how to handle common communications problems. After that, I'll show you how to make RS-232C cables and null-modem cables, so you can transfer data between your laptop and just about any kind of desktop computer.

If you like the products you see described in the book, you'll be pleased with the special "Shopper's Guide" section at the end of the book. Here, you'll find special offers and discounts from hardware manufacturers, software publishers, and online services.

■ ■ ■

Again, take this book with you when you travel. Write in it, underline important sections, and fill it with bookmarks. It is your personal guide to truly making the most of your laptop computer by putting it in touch with the world.

Part 1

...

The Basics

1
Defining the Field

It's appropriate that I define this book's areas of interest. So this chapter serves as an introduction to portable computers and their telecomputing applications.

In the Beginning: Homemade Hardware Hacks

I saw my first portable computer early in 1980. This was at a time when most personal computer users were too busy figuring out what to do with a computer in their homes to think about what to do with one while traveling. The venue was a meeting of CinTUG (the Cincinnati Tandy Computer User's Group). A nameless computer hobbyist showed up lugging a Radio Shack TRS-80 Model I in a sturdy wooden framework that held the keyboard/CPU, 12-inch monitor, disk drives, and disk interface. This computer's chief claim to portability was the fact that all the components were in one unit. Otherwise, it was too heavy to carry around with ease, and it still had to be plugged in. The builder's talents were more mechanical than electronic, so he wasn't able to build a portable power supply.

A year later, I saw a more sophisticated hardware hack by an Australian computer user named Eric Lindsay. Lindsay wanted to use his TRS-80 Model I during long flights between the U.S. and Australia, so he put together a setup that included battery power, and replaced the Model I's standard monitor with a 5-inch monitor. It worked—and may well have been the first personal computer used aboard an airplane.

Those desktop adaptations were a far cry from today's three-pound wonders, especially when you consider the fact that modern portables are far more powerful than those early state-of-the-art personal computers. But it is interesting to see how the laptop boom of the 1990s was anticipated a decade earlier. While the unnamed computerist who crammed his computer into a barely portable box may have done so for the sake of having a portable computer, the Australian computerist (and others like him) put together a portable computer because he had a need for it.

In similar fashion, the evolution of laptop computers followed the pattern I saw in those two primitive portables. Portable computers, as you will learn in the following pages, were at first difficult to transport, and were limited to operating in the same environments as their desktop counterparts. Soon enough, portable computers became truly portable, transcending the limits of power supplies and available work space.

The evolution of portable telecomputing applications likewise followed this pattern. Early portable computer users sometimes added a modem simply for the sake of having a modem. Today, a modem is an essential portable computing tool—hence, this book.

Portable, Luggable, Laptop, or Notebook?

Most dictionaries define "portable" as "capable of being carried or moved about," or something similar. This doesn't quite define portable computers. For one thing, it does not exclude desktop computers, which you wouldn't normally categorize as "portable" even though they can be moved. A more precise definition of a portable computer might be along the lines of "a small computer, with all components in one compact unit; capable of being carried about by anyone of average strength; operating in environments where the normal requirements of a desktop computer, such as an electrical outlet, are not available." Or something like that.

Some portable computers don't quite meet all the requirements set forth in that definition, either—at least, not in a subjective sense. Consider the earliest portable computers. They weighed in at 40 pounds or more. Some people could carry them about, and some couldn't. Still, they were more portable than desktop computers. Other early portable computers were not battery-powered; but they could be moved about and all their components fitted together into one unit for moving. These early machines were probably better called "transportable," though they were as portable as computers got in their day.

All of which points to the loose definition of "portable computer" I'll use for the purposes of this book: A personal computer with all its components housed in one easy-to-transport unit. This excludes desktop computers, but includes portable computers that require a 110V outlet—though most portable computers you're likely to encounter nowadays operate on batteries or an AC adapter.

Note, too, that I'll concentrate on MS-DOS portable computers throughout this book.

That much said, let's take a look at the varieties of portable computers, past and present.

Categories and Evolution

Portable computers come in several categories: *luggable* (40 or 50 pounds, and larger than a briefcase), *laptop* (weighing 15 to 20 pounds), and *notebook* (small foldup computers that weigh four or five pounds or less).

Figures 1.1 and 1.2 illustrate laptop and notebook computers, respectively.

The categories match the evolution of the portable computer, from a condensed version of a desktop computer (luggable computers) to truly portable, full-function computers (laptops and notebook computers).

Luggable Computers

Luggable computers were the first mass-market portables. Sometimes referred to as "transportables," they were portable for their time, and in the sense that everything was in one package. The monitor, disk drive(s), CPU, keyboard, were all in one fold-out unit.

6 Portable Communications

Figure 1.1 A Laptop Computer

Figure 1.2 A Notebook Computer

The idea of a luggable computer was to pack a desktop computer into a (usually) metal case, with a tiny monitor designed to save space. (Not unlike the first homemade "portable" computers I described a few lines back.) The monitor was of the same type as desktop computer monitors—a vacuum tube, or CRT (cathode ray tube). The monitor was also very difficult to look at; imagine reading 80 columns of text on a 5-inch monochrome monitor.

Like desktop computers, luggables were equipped with parallel and serial ports, and could be expanded via slots for internal cards. This meant you could hook up an external modem, or add an internal modem. With the luggable's reasonably powerful CPU and floppy and/or hard disk drives, telecomputing was no problem.

To say the least, however, luggable computers were bulky, requiring at least two square feet of table space for the main unit. The detachable keyboard required about the same area as a desktop computer's keyboard. The weight made it a real chore to haul one around—thus the *sobriquet* "luggable," as to move a portable computer this size was to lug it.

Once a luggable computer was set up, however, it offered pretty much the same capabilities as a desktop computer, save for the tiny monitor.

The first luggable to be marketed on a large scale was the Osborne, a CP/M machine. Named after its designer, the Osborne was lauded by the computing public as a work of genius. However, the idea behind the luggable computer was nothing new, nor a matter of genius, as demonstrated by the portable computers I described a few pages back. Apparently, all it takes to be a "genius" in Western society is to get something to market or in the public eye first.

Luggable computers have just about disappeared from the marketplace. You can, however, find used luggables for sale. Examples of luggable computers are the aforementioned Osborne, Kaypro CP/M and MS-DOS systems, and Zenith MS-DOS systems.

Laptop Computers

Fortunately for many computer users' aching muscles, the laptop computer came along not long after the luggable computer. The first true laptop computer was the Tandy Model 100, which made its debut in 1983. The Model 100 was lovingly referred to as a "slab" computer because of its shape. Everything was built into one package, with no unfold or setup required. The Model 100 had a standard QWERTY (typewriter-style) keyboard, an 8-line LCD display, and connectors for a printer, external modem (a standard serial port), an acoustic coupler, direct phone line, a cassette or disk drive, and bar code reader. All this was packed into a three-pound package roughly 8-½ by 11-¾ by 2 inches.

The Model 100 did not accommodate internal disk drives. Instead, you had to use a relatively slow cassette recorder or an expensive, specialized hard drive and interface for mass storage.

The Model 100 came with an internal 300-bps modem, and faster modems could be attached to the serial port. This was, not incidentally, the first portable computer to come with a modem as standard equipment. A set of applications was included (word processing, telecommunications, etc.). The operating system was not MS-DOS, but something similar from Microsoft—though not similar enough to let the machine run MS-DOS software. (And certainly not in its limited RAM.)

In its day, the Model 100 was the ideal system for on-the-road telecomputing. Its full-size keyboard, light weight, and built-in modem made it popular with anyone who had to produce text while traveling. Newspaper reporters in particular put it to good use. Many of them could dial up their newspapers' computers and upload stories while on location. Or the reporter could work off-site and dump his stories into the newspaper's computer later in the day, using a direct serial port connection. (The Model 100 stored data in battery-backed RAM—up to 32K—which was shared with the applications programs.)

Tandy brought out a slightly updated version of the Model 100, the Model 102, not long after it introduced the Model 100. Shown in Figure 1.3, the Model 102 is still marketed, billed as an "executive workstation." (The Model 200 and the Model 600, two other enhanced versions of the Model 100, are no longer

*Figure 1.3 The Tandy Model 102—
An Early Laptop Computer*

produced. This is largely because these systems could not run MS-DOS software.)

Newspaper reporters continue to use the Model 100 and Model 102 today. Many have become so accustomed to the machine and its applications that they'd rather not switch to something new. I suspect the main reason Model 100 users don't switch is because the computer has virtually unlimited battery life—as much as 20 hours on a single set of inexpensive batteries. Rather than using bulky rechargeable batteries like newer laptop machines, the Model 100 uses four AA batteries. (I have a Model 100, myself, and still use it on occasion. I prefer to use several sets of rechargeable AA batteries and an external recharger, for long-term cost savings.)

The issue of battery life is quite important, as you will learn, and there are few contemporary laptops that can match the battery life of the Model 100. Most laptop batteries are limited to two, six, or eight hours, and require 12 hours or more to recharge. The reason the newer machines' batteries have such a short life is because they have to power stepper motors for disk drives, and because they drive larger screens that require more power. Thus, we find some trade-offs. The old Model 100 has a display of only eight lines by 45 characters, and no internal disk drives; in return you get longer battery life. Also, the characters are much larger than a typical desktop computer's display.

Even though the Model 100 was a tremendous success, computer users were looking for something more like their desktop machines to carry with them. As soon as the technology became available, laptop computers with near full-size screens (80 columns by 25 lines, albeit somewhat skewed in aspect ratio because of the relatively low height of the displays) hit the market.

These machines gave the computer user more of the advantages of desktop computers, without the limitations of luggable machines and computers like the Model 100. With laptops such as early Zenith and Tandy machines (*circa* 1985), the user had the benefits of MS-DOS, floppy disks, hard disks (at a pretty price), and internal expansion—with a weight of 20 to 25 pounds. The size was somewhat larger than the Model 100, in the neighborhood of 12" by 14" by 3" and necessary to accommodate folding displays, larger batteries, internal slots, and disk drives.

These machines eventually gave way to smaller and lighter laptop machines, such as that shown in Figure 1.1.

Notebook Computers

By the end of the 1980s, new technology and competition brought still smaller machines, called notebook computers, to the marketplace. A typical notebook computer is shown in Figure 1.2.

The idea of notebook computers is to provide as lightweight a unit as possible, in a package that is as thin as possible, if not tiny in other dimensions. (The width and depth of a laptop or notebook computer are determined in large part by the size of the keyboard and the display.)

Notebook computers are actually just the latest wrinkle in, and the future of, laptop computers: thinner and lighter. The term "notebook" itself is mainly a marketing device, used to distinguish low-profile machines from their stockier cousins.

The use of the word "notebook" in describing a computer seems to hinge on the computer's thickness, in any event. I'll use the term as it applies to specific models of computers, but "laptop" and "notebook" are often used interchangeably.

Palmtop Computers: Is Smallest Best?

A new category of portable computer has emerged in recent years: The *palmtop* computer. Palmtop computers are hand-held units with a size in the neighborhood of 4" x 8", folded. They unfold to double the 4" width, and reveal a tiny QWERTY keyboard and an equally tiny display. Figure 1.4 shows a typical palmtop computer, a Poqet.

Figure 1.4 Poqet Palmtop Computer

The "Wizard" from Sharp Electronics is another popular palmtop computer.

Although palmtop computers have several built-in applications, and can be expanded with add-on programs (either via file-transfer or plug-in ROM packs), they have minimal telecomputing applications. Most offer some sort of serial interface, but these are intended more for sharing data and programs with larger computers than for modem communications. Going online with a palmtop computer is a novelty that quickly grows stale; the limitations of the tiny keyboard and screen, and the lack of mass storage, make E-mail and file-transfer fairly impractical.

Palmtop computers are nothing new, by the way. Computer hobbyists will recall the "pocket computers" manufactured by Sharp and marketed by Radio Shack in the early 1980s. Dubbed PC-1, PC-2, and so on, these computers were superficially similar to today's palmtop computers. Like their modern cousins they had few built-in applications, least of all telecom programs.

In any event, you might use a palmtop computer with a serial port for telecomputing—but it won't be easy. And using a palmtop computer with a modem is usually a novelty or a last resort.

■ ■ ■

So much for the basic hardware, for now. We'll examine laptop computers and their peripherals in a more in-depth manner in Chapter 2. In sum, though, the traveling computer user usually carries (in addition to the computer itself) a plug-in power supply, perhaps an extra battery pack, and maybe a portable printer. That's about it—until you get into telecomputing on the road. Portable telecomputing, of course, requires a modem, and may require that you carry other sorts of hardware, which we'll examine in Chapter 3, as well as in Chapter 2.

Now, a quick overview of computer communications via modem, or telecomputing.

Telecomputing: An Introduction

Computer telecommunications, or "telecomputing," is no longer the exclusive province of "techies," hackers, and professional engineers. The only physical requirements are a home computer, a modem, the appropriate software, and a telephone line—nothing that's beyond those of at least average means. The level of technical sophistication required is little more than that necessary to operate an automatic bank teller or your own computer—which is to say that if you can handle a personal computer you can telecompute.

Combined with portability, the social, cultural, and other implications of this are staggering, and won't be completely realized for decades. Entire electronic subcultures have already evolved on and across computer bulletin boards and online services, and I've no doubt we'll see more of this in coming years.

On a practical front, we find ourselves on the verge of a new communications and information age. Telecomputing power is now available to the people at large, and a new world is being opened for exploration.

The following is an overview of telecomputing activities and applications. This section introduces concepts and terms used throughout this book. If you're completely new to telecomputing, it's especially important for you to read this.

First, we'll examine the major categories of online activities:

- messaging
- real-time conferencing
- file transfer
- online research
- online transactions

Then we'll take an introductory look at your two major links to telecomputing—bulletin board systems and online services.

Messaging

Electronic messaging is easily the most-used feature of BBSs and online services. (A message in this context is a note, letter, announcement, or other private or public textual communication.) It's also the most frequent application for portable PC communications.

Messages are exchanged online in a number of ways. The main distinction in how messages are exchanged is that some are private and some are public.

Public Messages

Public messages are posted on what are usually called "bulletin boards," but sometimes called "conferences."

Getting the Words Right

Having introduced those two terms in this context, I'd best take a few lines to distinguish their meanings from those in other contexts.

Strictly speaking, a "bulletin board" is a public place where messages, announcements, etc., of general interest are posted—in short, a public system for written communications. Unfortunately (in linguistic terms), certain types of small-scale computer systems you'll be dialing up are called "bulletin boards," too—and most of these offer far more than just message reading and posting. (You'll find more information on these systems at the end of this chapter.) The appropriate terminology for such a dial-up system is "bulletin board system" (usually shortened to the acronym "BBS"). To avoid confusion, I'll use "bulletin board" only when I'm referring to an area on a BBS or online service where public messages are posted. I will not use the term to refer to commercial online services, as so many erroneously do.

Similarly, "conference" has two meanings in the lexicon of the online world. As mentioned a few paragraphs back, the term sometimes refers to an area where public messages are posted; but it usually means real-time, face-to-face (or, keyboard-to-keyboard) online chatting (typing and reading in lieu of talking and listening).

To simplify matters, I'll usually use the word "conference" to mean real-time chatting. You should be aware, however, that certain systems (the BIX online service, to name one) use "conference" to refer to a public bulletin board-type message area. Actually, when used in this context, "conference" usually refers to a very specific and sophisticated type of public messaging system in which messages are organized and linked for access by subjects. Fortunately, you'll know which kind of "conference" I'm referring to by context (ditto for any systems you're on that mention "Conference").

Now, back to the topic at hand . . .

Bulletin boards. Bulletin boards are found on BBSs as well as online services, and they go by several different names—"Forum," "Conference," "board," "Classified Ads," and "Post," to name a few.

The idea behind bulletin boards is the same as that behind the cork boards found in laundromats, apartment complex rec rooms, meeting halls, or other public areas: to share information. Messages are grouped in categories or subjects (such as "For Sale," "Jokes," "News," or "Wanted").

Public messages can be read and (usually) replied to by anyone with access to the system (and any such replies will, in turn, be public).

You can read and post messages by category, but the more sophisticated online message bases allow even greater control and definition of messages. DELPHI's Forum, for instance, allows you to view messages based on any combination of the parameters of subject, sender, addressee, and date, if you wish. Other online services' message bases provide similar control, and often allow you to limit access to a message to a select group of people. BIX's conference system allows for the division of each conference subject into various subtopics, and for some subtopics to be read-only.

Public messages may or may not be addressed to individuals. Usually, if a message is addressed to you, you have the privilege of deleting it. You can also delete messages you have posted. A system may also allow you the option of making a message readable only by the addressee, providing, in effect, a private messaging service.

As you'll find when you're online, a typical bulletin board message is brief (a couple hundred words long, at the most), and to the point. The length of a bulletin board message is limited on some systems.

Private Messaging

Private messaging is commonly called "Electronic mail," or "E-mail," and exists quite apart from bulletin boards. In E-mail, text messages are stored in what is referred to as your "electronic mailbox," which is analogous to a mailbox to which only you have the key. (This is actually a private file or portion of a file area to which only you have access, as it is tied to your online ID or username.)

Replying to an E-mail message involves simple commands, and you can delete messages to and from you, if you wish. A system may provide additional E-mail functions, such as the ability to forward an E-mail message to other users, or to send the same message to multiple users.

Real-Time Conferencing

Real-time conferencing is probably the most popular (and "addictive") of telecomputing activities. In basic terms, real-time conferencing is one-to-one conversation—though on the majority of systems it's not limited to just two people.

Imagine, if you will, a CB or ham radio conversation in which you type and read, rather than speak and listen. This will give you a good picture of what real-time conferencing is all about. In fact, some services call their real-time conversation facilities "CB Simulators." (You may find real-time conferencing called "Chat," "Speakeasy," or other names, depending on which system you use.)

You'll find real-time conferencing on very few BBSs (although nearly all have a provision for the person operating the BBS to "break in" and chat with you at his discretion, and most allow you to page the system operator). But the majority of online services offer a real-time conference feature.

Online services offer an astonishing variety of enhancements to real-time conference, ranging from the ability to make an automatic transcript of a conference to creating private conferences. You may or may not find this kind of communications useful for your communications needs while traveling; many portable computer users do.

File Transfer

File transfer is, as you might guess, the process of transferring files between computers. Next to E-mail, it is probably the most pragmatically useful aspect of telecomputing for business and personal users. With the right software on each end, files of all types—from manuscripts to database and spreadsheet files to programs—can be transferred between computers. File transfer is going to be very important to you if you have to deliver reports or data files of any type to someone else while you're on the road, be it to that person's electronic mailbox, or to a desktop computer at your office or in your home.

A major advantage of file transfer is that—with text files, at least—you transcend the differences in format between computers; thus, if you have an MS-DOS laptop and need to make a long document available to someone who has a Macintosh, you can use your computer and modem to give him the file in a format his machine can read.

File transfers work in two directions—from your computer and to it. The terms used to describe which way a file is going are relative, and easy to remember: if you are sending a file, you are uploading it; if you are receiving a file, you are downloading it. (And, in case you're wondering, when a file is sent from one computer to another, it is actually copied; the file being "sent" is not deleted.)

Files may be transferred using any of several protocols—ASCII for straight text, and Xmodem, Ymodem, Zmodem, and other error-checking protocols for transferring program, data, or text files. Not all systems offer all of these protocols; refer to the sections of this book on various systems and to the systems themselves to find out which protocols are available.

By the way, you'll find "free" software among the major benefits of file transfer. BBSs everywhere (as well as consumer-oriented online services) offer thousands of public domain or "shareware" programs for download. (Public domain programs are programs which have been made available to the public at no charge by their creators. Shareware programs are programs for which the user is asked to make a contribution if he or she finds them of value.) Most of the online services host special areas for laptop users, wherein you'll find utilities of particular interest.

Online Research

Talk with many business and professional modem users, and you'll come away convinced that the sum total of human knowledge can be found online.

That's almost true. Sophisticated services like the DIALOG Information Service provide access to a wealth of general and specialized information that is nothing short of staggering. Information utilities such as NewsNet and Dow Jones News/Retrieval offer the latest information in a variety of special-interest areas, as well as updates on current and recent events, and business news. Business, economic, and general news from AP, Reuters, *USA Today*, and other sources are available on a variety of online services, and some magazines publish limited online versions or, as is the case with a number of publications from Ziff-Davis and McGraw-Hill, all the articles, columns and reviews from every issue.

Comprehensive encyclopedias (in particular, the electronic version of Grolier's Academic American Encyclopedia) with sophisticated search and cross-referencing capabilities can be found on several services, too.

Suffice to say, whether you're working on an economic forecast, a technical paper, or just browsing for information on a specific topic, you'll find online research beneficial. It's also convenient for travelers. There's no need to seek out a bookstore or library in a strange city; just dial up the appropriate online service and plug in to the information resources you need.

Such services do not come free, of course. You pay for the convenience of home access, as well as for the specialized knowledge you won't find elsewhere. Thus, services such as DIALOG and NewsNet cost more than the average online service, and "gateways" to these databases from various online services bear a surcharge. The same is usually true of encyclopedias and magazines available on consumer online services.

Online Transactions

It is now possible to purchase a surprising variety of goods and services online, as well as undertake other kinds of financial transactions.

Although banking promised early on to be one of the most-used features offered by online services, very little online banking took place until recently. Now, online banking is a hot product, and another service of convenience for travelers. (Forget to make your house payment before you left on that trip? Do it via computer.)

Online shopping is booming. Virtually all online services offer shopping of one sort or another, from merely selling their manuals to sponsoring computer software and hardware marketplaces. There are also special services (such as Comp-U-Store and American Express) that offer a variety of general, non-computer merchandise. As might be expected, however, the mainstay of online shopping is computer products. The traveling computer user won't find this area of online activity of much interest, but it is there. (And, while you may not order goods while traveling, online catalogs can be a great tool for comparison shopping.)

In the service category, stock and commodity quotes, stock brokerages, and full service travel information and booking agencies are online. These are especially useful to the traveler because they give up-to-the-minute information that may not be readily available elsewhere.

Channels of Telecomputing

Broadly defined, telecomputing is communication via computer. More specifically, it is the transfer of data between two or more computers. Telecomputing can be as simple as connecting two microcomputers sitting side by side, or as complex as accessing a mainframe computer several thousand miles away with your personal computer, via a packet-switching network computer and telephone lines.

Later chapters provide a close look at the whys and hows of telecomputing—it's a layman's guide to the technical side of things—but we'll briefly survey the major channels of telecomputing here.

Local Versus Remote Systems

Note that two computers connected in a telecommunications link are distinguished from one another by the terms *local* and *remote*. These terms are strictly relative (i.e., dependent upon the viewpoint of the operator).

From your viewpoint, your personal computer or terminal is the local system, while the computer you dial up is the remote system. To a person who operates a BBS or online service, his computer is the local system, while yours is a remote system dialing in.

Modems

A modem is required for all but direct connect communications (explained below); any communications via telephone lines require a modem to "translate" digital computer data into a format (analog) that can be transmitted by wire. The modem translates incoming data back to the digital format the computer understands.

Direct Connect Data Transfer

Data transfer between computers that are within a few feet of one another is most often accomplished without a modem, using what is called a null-modem cable (also called a "reversed" or "flipped" cable). This type of connection is known as a "hard wire" or "direct" connection and is far easier to set up and use than a modem-to-modem connection between two adjacent computers.

A null-modem cable simply reverses the way the wires are connected at the serial port (RS-232C) of each computer, so that computer A's "data send" wire is connected to computer B's "data receive" wire, and vice versa.

A common application for direct connect data transfer is transferring data between two incompatible computers (such as a Macintosh and IBM PC). Another application is to connect computers in close proximity which must share data and/or common peripherals in what is known as a "Local Area Network" (LAN). Yet another application is of special interest to laptop owners: transferring data and programs between a laptop and a desktop machine. (By the time you've finished reading this book, you'll be an expert at this!)

Modem transfers can be conducted using conventional communications software, or using special computer-to-computer file-transfer programs, like LapLink, detailed in later chapters.

Dialing Another Computer Direct

An increasingly common scenario has a company setting up a computer and modem, and having sales and other employees in the field transmitting data from laptop computers. Many laptop computer users find it more than convenient to be able to dial up their desktop machines to get files or leave messages. There are often problems with this kind of communication because desktop systems aren't always set up to communicate with just any caller. However, with the right software and enough knowledge (supplied by this book), you can connect with just about any computer whose modem and communications software will answer the phone.

Incidentally, many communications programs let you set up the equivalent of a mini-BBS system, a la those discussed in a couple paragraphs. With the proper setup, you can dial up your desktop computer from your laptop, and read and leave E-mail, or transfer files, all with the benefit of password protection. More specialized programs let you dial up a desktop computer with another computer, then access the desktop computer's hard and floppy disks as if you were at its keyboard. You can see some of the applications for a laptop user who needs to get at his "main" desktop machine, I'm sure.

Bulletin Board Systems

If you're like most modem users, your first experience with telecomputing may be with a local BBS. This is because BBSs are so readily accessible. They exist in virtually every region of the U.S. and Canada, and usually don't require you to set up a membership or account in advance. Nor do the majority of them charge a fee. Many laptop users use bulletin boards to "park" files uploaded while they're traveling, for later download to their desktop machines.

You'll find two main differences between dialing a friend's computer and a bulletin board system:

1) A BBS does not have to be attended.

2) When you call a BBS you have access to a limited—but extremely useful—range of services. On most systems, you can post and read messages, upload and download files, and participate in other activities.

As I mentioned a few lines back, a few BBSs charge for access. Those that do normally charge a nominal annual rate for access—perhaps $20 or so—to help the sysop cover the cost of a dedicated telephone line and computer equipment. The majority of calls to a BBS are from the board's local calling area; for obvious reasons, computer users prefer to find what they want locally rather than spend money on long-distance telephone charges.

Commercial Online Services

Commercial online services may offer some or all of the same features of the average BBS (E-Mail, public message areas, and downloadable files), as well as any number of unique services.

Online services differ from BBSs in several ways. First, online services cost money. In contrast to the vast majority of BBSs, an online service is in business to make money. Online services operate on expensive mini- or mainframe computers (often more than one), and employ programmers, customer service representatives, and other specialists to keep things running smoothly.

Typically, an online service bills by the minute (which isn't as bad as it sounds; billing for non-prime time on an online service is quite often less than per-minute rates for a long-distance voice telephone call). Certain kinds of online services bill by the access—a flat rate for a data base search, for example.

Second, online services provide services and features offered by few (or no) BBSs: multiple-user real-time conferencing, personal file areas, and access to FAX and Telex service, databases, news services, and other services.

Online services are national in scope, and are often accessed via packet-switching networks (SprintNet, Tymnet, and/or the service's own private network). A packet-switching network is nothing more than a nationwide (or worldwide) network of computers, strategically located in various cities, whose job is to route data between your computer and a "host" computer (an online service's computer).

Packet switching networks provide a way for you to call a distant host computer without incurring long-distance charges. In practice, you dial a local telephone number, connect with the packet network computer and tell it to which service you wish to be connected, and the packet network computer connects with the online service via its own system of dedicated phone lines. There is a charge for such access, but it is normally built into an online service's fees.

■ ■ ■

As should be obvious now, portable PC communications can make your work, hobby, and personal activities more efficient in many ways. And no matter how you approach it, you'll find telecomputing fascinating—and just plain fun.

Now, on to Chapter 2, where we'll take a look at what you need to get started.

2

Laptop Basics for Portable Telecomputing

This chapter addresses various elements of a laptop computer's configuration. Although laptop computers and their overall capabilities are not the focus of this book, I'll cover some basics for the sake of discussions later in the book. I'll also offer advice regarding laptop features and telecomputing, for those who may be contemplating buying a laptop for the first time, or replacing an older unit.

Operating Systems and CPUs

Operating Systems
Your computer's operating system is among its most important elements, because it dictates the kinds of programs you can run. This book concentrates on MS-DOS computers. This is no accident; most laptops are MS-DOS computers. It also happens that MS-DOS computer users constitute a majority in the online world. This means there are more online products and services for MS-DOS computers than other systems.

In support of the preceding, at least one major online service, GEnie, tells me that more than half its members use MS-DOS computers—a decided majority. Usage on most other systems—including microcomputer-based BBSs—seems to mirror this.

The preponderance of MS-DOS computers online is supported by the fact that front-end programs for specific services (CompuServe's CIM and GEnie's Aladdin, among others) are almost always made available for MS-DOS computers first. Sometimes such programs are available only for MS-DOS computers. Then there are the online services that can be accessed only with front-end programs. Most are limited to certain kinds of computers, and most accommodate MS-DOS computers.

All of which is not to say you can't be happy telecomputing with, say, a Macintosh PowerBook. (And, I should add, you will find this book useful no matter what kind of equipment you have. Much of the information herein applies to portable telecomputing in general.) But you will find a greater variety of online products and services, and a broader selection of telecomputing hardware and software for MS-DOS machines.

Within the DOS world, there are schisms over the various operating systems available: MS-DOS (or PC-DOS for IBM's machines), OS/2, CP/M, UNIX, OS-9, and DR DOS. Unless you like tinkering with software to get it to work properly, or tracking down obscure programs from obscure sources, MS-DOS or PC-DOS is the way to go. More software is written to operate under MS-DOS than any of the other operating systems.

Which Version of MS-DOS? When it comes to deciding which version of MS-DOS to use, the best answer is generally "the newest." However, if your laptop doesn't have a newer version of DOS, don't worry—as long as you have at least Version 3.3 of MS-DOS, you can use most DOS communications programs.

MS-DOS Version 4.1 adds a few advantages, paramount among them the ability to recognize more than 32K of disk space. This means you don't have to partition a large hard disk into two or more disks. Version 5 provides more advantages, mainly related to multitasking and the command environment.

Overall, the version of DOS you use is a matter of taste, and shouldn't affect telecomputing all that much.

I should note that some laptops have MS-DOS "built-in," in ROM, and upgrading involves replacing ROM (no upgrade is available for some such machines). If the laptop has a hard disk, however, you should be able to install a newer version of DOS on the disk and set the machine up to boot from the hard disk rather than ROM.

Which CPU is Best?

A computer's CPU is an integral part of its operating system, and the CPU in your machine dictates your system's speed, how it uses available memory, and sometimes whether you can use certain programs.

CPU speed is an immediate consideration. An 8088- or 8086-based computer has a much slower operating speed than a machine based on a 80286, 80386, or 80486 chip (commonly known as 286, 386, and 486, respectively). Speed is a critical factor with very large communications programs. Slow processing can mean long waits while program overlays or modules are loaded. It can also slow down file-transmission and disk read/write operations. If you use a front-end program for a graphics-based online service of the sort I'll be discussing later, you may be in for excruciatingly long waits for screens to be displayed with slow systems.

The operating system and programs you can use may be limited by the CPU. You won't be able to run Windows 3.1 or DESQview 386 on an 8088 laptop, for example. And some newer communications programs are designed with a 386 or 486 processor in mind. Also, low-end processors may not be able to handle communications programs and memory-resident programs together.

Also of importance is the fact that 80386, 386SX, and 80486 machines have memory management features that let them address more than the simple 640K of RAM that the PC, XT, and AT computers (8088 and 80286) recognize. (More on memory in a few lines.) In practice this means that, if you have a 386 machine, there doesn't have to be any practical difference between extended memory and expanded memory; the 386 is perfectly capable of operating the same with either, or both. (DESQview on the 386, for instance, can not only swap programs into extended memory, but can also run them from there. You'll need a 386 memory management program such as Quarterdeck's Expanded Memory Manager 386 [QEMM], but that's a detail.)

Obviously, the answer to "Which processor...?" is "The newest and fastest," if you want to use the newest and fastest software and/or multitasking and graphical interfaces. But, as with DOS and other elements of your system, you don't have to have the newest and fastest CPU—one of the reasons this book exists is to show you how to get the most out of what you have.

Memory

In the DOS world, it sometimes seems that RAM is everything. When you look at the programs you run on your desktop machine, you may feel you'd be helpless without at least a couple of megabytes of extended memory in your laptop. But this isn't the case; you probably won't use all those memory-intensive programs on your laptop. The standard 640K of RAM (known as "conventional memory") that low-end laptop computers offer is fine for most telecomputing applications. Most popular DOS communications programs require less than 640K, and the low-end graphical user interfaces, such as DeskMate and GeoWorks Ensemble, are designed to operate in a 640K-or-less environment.

Similarly, dedicated front-end programs for online services (Prodigy, America Online, etc.) are designed to work with a minimal system.

Unless you have to run Windows or applications that require extra RAM to run efficiently, you can get by fine with 640K of RAM. If you have extended or expanded memory, however, you can take advantage of programs that use RAM for swap files, as well as memory-resident programs and utilities that speed up operation.

Extended Memory Many MS-DOS laptops come with 1024K of RAM—640K of conventional memory and 640K of what is called Extended Memory, or XMS for short. Not many programs use that extra 640K, however. Extended memory can be useful for print spooling and as a RAM disk, but it is not managed, which is to say that programs cannot grab and reserve areas of that extra memory. The result is that programs can, in theory, use extended memory, but you can run only one such program at a time. Memory-resident programs ("terminate-and-stay-resident," or TSR programs) can use XMS, but there are often difficulties.

In operation, XMS fools the computer (which doesn't know the memory is there) into looking at a particular area of extended memory when it thinks it's looking at a chunk of its own conventional memory. If that's confusing, don't worry about it; the upshot is that it works—in some applications. In practical terms, the only useful things you can do with extended memory are disk caching and making RAM disks, and perhaps running TSR programs.

Expanded Memory A more useful memory development is expanded memory, also known as Expanded Memory Specification, or EMS. Expanded memory is RAM above and beyond the 1024K provided by conventional memory and XMS. EMS lets you run programs in high memory (i.e., above the 1-megabyte or 1024K address area). Many newer communications programs make use of EMS (GEnie's Aladdin front end is one that comes to mind). Such programs run faster, and there's plenty of room for TSR programs.

EMS is pretty much a requirement for DESQview or Microsoft Windows, which use the memory to store parts of themselves or their applications. This speeds up and enhances multitasking and task-switching.

Displays

If you've spent much time using a laptop computer, you know how important the display can be. Your laptop's display is particularly important in telecomputing, because when you're online you have to look at a lot of scrolling text. In the case of graphic front ends, you'll be dealing with rapidly changing graphics and text. If the display has slow decay (slow replacement of an existing image with a new image), you may find that it seems much slower when you're online because you have to wait for the "ghosts" of old lines of text to fade before you can see new lines clearly.

Due to size, weight, and cost constraints, laptop displays are generally of lower quality than those of desktop computers. The resolution is not as fine, and the skewed aspect ratio of some screens may distort familiar applications. This is something all laptop users have to live with, but there are several things you can do to make a laptop screen more readable, as you will learn later.

Resolution

A display's resolution depends in large part on the number of picture elements it uses per square inch. (Or, if you're considering text only, the number of picture elements in the width and height of a character.) A picture element, or "pixel" for short, is the smallest possible element on the screen; a single pixel will appear as a dot. (To give you an idea of a pixel's size, a period is typically composed of two or four dots on CGA or EGA monitors, respectively.)

The basic idea is the same used to display text and graphics on your desktop computer's monitor. The tiny pixels are activated in certain patterns that correspond to letters and numbers, specific shapes, and graphic characters and images. The image is not as fine as that displayed on a regular monitor, however, because the pixels are larger and not as close together. As far as resolution is concerned, the comparison is similar to the outputs of a 6-pin and a 24-pin dot-matrix printer. The more pixels, or dots, in a given screen area, the higher the resolution.

A monitor's resolution is more often measured by the number of pixels it can display horizontally and vertically (rather than by pixels per inch or the number of pixels in the width and height of a character, as is the case with printer output). For reference, here's a sampling of the numbers of horizontal and vertical pixels various PC displays offer:

- Monochrome: 720 × 350
- CGA: 320 × 200, or 640 × 200
- EGA: 320 × 200, or 640 × 200, or 640 × 350
- VGA: 320 × 240, or 320 × 400, or 640 × 320, or 640 × 480, or 720 × 480
- Super VGA: 800 × 600

Other resolutions are possible with most display types. (Note that the majority of monochrome laptop monitors emulate

CGA, which means you should set up your communications software for a "CGA monitor." More on how this works later.)

Display Size and Aspect Ratio

The size of a display, of course, dictates the size of the characters it can display. Obviously, you'll want as large a display as possible, for ease of viewing. The average laptop's display is around 8 inches by 5 inches, which means the characters it displays are somewhat smaller than those displayed on the average 14-inch monitor, with both displaying the standard 25 lines by 80 columns.

You can compensate for this with certain software I'll discuss later in this chapter, but that software won't work with all programs you wish to use.

Roughly defined, the aspect ratio is the ratio of the width to the height of an image. Generally, laptop displays "squash" an image. They provide an image width and height that do not have the same relative proportions as those of a standard desktop monitor. While the width is near that of a desktop monitor, the height is less, by 25 percent or more. Thus, a circle would appear somewhat flattened. This generally doesn't affect the readability of text, beyond giving the lines the appearance of being crowded.

Display Types

There are several types of displays, in terms of the technology used. I'll describe several here, in brief.

Liquid-Crystal Displays Most laptops use a liquid-crystal display, or LCD. This is the same basic technology that's been used for watch and pocket calculator displays for years. LCD displays are lightweight, and have relatively low power requirements—perfect for use with laptop computers.

Most LCD displays are monochrome, meaning they have basically one color—a dark foreground color displayed against a light background. The typical LCD display works by darkening pixels on a light background. The nature of the liquid crystals is such that they darken when an electric current passes through them.

All but the oldest LCD displays vary the intensity of the darkening based on the amount of current applied, to create shades of the foreground color. LCD displays use various shades the same way a green or amber monochrome desktop monitor shows different "colors."

The resulting image is fairly easy to see if the display is large enough, and if you have good lighting. You can change an LCD display's contrast (lighten or darken the background or foreground) by moving a contrast adjustment wheel, or by changing the viewing angle. However, a normal monochrome LCD display emits absolutely no light, so you cannot use it in low light conditions. Such a display may be difficult to view under certain other lighting conditions—like bright sunlight. Early laptops that used black-on-gray LCD displays, like Toshiba's T-1100, are perhaps the most difficult to view.

Laptop manufacturers were quick to address the lighting problem with a newer technology that enabled what are called "backlit" LCD displays. A backlit display adds liquid crystals that emit light, for either the foreground or the background. Thus, you can see a backlit display, even in the dark.

Nowadays, most LCD displays use a refined LCD technology (called *supertwist*) that makes for lighter and smaller displays that deliver greater resolution. The greater resolution is accomplished by putting more pixels in a given area on the screen.

Figures 2.1 and 2.2 show normal monochrome and backlit monochrome LCD displays on laptop computers.

There is a further distinction among LCD technologies, involving how and how quickly pixels are switched on and off. The older, slower technology is passive-matrix, in which pixels are switched one row at a time to reflect changes in the image transmitted. This can result in slow decay and difficulty in reading scrolling text. The newer technology is active-matrix, with individual controllers (diodes or transistors) to switch pixels on and off. This is faster, but a more expensive proposition.

Color LCD Displays Color LCD displays are available, and have generally good resolution (pocket-size television receivers use them), but until recently they were rare in laptop computers,

Laptop Basics for Portable Telecomputing 33

Figure 2.1 Monochrome LCD Display

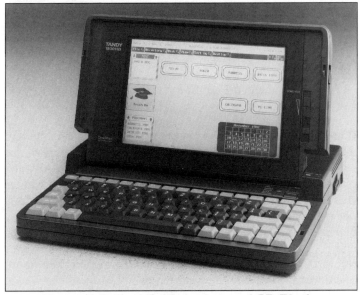

Figure 2.2 Backlit Monochrome LCD Display

largely because of cost. Expect color LCD displays to become very common as increasing demand results in lower costs.

Color displays use both passive- and active-matrix displays. As with monochrome displays, active-matrix delivers the best quality, but at a higher cost. Figure 2.3 shows a color LCD display.

Figure 2.3 Color LCD Display

Gas-Plasma Displays Gas-plasma displays were a hot item in the mid-1980s, being the only alternative to LCD displays for laptops, and offering much higher resolution. Gas-plasma displays use an ionized gas and a grid of electrodes to produce sharply defined pixels. These displays also allow more pixels per inch, which means letters and graphics are smoother and better-defined. When current is applied to an electrode—one electrode constitutes a pixel—the gas at that point glows, or fluoresces. The intensity of the glow can be varied by the amount of current applied, to achieve different shades.

Laptop Basics for Portable Telecomputing   35

Gas-plasma displays are widely available in monochrome, the foreground color being orange. They are rather expensive, and some require much more power than LCD displays. Color gas-plasma displays are hitting the market, but will probably not be as common as color LCD displays for some time, due to higher cost and power requirements.

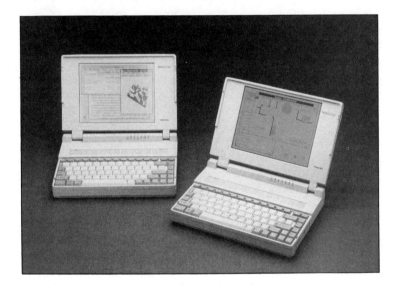

Figure 2.4 Gas-Plasma Display (right)

Improving the View

The photos in Figures 2.1, 2.2, 2.3, and 2.4 are provided by the respective manufacturers, and of course show the displays at their optimum. Lighting conditions, contrast settings, and viewing angle can be altered to improve the clarity of a laptop's screen. Still, it is difficult to see the cursor on many LCD screens. For those who have difficulty finding the cursor on laptop displays, I suggest two programs: No-Squint II and REDline. (Windows users can't use those—but I've an answer for Windows.) Those who have difficulty with the relatively small characters on a laptop display will find some relief while word processing with a program called Eye Relief.

No-Squint II No-Squint II lets you adjust the cursor's blink rate (laptop cursors are notorious for having a fast blink rate) and toggle it between an underscore or a solid, one-character size block. This saves you the aggravation and time you might waste looking for the cursor while running an application. You'll thank yourself for getting No-Squint, or any of several other commercial, public domain, or shareware programs that perform the same function. I recommend No-Squint in particular because it is compatible with more programs than any of its competitors. (No-Squint II is a product of Ken Skier's SkiSoft Publishing Corporation.)

Redlining Text DynaCorp's REDline takes another approach to making the cursor easy to spot. It highlights the entire line where the cursor is in inverse video, and then highlights the cursor in a lighter shade, or none at all. The dark line-highlight lets you find the cursor fast, though it may be obtrusive in some applications.

And a Better Cursor for Windows . . . Windows users cannot, of course, use a program such as No-Squint II or REDline. For Windows, I recommend a nifty shareware program that lets you design your own cursor for use within Windows: Jim Seidman's CHANGE CURSOR utility. You can download this from any of the major online services or a local BBS, or (better yet) contact Seidman directly at the address in Appendix B.

Eye Relief Eye Relief is a word processor that lets you magnify the text on your screen to two, three, or four times normal size. What's more, Eye Relief produces standard ASCII text files, which you can easily import into another word processor, upload to another computer via modem, or transfer via null-modem. It also works with existing ASCII text files—E-mail messages you've captured on disk, for example. The number of characters across and lines on a given screen are limited as you increase the magnification, but it's no big deal to scroll through more screen pages when you have the benefit of being able to see everything clearly. Eye Relief is published by SkiSoft, publishers of No-Squint II.

Hard and Floppy Disks

An expensive rarity just a few years ago, a hard disk is a common feature of today's laptop computers. Note that a hard disk is not an absolute necessity. You can run many programs on a single floppy disk, and I'll show you how to minimize a program to do just that in a later chapter. But, while you can get quite a bit done with one or two 720K floppy disks, everything is so much easier if you have a hard disk. The major benefits of a hard disk versus floppies are probably what you might expect:

- Faster disk access.
- You don't have to swap disks.

Not having to swap disks also means you don't have to carry a lot of floppy disks when you travel. That's probably the most important consideration for travelers.

If you do go with a floppy-disk-based laptop, get two drives; you'll need one for programs and the other for data disks. (While you can trim many programs to run on a single floppy, as I mentioned, that doesn't always leave room for data.)

Internal Versus External Hard Disks

If you don't think you need a hard disk at the time you buy a laptop, but may later, go ahead and buy the hard disk. If you can't do that, have an internal hard disk installed when you do get around to getting a hard disk. There are external hard disks available for laptops, but they are a chore to carry around and hook up.

Certain laptops can't accommodate an internal hard drive; there are external hard disks designed for such machines, and you'll find them listed in Appendix B. Otherwise, the only advantage of a portable external hard drive is being able to share it and its data between your laptop and desktop machines.

RAM Disks

A RAM disk is a fictional disk drive (also called a virtual disk drive) that exists only in your computer's RAM, and only when the computer is turned on. (An exception to the latter can be found in computers that have battery-backed RAM.)

RAM disks are built into many laptop computers. For instance, computers that have 768K of RAM use 128K of dedicated RAM for a RAM disk. All PC laptops come with a RAM disk, in any event—it's included in the DOS utilities, as RAMDRIVE.SYS or VDISK.SYS. This utility lets you allocate a specific area of the standard 640K RAM or expanded memory as a RAM disk. So, no matter what kind of PC laptop you have, you can have a RAM disk. (These are easily activated by a line in your computer's CONFIG.SYS file, and you can change the size of the virtual disk. See your DOS manual for information and instructions on using these.)

RAM disks have a few drawbacks. They seem like a good idea for many applications, but they aren't a good place to store data on a routine basis. If you use a RAM disk to store data, the data are vulnerable to power losses, or (more likely) to your forgetting they are there when you turn off your computer. Too, RAM disks use memory that a program might require, or which might enable a program to perform better.

If you have a lot of RAM, in extended or expanded memory, you can set up a virtual disk drive and copy your communications program's files to it. This will speed up the program's operation considerably.

The major application for a small RAM disk (like the 128K dedicated RAM I mentioned earlier) in telecomputing is in file transfer (this is the only thing for which I use a RAM disk in my laptop). For the same reason a program runs faster from a RAM disk (disk "reading" and "writing" isn't bogged down by drive mechanics), files transfer faster.

Power Supplies

Power supplies and battery life are items of major interest to laptop users. The requirements for laptop AC power supplies are simple: They should be lightweight and easy to connect,

Laptop Basics for Portable Telecomputing 39

have long cords, and designed so they recharge batteries as quickly as possible.

Battery requirements for laptops are a little more complex. The days when you could pop four low-cost AA cells into a laptop and work for days are long gone. Disk drives and displays are real power eaters, and conventional throwaway or rechargeable chemical batteries just don't provide the power a laptop needs to run for hours. Virtually all laptops use internal rechargeable batteries, each designed for a specific type of machine. (This helps the aftermarket business; many laptop power-users like to carry a spare charged battery to extend their computers' portable life. You may also want to invest in a battery charger—but make sure it will work with your computer's batteries first.)

In any event, rechargeable batteries are something of a two-edged sword; they free the laptop user from power supplies, but for limited periods (two to eight hours) and at a cost. The cost is the time it takes to recharge a battery—anywhere from six to fifteen hours.

Because laptops are often used where there is no AC power source, the time you get out of a rechargeable battery is an important issue in selecting and using a laptop. Battery life is determined by three factors: the battery technology, power-management features and peripherals in use, and how you use your laptop.

Battery technology improves yearly, amidst some controversy over whether NiCad or lead-acid batteries are best. I'll refrain from comment on that issue, but observe that performance is getting better and better, no matter what kind of battery is used. Where the Tandy 1400 HD I bought in 1990 has a battery that gives two hours per charge and requires fifteen hours to recharge, newer laptops with hard drives boast double the battery life and half the charging time. I expect we'll see similar improvements in laptop battery performance over the next two years.

Note that manufacturers' battery life claims are based on optimums. This means the length of time a manufacturer says its laptop will operate on a fully charged battery is based on certain minimum number of disk accesses, and with power-management features active. How much time you get will vary, based on your system's configuration and how you use it. In general, though, you can figure on a battery lasting at least 80 percent of the optimum time a manufacturer specifies.

Saving Battery Life

The only way to be completely independent of electrical outlets is to buy several extra batteries, and recharge all well in advance of the planned sessions away from electrical outlets. This is time-consuming and expensive, but it's the only way. (I do recommend that you carry one extra battery—fully charged. This can be a real lifesaver when it comes to unexpected demands or a problem with a battery.)

Power-Management Features Otherwise, plan on maximizing your system's battery life in several ways. First, make sure the laptop you buy has power-management features to reduce battery drain. These include:

- An automatic screen blanking feature that turns off the display after a set number of minutes pass with no keyboard activity. (You can get commercial and shareware programs to do this, as well.)

- If your laptop has a hard drive, make sure it has a "power-down" feature to shut off the hard drive's motor after a set time with no access. You'll have to wait a second or two for the hard drive to come back to speed after sitting idle, but the savings in battery life will be worth it.

- System power-down. A number of laptops offer this battery-saving convenience, which shuts down your display, hard drive, and certain other elements after a set time with no keyboard or disk activity. The CPU is still "alive" and all your data and programs are still in RAM, but these require minimal power.

- "Trickle charging." A few laptops do not recharge their batteries when the computer is connected to its AC power supply and turned on. Avoid such laptops; make sure your machine does a trickle charge, sending a small amount to the battery to recharge it while you are using the computer.

Personal Power Management Become a power-conscious user: Don't leave your laptop on for long periods without using it, and see what kinds of activities involving disk activity you can cut down on (directory scans and the like).

Monitoring Battery Life There are several products on the market that monitor battery life. I can't speak for shareware programs of this type, although I've heard good things about one called "GASGAUGE." On the commercial side, Battery Watch II, from Traveling Software, is about the best available, in terms of the systems it works with and what it does. In addition to monitoring your batteries and telling you how much time you have left, Battery Watch II eliminates the "memory" that NiCad batteries have, so each recharge is a complete recharge. It has several other interesting features, as well.

Modems and Batteries It may or may not come as a surprise to you to learn that an internal modem is an extra drain on a battery. Internal modems draw their power from the host computer, and can reduce battery life by 25 percent or more (external modems are another matter, having their own power supplies). So, figure on an internal modem reducing the time you have between battery recharges.

■ ■ ■

Those are the basic considerations for using a laptop computer for communications. Now, on to communications hardware and communications and support software in Chapters 3 and 4.

3
Portable Communications Hardware

Modems: An Introduction

Personal computer communication via modem is commonly referred to as "dialup" communication. For this, you need a dialup modem. (Dialup modems are technically known as *asynchronous communications adaptors*. The "asynchronous" part has to do with the fashion in which they exchange data; dialup modems don't use the precise timing to synchronize data bits being sent that more expensive leased-line modems use. Hence, "asynchronous," which means not synchronous.)

Dialup modems are serial communications devices. This means you connect a modem to your computer's serial port. (Fortunately, it's rare that a PC laptop computer doesn't come with a serial port.)

How Modems Work—In Brief

It's not the purpose of this book to provide a complete technical background in telecommunications, but you might benefit from some basic knowledge of how modems work.

A modem is a device whose primary job is translating data. When a modem sends to another modem, it translates computer data into a form suitable for transmission over normal, voice-grade telephone lines. When it receives, it translates data into a form compatible with its computer's internal operating system.

For future reference, data inside a computer are in *binary* format; when they are transmitted over a phone line, the modem translates the data into what is called *analog* format.

V.32 and All that Jazz: Modem Standards Of special importance here is how modems convert and communicate data via phone lines. Data translation and communication techniques involve several factors, paramount among them speed, error checking and retransmission, pseudofile compression, and how a modem modulates (puts data on) a signal.

There are standards for each speed, and for error-checking and other modem features. Note that the speed at which a modem transmits data is measured by the number of data bits it transmits each second. This is commonly referred to as "bits per second," shortened to *bps*. Bps is often and erroneously referred to as "baud."

The first modem standards used in the U.S. were Bell 103 and Bell 212A. These were established by Bell Laboratories for 300- and 1200-bps modems, respectively. At the same time, an international organization called the CCITT (the Consultive Committee on International Telephony and Telegraphy) had established settings in use in Europe and elsewhere outside the U.S. By the time 2400-bps modems came on the scene there was enough of a demand for modems that could be used to communicate with systems overseas that American manufacturers began following the CCITT's standards.

These standards, which are referred to as V.xx (where xx is a number, as in V.32) and V.xx *bis* are the source of quite a bit of confusion among modem buyers. Some standards refer to the modem's highest operating speed, others to error checking and file compression.

Modem standards are misunderstood by many computer users. If you don't understand what is meant when a modem is billed as complying to or using a particular standard, you can end up buying the wrong modem. Thus, the explanation of modem standards in Table 3.1:

Table 3.1 CCITT Modem Standards

Speed	Domestic (U.S.)	International
300 bps	Bell 103	V.21
1200 bps	Bell 212A	V.22
2400 bps	V.22bis	V.22bis
9600 bps (& 4800)	V.29	V.29
	V.32	V.32
	V.32bis	V.32bis
Error-checking	V.42	V.42
Pseudo-file compression	V.42bis	V.42bis

Note that the domestic and international standards for modems operating at 2400 bps and up are the same. Also, a modem typically operates not only at its highest rated speed, but also at all lower speeds.

A few words of explanation on V.42 and V.42bis are in order. Neither has to do with a modem's speed. V.42 is a standard that specifies the kind of error correction a modem uses (in this case, a technique referred to as LAP/M, with some modems using MNP 4 for a backup). With V.42bis, the suffix *bis* denotes the ability to use pseudofile compression during transmission, which makes for effectively higher data-transfer rates.

It is important to know that V.42 and V.42bis can apply to 1200-bps and 2400-bps modems, as well as to 9600-bps modems. Thus, V.42bis does not necessarily imply a V.42, 9600-bps modem.

By now, you're probably wondering what "pseudofile compression" might be. Basically, it's a data transmission technique that involves reducing the amount of data that have to be sent to transfer a file by eliminating redundant data. This usually quadruples the transmission speed. (MNP 5 is an alternate technique used to reduce redundant data. Although not a CCITT specification like V.42bis, it is fairly common.)

The actual increase in speed depends on how much redundant data there is. (An exception is when you're handling files that have little or no redundant data. An archived file—one created with PKZIP, for instance—has little or no redundant data. Trying to transmit such a file with this technique can slow down the file transfer.)

Again, as noted in Table 3.1, V.42 and V.42bis do not automatically mean 9600 bps! V.42 and V.42bis can be used with a 2400-bps modem. So, beware of V.42bis modems offered at ultra-low prices; some are 2400-bps modems, rather than the 9600-bps modems that advertising would imply. These modems will communicate at 9600 bps—but only when connected with a similarly equipped modem. (They can achieve an effective data transmission speed of up to 9600 bps by removing redundant data.)

In any event, your modem should follow one or more of the domestic or international standards in the table, as appropriate for its communications speed. If a modem doesn't use the appropriate standard for the speed and other parameters at which you wish to communicate, it may not be able to communicate with many systems.

Beware, too, of modems that use "proprietary" communications protocols. Companies such as USRobotics, Hayes, CompuCom, and others have all marketed modems that use their own standards to communicate at high speeds. Such modems may advertise 9600-bps operation, but achieve it *only* when communicating with another modem from the same manufacturer. If a high-speed modem uses a proprietary standard, as is the case with USRobotics' HST modems, be sure it also uses a "conventional" standard, so it can communicate with other manufacturers' modems. (For example, the "dual-standard" version of the USRobotics HST modem also offers more conventional V.32 operation.)

To sum all this up, when you buy a modem, it should conform to the standards listed in Table 3.2.

Table 3.2 Buying a Modem: Standards

Speed	Applicable Standard
9600	V.32
2400	V.22bis
1200	V.22 and Bell 212A
300	V.21 and Bell 103

The modem may have *features* such as those specified by the V.42 and V.42bis standards, and proprietary communications protocols—HST, for example—but it must conform to the appropriate CCITT standard for its speed.

Most modems operate at all standard speeds below their maximum speeds. Thus, a 9600-bps modem also operates at 2400, 1200, and 300 bps.

Modems for Laptops

The most important considerations when buying a modem for a laptop computer are:

- conformance to standards;
- operating speed;
- error-checking and file-compression features; and
- whether the modem is internal or external.

The preceding discussion of standards gave you a guide of what to look for in that area. As for the other considerations, read on.

9600 or 2400?

As of this writing, the majority of BBSs in the U.S. operate at a maximum speed of 2400 bps. That will change by mid-1993, when demand reduces prices for 9600-bps modems to a level that most BBS sysops can afford. At the same time, most online services are upgrading to maximum operating speeds of 9600 bps. There's a catch, however; 9600-bps access is surcharged, meaning users pay (as of this writing) anywhere from $8.00 to $12.00 per hour extra for it.

The majority of online services don't levy a surcharge for 2400-bps access, but once did. The surcharge for 9600-bps access will be eliminated, eventually, just as the surcharge for 2400-bps access was, and for the same reasons. 9600-bps, V.32 modems will replace 2400-bps modems, just as 2400- and 1200-bps modems replaced 300-bps modems in the 1980s. This will be the natural result of competition and technological developments lowering prices. As 9600-bps modems move to the fore, online services will do away with surcharges, just as they did with surcharges for 2400-bps access. At present, however, the commercial services are paying for new equipment to handle 9600-bps calls, and/or packet-switching network surcharges for 9600-bps access.

Considering the fact that it costs a good deal more to use a 9600-bps modem with a commercial online service, and will for a couple years, do you want to buy a 9600-bps modem? The answer is "Yes." As I just showed, those 9600-bps access surcharges will eventually go away, and there will be a lot of BBSs you can call at 9600 bps. Also, if you intend to call your desktop computer with your laptop, putting a 9600-bps modem at each end of the connection makes sense; you're going to save more than a little in long-distance telephone charges.

It does makes sense to use a 9600-bps modem with a commercial online service when transferring files. When you're uploading or downloading files, a 9600-bps modem reduces file-transfer time by as much as 75 percent. So, even if you're paying double the normal access rate, you come out ahead.

Error Checking and File Compression

In its simplest form, data error checking by a modem involves a receiving modem checking groups of data bits against information transmitted about those groups by the sending modem. If a group of bits doesn't check out, the receiving modem asks the sending modem to retransmit that group of bits. The ins and outs of this and related components of error checking are fairly complex, so we won't get into all that here. However, you should know that the two most popular error-checking protocols used by modems are MNP 4 and LAP/M.

MNP 4 (an acronym for Microcom Networking Protocol) is the latest in a series of semistandards for error-checking by dialup modems. (There are others for cellular communications and other purposes.) It is implemented on more modems than not.

LAP/M (Link Access Procedure for Modems) is the error-checking protocol specified by the V.42 standard. Because not all 2400- and 9600-bps modems use LAP/M, modems that do use LAP/M have MNP 4 as a backup.

It is important to emphasize here that LAP/M and MNP 4 work only if modems at both ends of the connection have these features. V.42 modems with LAP/M are not very common at present, particularly among commercial online services, so you may not be gaining anything by buying a V.32 modem with V.42. However, considering the preponderance of MNP 4 on commercial online services and BBSs, you will probably find some advantage in having MNP 4. If you want to buy a V.42 modem, it won't hurt—just make sure it has MNP 4 as well as LAP/M because MNP 4 is a semistandard, thanks to its ubiquitousness.

I've already explained V.42bis pseudofile compression. But I do want to re-emphasize the fact that V.42bis doesn't work unless both modems in a connection are using it. Like LAP/M, V.42bis file compression is not all that common. So, you probably won't be missing much if your modem doesn't have V.42bis.

Internal or External?

Like modems for desktop computers, modems for laptop computers can be either internal or external. I highly recommend using an internal modem with a laptop computer, but this isn't always possible because of price constraints, lack of internal space, or the fact that no modems are made for a particular laptop.

(Note that many laptops have proprietary, nonstandard internal connections, or buses, which make it difficult or impossible to use just any modem card. Such laptops require an internal modem designed especially for them. This is the case with one of my favorite old laptops, a Tandy 1400 HD; it requires a modem sold only by Tandy. Similarly, Toshiba laptops require a specific internal modem—and not all Toshiba laptops use the same modem.)

Internal Portable Modems Internal portable modems are generally the same as their counterparts for desktop computers. They consist of a circuit board that connects with the computer via card-edge connectors, as shown in Figure 3.1.

An internal modem draws its power from its computer. Any other disadvantages aside, an internal modem is an additional

50 Portable Communications

Figure 3.1 Internal Modem

drain on a laptop computer's batteries. It's something of a trade-off—convenience in exchange for shorter laptop battery life.

On the other hand, an internal modem can be really convenient when you're in a situation where you don't have an extra plug for an external modem's power supply.

A big advantage of having an internal modem in your laptop is that you have one less item to carry around (or two or three fewer items, if you count a power supply and/or batteries). And you won't tie up your computer's serial port—an important consideration if you use a serial mouse. Also, you won't need a connecting cable with an internal modem. (Note that some external modems don't use cables, in any event; rather, you can plug them directly into your computer's serial port—provided the connectors match. More on this in a bit.)

NOTE: If your laptop computer has a serial port—and it should—you will most likely have to set up your communications software to communicate with a port other than COM1 (usually COM2, for an internal modem). This is because COM1 is the default serial port, and communications pro-

Portable Communications Hardware 51

grams try to communicate through COM1 by default. If you don't make this setup change, your software will try in vain to communicate with a port to which nothing is connected.

External Portable Modems External portable modems are less costly than internal portable modems, but, as mentioned, require their own power sources. Actually, if you have a place to plug in a modem's power supply when you're traveling, your desktop modem will serve as well as a portable modem. Of course, desktop modems are much larger than portable modems, as comparing the modem in Figure 3.2 with the average desktop modem will indicate.

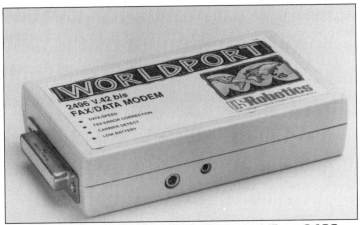

Figure 3.2 Touchbase Systems' WorldPort 2400 Portable Modem

Then there's the bother of removing and replacing the modem on your desktop, which you can avoid by buying a portable modem.

Almost all portable modems are battery-powered, in addition to having plug-in power supplies. This can be more than a convenience in some situations. Note, however, that portable modems are notorious "battery-eaters." A typical portable modem will drain a 9-volt battery in two hours or so.

Few portable modems have external indicators (an exception is the modem in Figure 3.2). These may be important; being able to see whether or not you have a carrier can be vital when you're having trouble getting a portable modem to make a connection.

Modem Features and Options

Many features and options are available with modems. Among the more useful are:

- the ability to dial phone numbers;
- tone- or pulse-dialing capability; and
- call status indicators (external modems).

Modems that offer dialing capability and other advanced features are called "intelligent." The number of features that a modem has isn't necessarily an indication of its quality, but the better-quality modems usually have more features than the bargain-basement kind.

The majority of dialup modems offer pretty much the same basic set of features, which also happen to be the features you want or, in some cases, must have. The following features will save you a lot of trouble. Make certain your modem has them.

- External dip switches, on an external modem. Dip switches are small switches used to set certain important operating parameters. Most operating parameters can be set internally with commands, but it's far easier to use dip switches, especially for settings you don't intend to change, like carrier detect.

- Variable communications parameters. This is almost a given; virtually all modems allow you to set the communications speed and other operating parameters. (Your software takes care of setting the modem's parameters, based on your software setup.)

- Autodial and auto-answer capability. These features let the modem dial a number without a telephone set by generating its own tones, and answer an incoming call.

- Tone- and pulse-dialing capability. These give the modem the ability to generate the tones used by Touch-

Portable Communications Hardware 53

Tone phones, and the pulses used by older rotary style phones.

- Compatibility with the AT or "Hayes" command set. The AT command set is a *de facto* standard among modems. It's used by almost all PC communications programs, too. If a modem doesn't use that command set you may find yourself stuck with entering commands manually, unless the program you're using is set up to accommodate the modem's command set. Commercial programs can handle a variety of modems, but it's a good idea to make sure the modem you're buying is either supported by your program or uses the AT command set.

  Note that almost no non-Hayes modems are 100 percent compatible with the Hayes command set; most manufacturers have devised their own "extended" command sets to handle things like storing number and parameter sets, enabling or disabling error correction, and other tasks.

- Dual telephone jacks. If you intend to set up your laptop for extended use with a phone line it will share with a voice phone you're using (say, in a hotel room), you will want dual telephone jacks on the modem. This lets you use either telephone or modem without plugging and unplugging phone lines. Plug the incoming phone line into one jack, and the telephone set into the other jack, and you're in business.

- Automatic hangup on carrier loss. This means the modem hangs up the telephone if the carrier tone generated by the modem to which it's connected stops. With this feature, you don't have to hang up your phone or send a hangup command to the modem manually before you can dial out again.

  I also recommend that you get a modem with a speaker you can turn down or off—either with an external control or through software commands. (Unless, that is, you don't mind hearing annoyingly loud dial tones every time you use your modem.) Most modems let you turn off the speaker with the command **ATM0**.

Additional features that may make telecomputing easier for you include:

- Automatic parameter and speed matching, which enables the modem to adjust its operating parameters and speed to match those of the modem it's calling. (This includes negotiating with the other modem which speed to use—normally the maximum speed of the slower modem, and which error-checking and data-compression protocols to use, if any.)

- Result codes, which the modem uses to report the status of a call—connection, ringing, voice answer, and other responses. The modem may use one- or two-word messages, or numeric codes. The kind of responses you get (verbose or numeric codes) should be settable.

- Changeable S-register values. S-registers store values that define various operating characteristics of a modem, such as whether result codes are displayed, various timeout periods for calling, how long the modem waits after carrier loss before hanging up, etc. When you're dialing through long-distance services, hotel or other switchboards, or making international calls, you'll sometimes need to change how your modem operates. Being able to set how long your modem will wait for a dial tone and how long it will hold the line when the remote system's carrier is interrupted are particularly important.

- Adaptive dialing, a feature that lets the modem know whether to use tone or pulse dialing.

- Built-in error checking and data compression, via MNP or other protocols.

EEPROM storage for telephone numbers and parameters is offered with many modems, but this is a bit overrated. You can store numbers and settings for recall with your software as easily as you can with a modem.

What You Need: Cables, Phone Hookups, and More

As noted earlier, a modem connects with your computer's serial port. Your laptop's serial port will have either 9 or 25 pins, configured in a D-shape. These are referred to as DB-9 and DB-25 connectors, respectively. Their configurations are shown in Figure 3.3.

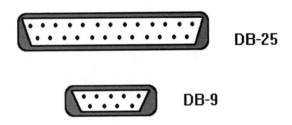

Figure 3.3 DB-9 and DB-25 Connectors

DB-9 and -25 connectors come in two varieties: male and female, distinguished by whether they have pins or sockets. To connect an external portable modem to your serial port, you need the same kind of connector (DB-9 or DB-25) on your modem cable and serial port, with one "male" and one "female."

Pin Adaptors and Gender Changers If your cable doesn't match the number of pins on your modem or your serial port, you can buy an adaptor. These have a DB-9 connector on one end, and a DB-25 connector on the other end, as shown in Figure 3.4.

You can get any combination of male/female connectors in this kind of adaptor.

If your cable type matches (DB-9 to DB-9 or DB-25 to DB-25), but the connectors don't match, you can fix the problem with what is called a "gender changer," like that shown in Figure 3.5.

Like adaptors, gender changers are available in any pin combination, so you can link two female connectors or two male connectors, as necessary.

56 Portable Communications

Figure 3.4 DB-9 to DB-25 Adaptor

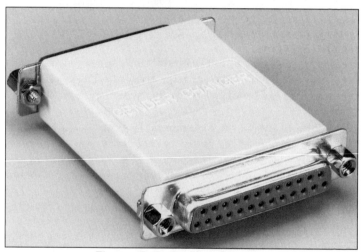

Figure 3.5 Gender Changer

Modem to Phone Connections In terms of how they connect with telephone lines, modems come in two basic types: acoustic and direct connect. Acoustic couplers connect with a telephone via rubber cups that fit over the telephone handset's earpiece and mouthpiece. An acoustic coupler is shown in Figure 3.6.

Figure 3.6 Acoustic Coupler

An acoustic coupler isn't a modem as such, but a conversion device. It converts incoming audio signals into analog data signals, which are in the format a modem expects. It does the reverse with outgoing data signals. Some modems come with an acoustic coupler, and you can buy a coupler to work with just about any kind of modem.

Direct connect modems connect with the telephone line directly, via a jack that accepts the common RJ-11 phone plug. Direct connect modems may be internal or external.

Each has its advantages and disadvantages, but for most applications a direct-connect modem is superior to an acoustic modem. In fact, your modem will probably be direct connect. It may come with an acoustic coupler. Or, you may have to buy an acoustic coupler for use with phones that don't offer RJ-11 jacks that you can plug into your modem. I'll discuss this in more detail in Chapter 5.

Portable Fax

Portable FAX is more than convenient for many PC users, with so much of today's business communications depending on FAX. While there are alternatives, one of which we'll explore in Chapter 7, many laptop users are adding FAX capability to their computers. Most portable PC FAX activity involves sending text, since few laptop users carry a scanner. This works out well, as portable PC FAX devices are geared toward creating and sending text (though they receive graphics easily enough). I should note that I'm referring to sending text from a text file here, as all FAX messages, even those containing only text, are graphic in nature.

What FAX is and How it Works, in Brief

FAX is verbal shorthand for "facsimile," which alludes to the process of electronically copying and transmitting textual and/or graphic images via telephone lines, and sending them as graphical data. The word FAX is also used to describe documents transmitted by facsimile machines, as well as the machines themselves.

FAX transmission is accomplished in a manner similar to that used by dialup modems. Digital data, provided by a scanner or by software used with FAX machines, is converted to analog data by a modem. The data are transmitted via telephone line to the receiving system, whose modem converts data back to the digital format used by the FAX machine or host computer, then printed or stored.

FAX modems use the same principles as dialup modems (varying frequencies and other signal elements to modulate, or place data on, a signal). However, they are not compatible with dialup modems. FAX modems, which operate at a maximum speed of 9600 bps, use a set of CCITT standards that is different from any used for dialup modems. (This is why you cannot send or receive FAX messages using a dialup modem.)

It is important that any FAX machine, card, or portable FAX device you use be compatible with what are called Group 3 FAX machines. This is the standard in most common use throughout the world. It's a safe bet that any PC FAX card or FAX/modem on the market is compatible with Group 3 machines, but it doesn't hurt to check. (A newer standard, Group 4, exists, but this is mainly for use with digital telephone systems.)

Portable PC FAX Devices

As implied, a portable FAX must use a FAX-type modem to communicate with FAX machines; this is built into the portable FAX device. The FAX device's main external connection (i.e., connection with a device other than the host computer itself) is a telephone line jack—an RJ-11 jack into which you can plug a telephone line. Other external connections may or may not be present, but the telephone line jack is present on every PC FAX board, since FAX communication is via telephone line.

Portable FAX devices come in two varieties: internal PC FAX boards and external portable FAXes. Figures 3.7 and 3.8 show a PC FAX board and a portable computer FAX.

A FAX board or portable FAX may come equipped with a dialup modem. This is almost always the case with external units, so I'll refer to that kind of unit from here on as a "FAX/modem."

FAX cards and portable computer FAXes work in conjunction with special software to convert computer-generated text and graphics into the format used by dedicated FAX, and to convert FAX transmissions it receives into the format used by its host computer. The software is normally provided with the FAX board or FAX/modem.

Figure 3.7 PC FAX Board

60 Portable Communications

Figure 3.8 Worldport 2496 Portable FAX/Modem

Internal or External? Whether you use an internal or external FAX device depends in large part on your laptop. As noted earlier, many laptops have special, not-quite-standard internal connections or buses. So you have to find a FAX card or FAX/modem card that is designed for the computer. Sometimes, you have to find a card that is designed for the specific model of a laptop you have. An example of this is the Holmes FAX'EM, which is a FAX card with dialup modem. This can be used with all Toshiba laptops, save for the T1000, T1100, and T3200.

As you might infer, you may not be able to find a FAX card for your particular laptop. In this case, you'll have to go with an external FAX/modem.

Other factors to consider in determining whether you use an internal FAX device include battery life (FAX cards draw their power from the host laptop, just like internal modems), the ability of your communications software to recognize another COM port (assuming you want a FAX card with a modem), and the importance of the convenience of not having to carry around an extra item.

If you use an external FAX/modem, be aware that battery life will be an issue; like portable modems, portable FAX/modems are real battery eaters.

Portable PC FAX Features and Options

One thing that's required to use a portable PC FAX device is a hard disk. The files that store incoming FAX messages can be up to 1 megabyte in size for 12 pages of text—more if graphics are involved. And the software that drives the FAX system takes up a good bit of disk space itself.

Software is of special importance when you're considering a PC FAX card or external FAX/modem. Software determines most of the features and options your FAX card offers. FAX software should come with any PC FAX you buy—it's far easier to use the FAX software you already know works with a particular FAX card or FAX/modem than it is to try to get software to work with a FAX. (This applies only to the software that handles FAX communications; I recommend that you use whatever communications software you like with the dialup modem.)

There are several basic features that FAX software should offer. These include:

- Being able to convert ASCII text files you've created with your favorite editor to send as FAX messages.

- A phone directory, in which you can store numbers for the FAX to dial up and communicate with.

- Printer interface, so you can print out FAX messages you've received.

On the hardware side, compatibility with your computer and with CCITT standards are of paramount importance. If you expect to switch between FAXing and using a voice telephone, dual telephone jacks will be of interest. FAX cards that offer a serial port and/or a scanner input port may be desirable for some users, too, although few people lug a scanner with them when traveling. And make sure the FAX device can receive as well as send; there are a number of send-only FAX cards and external FAX/modems on the market, but they won't meet your requirements if you need to receive FAX messages.

Among other desirable PC FAX features are:

- A built-in dialup modem, typically a 2400-bps modem with MNP 4 and 5.

- If you want background operation (true background operation, which lets you run other software and doesn't slow down your system) in a FAX card, it should have a co-processor.

- Multiple file format support, so you can read and forward incoming FAXes stored on disk, as well as graphic files you may have created in formats like .PCX. Support for .TIF files is important if you intend to send scanned documents. The software should either provide file conversion or be able to access files directly.

- Automatic cover sheets.

- The ability to send FAXes at a set time, and redial when the number called is busy.

- Software that can handle converting the text in a FAX message from graphics to a standard 7-bit ASCII text file.

Cellular Links

Cellular telephones are almost as ubiquitous as FAX machines, and like any telephone communications link, cellular phones provide a channel for data communications.

Cellular telephones offer a few specific problems. One is connecting with the hardware. Fortunately, the market is well-developed enough that modems and FAX machines designed for use with cellular telephones are available. These take care of the problems of physical connection (which can also be accommodated by special connection adaptors), as well as the problems caused by changes in line conditions.

I highly recommend that you buy a modem or FAX designed to work with a cellular telephone, rather than try to work with adaptors. If you decide to use your existing equipment, be aware that you will have to make some changes in your modem's setup so it will ignore dropped carriers. Cellular telephone systems transfer the communications carrier wave for a link from one antenna system to another—sometimes when you're not moving. This results in momentary carrier loss, of the kind which normally causes a modem to disconnect. I'll show you how to get around this and other cellular data communications problems in Chapter 5.

■ ■ ■

We'll discuss additional hardware for portable computing in general and telecomputing in particular in later chapters. For now, though, it's on to Chapter 4 and a close look at telecomputing software.

4
Portable Communications Software

You can't use a modem without communications software, but communications software isn't the only kind of software you need to think about. There are several kinds of support software to consider. Some are vital to certain operations, while others are conveniences. We'll discuss these, as well as communications software, in this chapter.

Communications Software: An Introduction

A communications program enables and enhances modem communications. It is a direct link between your computer and modem, which in turn is your pipeline to the remote system to which you're connected.

A communications program's primary job is to initiate and maintain a connection with another computer system through the computers' modems. Other basic tasks include taking care of such chores as setting communications parameters, displaying characters on the screen, and handling data transfers to and from a remote system. (The term "remote," by the way, always refers to the computer you're calling. Your computer is the "local" system. To someone on the other end of the connection, the terms are reversed.)

Often called terminal emulation software, or terminal software, communications software routes data and commands to and from the modem and instructs the modem, via communications parameter settings, to use proper protocol in communicating with another system. (Simply put, protocol is an agreed-upon procedure for *how* data are to be transferred.)

Communications software comes in three varieties: conventional communications programs, front ends for specific online services, and proprietary front-end programs required to access graphics-based online services.

Systems that display only text or limited graphics using IBM graphics characters are called "text-based." Systems that display bit-mapped graphics (graphics in any of a variety of shapes, like those sophisticated computer arcade games) are referred to as "graphic-based" systems. Text-based systems may be accessed using conventional communications programs or front ends; graphic-based programs require proprietary front-end programs.

Depending on the online service you're accessing, you may use "conventional" DOS communications software or a front-end program with text-based services, or a dedicated front-end program with graphics-based services. Text-based services include online services such as BIX, CompuServe, DELPHI, and GEnie, as well as BBSs. Examples of graphics-based services are America Online and Prodigy.

I'll take a closer look at front ends for both text- and graphics-based services in a few pages. For now, we'll concentrate on "standard" DOS communications software for text-based services. (Front ends perform many of the same tasks and have many of the same features as DOS communications programs.)

Using Communications Software: Operating Modes and Commands

Most communications programs offer two operating modes: command and terminal. In the command mode, anything you type is issued to the software. Most programs offer a command line or menus—or both—for typing or selecting commands (Mirror III and Crosstalk work this way). The kinds of commands you issue to a communications program include loading and running a command or script file, hanging up the modem, and setting communications parameters. You can issue or select commands while you're online, by pressing a command or attention key. The command key is a preset or assignable key (like Esc) or key-combination (like Ctrl-Z).

Some programs, among them Odyssey and PROCOMM PLUS, also let you use Alt- and/or Ctrl-key combinations to issue commands. Typical combinations are Alt-D to dial a number, Alt-H for "Help" or "Hangup," and Alt-X to exit the program. Several programs also make use of the PgUp and PgDn keys to initiate uploads and downloads, respectively.

In the terminal mode, what you type is sent to the modem. If you're offline, the modem looks for commands (typically "AT" commands) to tell it to dial (ATDT), hang up (ATH0), or set operating parameters. Once your modem has dialed up and connected with another modem, however, what you type goes *through* the modem to the remote system. The modem ignores anything you type—even recognized modem commands—unless you switch to the modem's command mode (typically by typing +++). This is not the same as the software command mode just described.

Communications Software Options

At the very least, your communications software should allow you to set communications speed and basic communications parameters. Communications parameters include the number of data bits (7 or 8), the parity for error-checking (even or odd), and the number of stop bits (normally 1). (The two most common parameter settings at any speed are 8/N/1 and 7/E/1.)

Your communications software package should also provide at least one binary file transfer protocol (such as Xmodem, Kermit, or Zmodem).

If you're entirely new to telecomputing, you may think you don't need certain features now, but you will as you spend more time online. So, it's best to find a program with as many features as possible, but still relatively easy to learn.

The better communications software packages offer a variety of enhancements, including:

- The ability to handle multiple uploads and downloads automatically, with batch-file protocols like Zmodem.

- Autodial and redial capability.

- Macros and function-key assignments, which you can use to send multiple commands to a remote system with one keystroke.

- Dialing directories, which store numbers and parameter settings.

- Autologon capability, which means a program performs all the steps necessary to dial up and sign on to another system.

- Script-file capability. Script files use a simplified programming language to let you write scripts, or sets of commands, that the program can follow to send and receive E-mail, transfer files, and perform other tasks without your interaction. Combined with a dialing directory (or a file with a similar function called a command file), from which it draws information for dialing up and signing on to a system, script files can completely automate your online sessions.

- A review and capture buffer, so you can look back at text that's scrolled by online, and capture it if you wish.

- A pop-up editor that you can use to create messages for upload, or to view text files while online. (This replaces the old TSR programs like Sidekick, uncluttering RAM.)

As I've indicated previously, your software selection is limited (or determined) in large part by the type of computer you own and its configuration, the modem you use, and by your budget. Thus, you may not be able to have all the gosh-wow features dreamed up for various software packages, but use the more common features just discussed as a guide in selecting your software.

NOTE: If you use certain communications programs, you may find some of what I say here about script and command files confusing. Different programs call the same things different names—a function of competition and trying to maintain a separate identity, I suppose. One program's dialing directory is another's command file, for example. Similarly, one program may split the duties of a command file between two kinds of files. I have no control over what software publishers call these files, nor how they design their programs, so I'll just provide some thumbnail descriptions of what various kinds of files do, by way of defining the names as I use them.

(Check your communication software's manual for the names and extensions of the files that do the jobs described below.)

Command Files. A command file stores information used by a communications program and its script files. Depending on how a program is set up, there may be one command file for all script files, or a separate command file to match each script file. A command file's initial function is to provide the information the main communications program needs to set communications parameters and dial a number. It may also send commands to the program to set screen color and other operating elements.

A secondary function of a command file is to provide information used by the script file in issuing commands. Except for the initial dial command, however, it does not issue commands as such; that is the job of the script file.

Setup File. A "setup" file stores data on system configuration and operating parameters. The information in a setup file tells a program how to interact with your computer's hardware, as well as how to perform certain operations. This information might be shared with a command file, or might be substituted for a command file. Setup files are often used by a program for source information when setting up a command file.

Parameter Files. Parameter files are similar to command files in that they store telephone numbers and communications parameters. They save you the trouble of setting communications parameters every time you dial a system, although you still have to issue the dialing command and go through the sign-on process manually.

A parameter file is usually created by saving to disk the current parameter settings and giving the file a descriptive name such as DELPHI.PRM or BIX.PRM. Some programs create parameter files by entering the parameters and telephone number in a listing. Such a file may contain parameters and numbers for one system, or for a group of systems.

Dialing Directories. A dialing directory may store telephone numbers and communications parameters, or it may store telephone numbers only. Numbers (and parameters, if included) are usually stored in a "directory" format, accessible by name. With the proper command, the program will retrieve a specified number from a directory file and direct the modem to dial it. (Some programs only retrieve the number, after which you must enter the dial command.) If your program uses a dialing directory, it may allow you to use an associated script file with dialing directory entries.

Which Communications Program?

Unless you use only one online service and its front end, you will need a conventional communications program. You'll probably use this program more than front ends, so the selection process is important.

As with computers and modems, I can't recommend one program over all others; there's just too much out there. However, I lean toward Crosstalk's COMMUNICATIONS and Mirror III for neophytes, followed by PROCOMM PLUS. Most intermediate and advanced users will find Crosstalk Mk.4, Mirror III, a newer program called Odyssey, or PROCOMM PLUS more than enough to meet their needs.

(Odyssey will be of particular interest for those who want to take advantage of the "try-before-you-buy" shareware concept. You can always find the latest version of this British program in the UKSHARE Forum on CompuServe; type GO UKSHARE. Shareware shoppers might also investigate PROCOMM, the shareware "version" of PROCOMM PLUS. It's widely available on online services and BBSs.)

You really shouldn't have to look any farther than the programs named. Each can be configured to require minimal disk space (you can even run these programs on a single 720K floppy disk). Each is easy to learn, and has the following important features:

- script files and dialing directories;
- the most popular binary file-transfer protocols (the Crosstalk programs and the shareware PROCOMM come up a bit short in this category, in that they don't offer Zmodem); and
- macro or function-key assignment capability.

Incidentally, several publishers of popular terminal programs offer online product support in the form of BBSs or special-interest groups on commercial online services. If you use a program that has a really large user base, you have the additional advantage of being able to contact other users online. You'll find most more than willing to share their experiences and answer questions. Some even upload ready-to-use script files. This is all the more reason to go with a well-known program. Your friends may recommend this or that program, but unless they're willing to teach you how to use it, you're better off with one of the "name" commercial or shareware packages.

Don't be surprised if you find yourself trying out several programs before you settle on one. Most modem users don't know everything they need in a terminal program until they've been online for a while. Needs often change in any event.

Also, some programs work better than others in certain applications.

Automating Text-Based Online Services with Front-End Software

Once you're comfortable using an online service, you'll start looking for ways to make it easier to use. There are several ways to do this, including navigation shortcuts and setting up macros and function-key assignments, as described later. However, for maximum efficiency and speed on a particular online service, your best bet is to get a front-end program for that service.

How a Front End Works

A front end not only makes using an online service more efficient, but also easier. The typical front end offers the equivalent of prepared script files to handle tasks like sending and receiving E-mail and public messages, as well as editors to compose messages, and more.

Most front ends are set up so you don't have to remember an online service's commands. Instead, you select a command by pressing a single key (as in Figure 4.1), by selecting a menu item (as in Figure 4.2), or by typing an easy-to-remember "plain English" command.

The overall "feel" of using such a program is more like using an applications program in your computer than accessing a distant mainframe or minicomputer.

Even if you're a novice or "plug-'n'-go" user and you don't want to take the time to learn to navigate an online service like CompuServe, don't want to memorize a lot of commands, or don't want to go to the trouble of writing complicated script files to mechanize online activities, front ends may be just what you're looking for. (Some, like Aladdin for GEnie, even have macro and scripting capability, so you can customize their operation.)

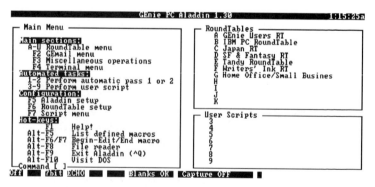

Figure 4.1 Aladdin Front End for GEnie

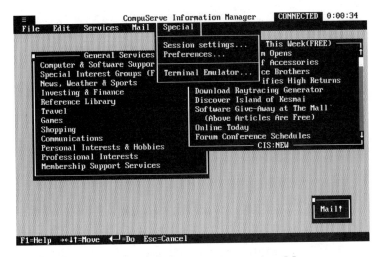

Figure 4.2 CompuServe Information Manager

Examples of Front Ends for Popular Online Services

Those are the bare-bones basics of online service front ends—enough, we hope, to give you an idea of what they're all about. Now we'll show you several online service front ends (by no means all of them).

CompuServe Front Ends CompuServe offers several software packages designed to make use of certain special CompuServe features and to make using CompuServe easier in general. The most popular of these, among MS-DOS users, are CompuServe Information Manager and TAPCIS. (For complete information on all CompuServe software, type GO CISSOFT at any CompuServe prompt.)

CompuServe Information Manager (CIM) is the newest CompuServe front end. Available for MS-DOS and Macintosh computers, CIM is the most powerful and feature-rich of any of the many front ends CompuServe has developed over the years.

As shown in Figure 4.3, CIM uses an environment with windows, dialog boxes, and pull-down menus.

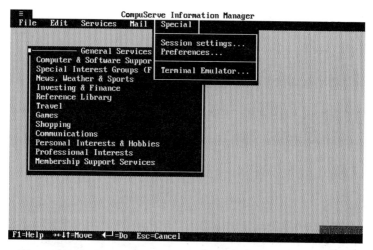

Figure 4.3 CompuServe Information Manager Screen

CIM is unique among other CompuServe software packages in that it uses CompuServe's Host Micro Interface for faster access and more efficient operation.

Among other features, CIM offers a variety of file-transfer protocols, including CompuServe's B+ Protocol. Of special interest is the fact that it lets you view certain GIF graphics as it downloads them. (Weather maps are in this category.)

CIM lets you create and edit messages offline, and provides such features as an E-mail address book, real-time conference color-coding (to identify speakers), graphic (GIF) support, mouse support, terminal emulation, and color settings. CompuServe also provides a support Forum for the MS-DOS versions. As of this writing, there are no connect charges while you are in the CIM support Forum. (Type GO CIMSUPPORT at any CompuServe prompt to access the MS-DOS CIM Support Forum.)

CIM lets you access all of CompuServe's services; many of them are built-in menu selections. If you like front ends and don't mind being one step removed from the actual online operations (you won't see commands on your screen as you will with some front ends, for example), CIM is an excellent choice for anyone who uses CompuServe. It's especially nice if you enjoy a window-type environment, and I recommend both the MS-DOS and Macintosh versions of CIM over other CompuServe front ends.

TAPCIS is the other major front end for CompuServe. Produced by a group independent of CompuServe, TAPCIS concentrates on Forums in its automation.

Among the program's many features are a split-screen editor for offline message creation, an E-mail address book, script files, and a variety of features devoted to sending, replying to, and filing E-mail and Forum BBS messages. TAPCIS handles Forum library functions such as keyword searches and unattended file downloads.

TAPCIS is menu- and command-key driven. It is available online for download in the TAPCIS support Forum (type GO TAPCIS), or from its publisher, Support Group, Inc. (Versions of TAPCIS downloaded from the TAPCIS Forum are for "shareware trial.") The program doesn't have an elaborate user interface like CIM, but it has inspired a fierce loyalty among those who use it regularly.

DELPHI Front Ends As of this writing, DELPHI is developing its own front-end program, presumably with a graphical user interface. It should be available by the end of 1992; to learn more about it, contact DELPHI's Customer Service, or type GO USING and select "What's New" at the menu.

In the meantime, there is another DELPHI front end available: The Messenger. Developed by the PAN network, Messenger automates E-mail, binary file transfers in E-mail, SIG Forum message base messages, and SIG databases. The program keeps track of billing, and can perform file transfers, E-mail, and Forum message transfer at preset times.

As shown in Figure 4.4, Messenger covers virtually every aspect of using DELPHI.

Messenger supports a mouse, and allows you to not only read and reply to E-mail and Forum messages offline, but also to browse entire SIG databases and set up uploads and downloads offline. (You can use the program to sign on and interact with DELPHI in real-time, too.) Binary file transfer is via Ymodem.

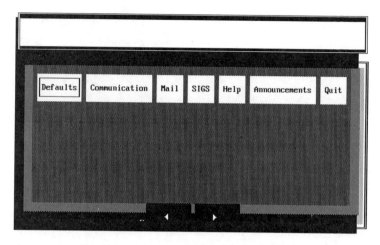

Figure 4.4 Messenger for DELPHI

The program is shareware, and available for download in DELPHI's Music SIG, and elsewhere on DELPHI.

GEnie Currently, there are two front ends for GEnie: Aladdin and EVA. Aladdin (whose full name is "GEnie PC Aladdin") is a program that automates the most frequently used features of GEnie. Among these are E-mail (including Xmodem E-mail), RoundTable BBS messaging, and software library file transfers. Like all front ends, Aladdin is designed to save you a considerable amount of time and money by reducing the time you're actually online.

Aladdin is a classic example of the ideal front end—one that acts as a buffer between you and the host service, while still letting you interact with the service at any time. Aladdin implements commands you select from menus. A RoundTable menu is shown in Figure 4.5.

Selections on this menu initiate actions or lead to detailed submenus, from which you can select actions (like downloading all new mail). This menu was reached by selecting a RoundTable from Aladdin's main menu (which was shown back in Figure 4.1). Other selections on the main menu let you set up Aladdin for your system and the sections of GEnie you use; write, read, and reply to mail messages; and more.

Portable Communications Software 77

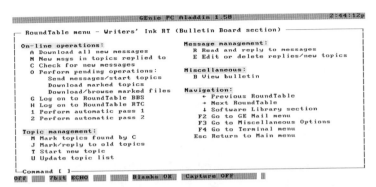

Figure 4.5 Aladdin RoundTable Menu

Aladdin allows you to do as much work as possible offline (reading and preparing mail messages, and selecting RoundTable files for unattended downloading, and other mail and RoundTable tasks). It also features script file and macro capability, so you can automate activities and functions not already covered by Aladdin. The program supports all file-transfer protocols that GEnie supports: Xmodem, 1-K Xmodem, Ymodem, and Zmodem.

Aladdin will work with virtually any MS-DOS machine that has 640K of RAM. It supports most all monochrome or color displays, including "long screen" EGA/VGA with more than 25 lines.

Worth noting, too, is the fact that you can use Aladdin as a "straight" terminal program to manually dial up any other text-based system (like DELPHI or BIX).

Aladdin is available in GEnie's Aladdin RoundTable for download (type Aladdin, or M110 4 to download the latest MS-DOS version). Note that it is neither PD nor shareware. It is free (save for normal connect time charges), and you can download the manual, although Aladdin's context-sensitive online help is more than sufficient for most users. (The average cost of downloading Aladdin is four or five dollars.)

EVA is a GEnie front end developed by Philippe Rabergeau (the author of the PROPLUS utilities). It can be a menu- or command-driven program, and supports a mouse. The program features pull-down menus, online "hypertext" help, multiple IDs, and E-mail management. E-mail features include an easy-to-use editor, spell checking, message forwarding and carbon copying capability, a built-in address book, mailing lists, and E-mail file transfers via Xmodem.

The program also offers automated CHAT/real-time conference features, system indexing, and Zmodem batch downloads. EVA was developed for color display systems. The program is shareware, and you can download it and related files in GEnie's GEnieus RoundTable (type M150 3).

MCI Mail Front Ends Several MCI Mail front ends are on the market or in the works. Most notable among these are Lotus Express, Norton Commander, and Messenger for MCI Mail. One feature that these front ends add to MCI Mail is the ability to transfer binary files. These programs require that you use a special telephone number (other than the regular numbers for MCI Mail), which dials into a node that takes advantage of their ability to transfer files using the X.PC file-transfer protocol. (The number is 1-800-825-1515.)

Lotus Development Corporation's Lotus Express is a dedicated front end for MCI Mail. Like AT&T Mail Access, Lotus Express is designed to work with one service and, as is the case with most programs designed around one application, it does its job fairly well. It is rather slow, however, and a memory hog.

Norton Commander is actually a sheaf of disk utilities, with an MCI Mail front end called Commander Mail built in. Even though it has some bugs, I prefer it to other MCI Mail front ends. It's imperfect, but very usable for MCI Mail management.

One of the nicest features of Commander Mail is that you can run it from a DOS prompt with the command MCI, in addition to accessing it from the Norton Commander program directly.

Naturally, the program lets you read, reply to, and create messages offline. It maintains a nicely organized file/folder system. All addressing and handling options are handled offline, as well. As noted, you can use it to transfer binary files, but this works only if the recipient is equipped with the same program.

Commander Mail will operate in background, supports a mouse, and lets you schedule events (like sending and receiving mail). Norton Commander is available from Symantec, or at your local software dealer.

Dedicated Front-End Programs

Some online services require that you use special software, which the service normally provides. These services are Prodigy, America Online and its affiliated services, PC-Link, and Promenade. With the exception of Promenade, all can be accessed with a laptop computer.

Online services that use dedicated front-end programs store part of the service itself in files on your work disk or hard disk. This means frequently displayed graphics and information do not have to be transmitted to your computer each time you use them, so the service is faster.

Each online service's front-end is designed to operate with a minimal system—i.e., they will work well enough with an 8088-based PC and a monochrome CGA display. Most are best used with a hard disk, but they can be run from a floppy disk.

I refer you to the online services in question (contacts are listed in Appendix C) for more information on their software, but I do want to tell you how to make three of them easier to use.

If you're using Prodigy, get either PROPLUS or Pro Master. These are shareware programs from Philippe Rabergeau's Gateway Software that provide all sorts of features that Prodigy doesn't offer—including screen and text capture, offline message composition and automatic replying, and more. (You'll find these available for download on CompuServe, GEnie, America Online, and elsewhere.)

If you use America Online frequently, you would do well to buy GeoWorks Ensemble. This will give you access to multitasking and all of Ensemble's applications. You won't be able to run DOS applications, but you won't have idle computer time while you're downloading files. The same is true of PC-Link; if you use it a lot, buy Tandy's DeskMate software.

Graphical User Interfaces and Telecommunications

I consider it worthwhile to use a multitasking operating environment when telecomputing, if you can. Remember that many online activities involve waiting—file transfer in particular. When your computer is engaged in such activities, you can't use it—unless you have a multitasking operating environment.

The front-runners in the DOS world are clearly Microsoft Windows and DESQview. You can run virtually any terminal program—and most front ends—under Windows, and several publishers offer Windows versions of their terminal programs. With DESQview, you can run just about any DOS-based terminal program. It may be possible to run all the proprietary front ends under Windows and DESQview, though I haven't been able to create PIF files for some of them. (PIF is an acronym for "program information files." A PIF tells a multitasking system how to manage a DOS program so it will run properly under the GUI in question.) In any event, both Windows and DESQview have very basic but decent terminal programs. Windows' terminal program is part of the Windows package; DESQview's is an extra-cost option.

A few other operating multitasking and task-switching environments are battling for the market share left over after Windows and DESQview. Tandy's DeskMate seems to have a very slight edge over the other major package, GeoWorks' Ensemble. Both have usable terminal programs, and a run-time version of each is used as part of a proprietary front end. (As noted earlier, DeskMate is the basis for PC-Link, and Ensemble is the foundation for America Online's PC software.)

Some laptops can't run operating environments like DESQview or Windows. For those machines, you can use DeskMate or Ensemble. Or, you can create a sort of poor man's multitasking system using TSR programs, discussed later. A communications program with access to DOS can expand your system in this direction, as can a program that runs in background.

Making Your Communications Software More Efficient: Do-It-Yourself Online Front Ends

One of the great benefits of using a computer is the ability to fully or partially automate a task. You do this all the time with various computer applications programs—formatting and spell-checking documents with word processors, sorting and searching out records in a database, and in automatically dialing up and signing on to BBSs and online services.

It's easy to extend the idea of automation to a BBS or an online service. Online automation can be accomplished in several ways—with script files and front-end programs covered earlier, and with macros and function-key assignments that you can put together yourself.

Each of these can not only automate your online sessions, but also make the services easier to use, as you'll see.

Making Your Own, Part 1: Macros and Key Assignments

Before we get into macros, function-key assignments, and other key assignments, I should mention that these are all basically the same thing: techniques whereby one or more commands are "recorded," assigned to a key or key-combination, then "played back" when the specified key or key-combination is pressed. (Script files are an expansion of this concept.)

One Touch Does it All: Macros

After you've been online a few times, you will find yourself using some commands more frequently than others. EXIT and BYE are two that are used in one way or another on virtually all online systems. As you get used to a system, you'll start using more specialized and complicated commands frequently. (Like SK TO LA, which I use on BIX to skip through messages in a conference topic when I've not signed on in a while and there are more new messages than I want to read.)

It's easy to see how this kind of program operation could simplify the use of many online services, even on a very basic level. As another example, consider the outmoded commands some systems require you to use, like LIST when you want to READ a message—which is how you think of the action. It would be nice if those systems would change their way of thinking to yours, but they probably won't. So, you're stuck with having to remember to type LIST when you want to read a message—unless, that is, you have assigned the string LIST to a key combination that you think of as READ.

(If you think about it, the ideal front end would allow you to use synonyms for virtually every command on the online service in question. At least one online service has that feature built in, by the way: BIX allows you to define nonconflicting synonyms for all of its major commands. This aspect of BIX functions as a front end in its own right.)

In operation, you can think of creating macros and key assignments as "recording" a series of keystrokes. When you press the key assigned those keystrokes, the keystrokes are "played back." For example you might assign an online service's sign-off command (BYE followed by pressing Enter) to F1, in which case you would get four keystrokes for the price of one. The number of keystrokes always has an upper limit, which limits the kind or number of commands you can issue with one key.

Such commands can be issued by pressing one or two keys, if your software has the ability to create macros. Macros are created by storing a series of keystrokes in a file, and designating one or two keys to recall those keystrokes from the file and send them as if you had typed them in terminal mode. (In many instances, macros can issue commands to your communications software, too.)

The key that issues the macro may be a function key, or a combination of keys. Key combinations include Ctrl-key (like Ctrl-Y) and Alt-key combinations (like Alt-H). The key in a Ctrl- or Alt-key assignment might also be a function key (like Ctrl-F1 or Alt-F1), or a shifted function key (like Shift-F1).

Using function keys alone and in combination with Ctrl, Alt, and Shift, you have 40 possible macros, which is more than enough for most applications.

If you need more than 40 function keys, you can go to Alt-key combinations using any other key on the keyboard. As previously mentioned, many popular communications programs use Alt-key combinations for commands. PROCOMM PLUS, for example, uses Alt-key commands almost exclusively, as illustrated by the command screen in Figure 4.6.

PROCOMM PLUS Ready!

```
┌──────────────────────────────────────────────────────────────────────┐
│              P R O C O M M   P L U S   C O M M A N D   M E N U      │
│         ┌──────────────→ COMMUNICATIONS ←──────────┬──→ SET UP ←─────┤
│         │──── BEFORE ────┬──── AFTER ────          │                 │
│         │Dialing Directory Alt-D │ Hang Up ........ Alt-H │ Setup Facility .. Alt-S │
│         │                │ Exit ........... Alt-X │ Line/Port Setup . Alt-P │
│         │──── DURING ────┤                        │ Translate Table . Alt-W │
│         │Script Files ... Alt-F5 │ Send Files ....... PgUp │ Key Mapping .... Alt-F8 │
│         │Keyboard Macros . Alt-M │ Receive Files .... PgDn │                 │
│         │Redisplay ...... Alt-F6 │ Log File On/Off  Alt-F1 │──→ OTHER FUNCTIONS ←──│
│         │Clear Screen .... Alt-C │ Log File Pause . Alt-F2 │                 │
│         │Break Key ....... Alt-B │ Screen Snapshot . Alt-G │ File Directory .. Alt-F │
│         │Elapsed Time .... Alt-T │ Printer On/Off .. Alt-L │ Change Directory Alt-F7 │
│         │──── OTHER ────         │                        │ View a File ..... Alt-V │
│         │Chat Mode ....... Alt-O │ Record Mode ..... Alt-R │ Editor .......... Alt-A │
│         │Host Mode ....... Alt-Q │ Duplex Toggle ... Alt-E │ DOS Gateway ..... Alt-F4 │
│         │Auto Answer ..... Alt-Y │ CR-CR/LF Toggle Alt-F3 │ Program Info .... Alt-I │
│         │User Hot Key 1 .. Alt-J │ Kermit Server Cmd Alt-K │ Menu Line Key ....... │
│         │User Hot Key 2 .. Alt-U │ Screen Pause .... Alt-N │                 │
│                    Press Alt-Z for extended help                     │
└──────────────────────────────────────────────────────────────────────┘
```

Figure 4.6 PROCOMM PLUS Command Screen

As noted earlier, the keys used with Alt often begin with the first letters of the command name—like Alt-H for "Hangup" and Alt-D for "Dial." This mnemonic combination makes the key-combinations easier to remember.

The mnemonic structure should give you an idea of how to think about command-key assignments. Many other communications programs rely on Alt-key commands, largely because it is accepted practice to assign online service commands to Ctrl-key combinations, so the communications programs seem to have "taken what's left" in the form of Alt-key commands. Thus, as a user, you are often left with only the 40 possible function key commands I mentioned a few paragraphs back. Again, 40 commands is probably enough for anyone to use and remember.

Function key assignment is fairly straightforward with most programs. Crosstalk Mk.4, for example, lets you view and set up function key assignments by pressing Alt-K (for keys). When you do this, you see the window shown in Figure 4.7.

84 Portable Communications

```
┌─ Crosstalk Mk.4 OFFLINE Menu ─┐
│  Make a call from the Phone Book  │
│ Add or change a Phone Book card (NEWCALL) │
│ Make a call without using the Phone Book  │
│    Change your user profile information   │
│    Change your equipment setup (CONFIG)   │
└───────────────────────────────┘

Normal function key definitions
 F1  EXIT!..................    F2  SCAN ALL!..............
 F3  READ INBOX!............    F4  NEXT!..................
 F5  @CApture toggle........    F6  @Browse·...............
 F7  ^S ....................    F8  ^Q ....................
 F9  FIND!..................   F10  NAME!..................

                            Press  .PgUp  or  PgDn  for others
```

Figure 4.7 Crosstalk Mk.4 Function Key Commands

(The other function key sets displayed when you press PgDn are Ctrl-, Alt-, and Shift-function key combinations.)

To assign a command string to a key with this program, you just tab to a function key's field and enter what you want issued when you press that key. A few special characters are used to insert control characters, specify a local command to the program, or send a carriage return (press Enter) at the end of a command string.

As you've probably guessed, macros can be used to issue IDs and passwords, as well as system navigation commands, file-transfer commands, etc., to the remote system. Basically, you can send anything you can type.

If the program allows internal commands, you can set up macros to open a capture file, transmit files, etc. With this capability, you can build your own sort of primitive front end for any text-based online service.

What's more, if you use more than one online service, you can unify the command structures for each through your macro/key-assignment-based front end. This is certainly a worthwhile endeavor; the commands used to navigate various online services are at times impossibly diverse. If you use more than one service you must spend a lot of time learning each service's commands. Even after learning all the commands, it's easy to confuse services and issue the wrong command while online.

The Key to Online Success

As you've probably figured out, you can avoid command confusion and make online navigation easy by assigning commands to function keys in such a manner that the appropriate command for the operation you wish to perform is sent to an online service when you press a function key. Assign the same type of command to the same function key for each service, and you will have a personal "front end"—rather like having an assistant who always remembers the right command, no matter which service you're on. For example, if you assign each service's log-off command to F1, you won't have to remember whether to type BYE, OFF, EXIT, QUIT, or whatever a service uses.

This, of course, requires a communications program that can save and automatically load different function-key assignments for each service.

NOTE: If your communications software package doesn't offer macro capability, you might investigate using a macro program that is compatible with your system and your communications software. If you're running under DESQview, you can, of course, set up macros that you can use with any DOS-based application you run under DESQview.

You can create a "function-key front end" with any of a number of conventional communications programs, including Windows' Terminal program.

Laptop-to-Desktop Communication: Null-Modeming

If you need to transfer data from your laptop's hard disk to your desktop computer's hard disk, or vice versa, there are several ways to do it. If both have serial ports, you might use your modem to upload the data from one computer to an online service or BBS, then download it with the other computer. Or you might copy data from the first computer's hard disk to a floppy disk, then copy the data from the floppy disk to the second computer's hard disk.

However, this is time-consuming, and—where an online service is involved—costly. Both machines already have what it takes to communicate with one another: serial ports. All you need to do is link them directly, substituting what is called a null-modem cable for modems and telephone lines. Such a direct link transfers data far faster than a modem and online service or BBS, in any event: Data are transferred at speeds of up to 9600 to 19,200 bps between directly linked computers!

Null-modem transfers can be conducted using conventional communications software, or with a program designed especially for that purpose, like LapLink II.

Using a Conventional Communications Program for Null-Modeming

Transferring files via a null-modem connection using a conventional communications program isn't that much different from transferring files via modem. It helps to use the same software on each computer, though. And you will, of course, need a null-modem cable. You can buy a null-modem cable at any computer store, or make one yourself, per the instructions in Appendix E.

Before you attempt the link, set up each computer's program to its maximum speed, and to the same communications parameters (8/N/1 or 7/E/1). You won't be communicating back and forth, so you don't have to worry about setting echo. Leave the terminal emulation at "None" or "TTY," whichever your program offers.

With the parameters set, go into terminal mode with each system, and type the command to go online—unless, that is, your program lets you set things up to assume it is already online.

You can verify the connection by typing a few characters on one computer's keyboard, and seeing if they appear on the other computer's screen.

Once you've verified the connection, switch to command mode on each computer and issue or select the proper file-transfer command (upload or download), select the same file-transfer protocol, and type the filename(s) to be transferred. Stop at the final step in the process with each computer, then initiate the upload (transmission) on the sending computer a second or so before initiating the download on the receiving computer. From there, the transfer will proceed as it would with a modem connection.

NOTE: When using Xmodem (and sometimes other binary file-transfer protocols) to transfer binary data and program files, use an archiving program like PKZIP to archive the file or files first. Some software's binary file-transfer protocols corrupt binary files by "padding" them with extra bits. This is a perfectly legitimate function as far as the program is concerned, but it can result in unreadable data files and programs that won't run. Archived files are not corrupted by this process.

It makes sense to archive all the files you intend to send, in any event. The reduced file size gives you a faster transfer.

Using a Null-Modem Program

Null-modeming is a lot easier if you use a program designed for computer-to-computer data transfer. The best all-around program of this type is Traveling Software's LapLink II. It not only provides a communications link and file-transfer protocol, but also comes with long null-modem cables that will fit any combination of DB-9/DB-25 connectors. It even copies itself from one computer to another.

Laplink and programs like it also let you specify directories from and to which files are copied. You can copy or move (copy and delete) individual files or groups of files within directories as you wish. If you do very much null-modeming, get LapLink; you won't have to worry about archiving programs, changing directories with your communications program, or copying programs from one directory to another on the destination disk.

Portable Communications Support Software

As noted earlier, communications software isn't the only kind of software you'll need for portable telecomputing. There are a number of utilities and TSR programs that are either necessary or useful enhancements to telecomputing.

Archiving and File-Compression Programs

Archiving and file-compression programs head the list of necessary support programs. Archiving programs are programs that combine several data and program files into one file. File-compression programs compress, squeeze, pack, squish, implode, or otherwise reduce files in size. (A few kinds of files, among them "GIF" graphics files, cannot be compressed using archiving programs.)

These programs perform two useful functions where file transfers are concerned. First, they make files smaller, thus reducing transfer time. Second, in putting more than one program into a single file, they make it easier to download a program that has multiple files—you get everything in one package.

The most commonly used programs in these categories do both. I'll call them *archiving* programs for the sake of this discussion.

Archiving programs are usually used to create files with an identifying filename extension (like .ZIP or .ARC), from which you can extract files using the same program. A few programs create what are called self-extracting archives. These are files with the extension .EXE which, when run, unpack themselves. The most popular of these is LHarc. (Note that you don't need the unpacking program to unpack a self-extracting archive.)

The most popular of the archiving programs is PKWARE's PKZIP/PKUNZIP package. You'll find files created with PKZIP.EXE (identifiable by the filename extension .ZIP) everywhere. An accompanying utility, PKUNZIP.EXE, is used to decompress and extract files from archives. The file is available for download as a self-extracting archive, usually with a name like PKZ???.EXE. (??? indicates the version number, as in PKZ110.EXE.)

ARC files (bearing the filename extension .ARC) are almost as prevalent. The ARC.EXE program handles both archiving/compression and dearchiving/decompressions. It can be downloaded as a self-extracting archive, with the name ARC???.EXE (as in ARC602.EXE).

PKZIP has a slight edge over ARC in how much and how quickly it reduces files. PKZIP also has an edge on many BBS systems, whose sysops took umbrage at a lawsuit involving PKWARE and will carry only PKZIP files. You'll need both PKZIP/PKUNZIP and ARC, however, as too many good programs can be found in either format. (If you can't download these programs, you can get them from their publishers. They're listed in Appendix A.)

A relatively new archiving program is ARJ. ARJ has a distinct advantage over both PKZIP and ARC in speed and compression. ARJ isn't in widespread use yet, but probably will be in 1993.

Other archiving and compression programs include .LZH, PAK.EXE (.PAK), ZOO.EXE (.ZOO), LU.EXE (.LBR), and NUSQ.COM (?Q?). You may or may not need all these. ZOO and LIB files are relatively rare nowadays. Files created with LU.EXE are usually not compressed, but may contain files that have been compressed with NUSQ.

Notepads, Calendars, and Other TSR Programs

TSR programs provide useful supplements to communications programs. The more common TSRs range from pop-up notepads, calculators, and calendars to ASCII tables and phone directories. (Borland's Sidekick provides all of these.) Some of these features may be provided by a terminal program.

The main disadvantage to using TSRs online is the fact that they use memory which the communications program may need (perhaps to run an external file-transfer protocol). Thus, you may limit your program's capabilities. Too, some TSRs conflict with some communications or other programs you may be running, which can have unpredictable results. (The conflicts occur when a program you've loaded wants to access an area of memory occupied by the TSR.)

If you need to access text files, a calculator, calendar, and other data when you're online, you might consider a multitasking or task-switching environment. If you want to run your own programs in each category, DESQview is probably your best choice in this area. (DESQview offers an optional notepad, calendar, and other features useful when you're online, too.) Windows 3 is also a good choice, since it provides all of the aforementioned applications, and more, all guaranteed to work in concert. The same is true of DeskMate and GeoWorks' Ensemble, which don't require a 286 or 386 for optimum performance.

Also on this topic, I should mention that you may find a memory-resident spelling checker useful—or you may find one maddening. These programs typically operate by scanning the preceding character string each time you press the space bar. If the string is in the program's dictionary as a word, it is ignored; if the string is not recognized, the program either beeps and/or pops up a window with suggested spellings.

RAMdisk Software

As explained in an earlier chapter, a RAMdisk can reduce file-transfer time, particularly if your system has slow disk access speed. If you can't use a multitasking system and do a lot of file transfers, you'll really appreciate the time a RAMdisk saves.

There are two drawbacks to using a RAMdisk. The first is it uses memory. The second is a RAMdisk that disappears when you turn off your machine. You have to remember to copy a downloaded file onto a real disk before you turn off your machine—and there is always the possibility you'll forget you downloaded something.

As already noted, you should find RAMdisk software included with the utilities that came with your computer. If not, there are endless RAMdisk programs out there to buy or download. (These programs allocate a specified number of bytes of your system's RAM to look like another disk drive to your computer.)

Macro Programs

If you use a terminal program that doesn't offer function-key assignments or macro capability, you can add this feature with a key-assignment program. There are a number of commercial, PD, and shareware macro programs available. Which you use depends on how much memory your computer has. There are also compatibility issues, since key-assignment programs are TSRs. (In the shareware realm, NEWKEY seems to have a fairly good compatibility record. You might also take a look at FUNCREDO and DKEY, among others.)

Although the better terminal programs and virtually all front ends for text-based services offer macro capability and/or function-key assignments, you may still want to use a keyboard-assignment program to extend the communications program's abilities. (Perhaps you can add Ctrl-, Alt-, and Shift-function key to function-key assignments.) Again, watch for compatibility problems—and remember that proprietary front ends do not generally tolerate TSRs.

Text-File Converters

Many modem users create text files offline for upload as message base postings or E-mail messages. This is fine, as long as the files are in what is called 7-bit ASCII format. Unfortunately, many popular word processors don't store text files in 7-bit ASCII format. Instead, they use an 8-bit format, which incorporates graphics and control characters. Or, they may store files in 7-bit ASCII, with 8-bit headers and formatting marks. If you try to upload a message created with such a word processor using ASCII upload, your system or the remote system will lock up because one or the other will interpret an 8-bit character as a command. (You can upload the message using a binary protocol, but it will be unreadable online.)

Nowadays, most word processors that use 8-bit characters in storing files offer a "print to disk" or ASCII storage option, Microsoft Word and WordStar among them. Still others, like WordPerfect, offer conversion utilities. However, a few offer neither. If your word processor can't "do" ASCII, you'll need a text-file conversion program. XWORD, by Ronald Gans, is among the best of the shareware programs of this type.

■ ■ ■

By the way, applications for the support software I've discussed thus far aren't limited to online activities. Archiving software is handy for freeing disk space. You can use TSR programs with word processors, databases, and other applications. The same is true of RAMdisks. Text-file converters are useful when you want to share text files on disk with someone who uses different word-processing programs.

Communications Utilities

A few specialized utilities for communications are circulated as PD or shareware programs. For openers, there are TSR programs that display the equivalent of modem indicator lights on your computer screen (useful if you have an internal modem but want to monitor call status). You'll also find at least one program (CALLWAIT.BAS) that you can use to make your modem more tolerant of interruptions from call-waiting and line noise.

There are an increasing number of modem setup programs online, too; these set your modem's parameters for optimum performance under certain conditions.

Among the more esoteric communications support programs are viewers that display GIF graphics files as you download them. There are also terminal emulation and download protocol "add-ons" for several PD and shareware programs. (These can be difficult to use. And, you might be a little suspicious of a program you have to build yourself—unless you like tinkering. The ostensible focus of a terminal program is to help you communicate, not learn to do patches and program.)

Communications Software: Making It Fit

Disk space is an important concern for you as a laptop user, whether or not your computer has a hard disk. This being the case, here are some guidelines for minimizing the disk space used by your communications software:

- When you install communications software on a laptop's floppy or hard disk, disable optional features, such as terminal emulation and text file editing, that you won't be using. This often results in the files that support those features not being put on your hard disk.

- Delete all help files. (Presumably, you will be using communications software with which you're already familiar.)
- Delete script files for services you won't be using.
- Edit dialing directories to minimal size.
- Delete video, printer, and file-transfer support files that do not apply to your system.
- Delete all "READ.ME" text files.

You'll save a surprising amount of disk space this way. And, pruning a program to the absolute minimum number of files required to use it may let you get the program on one floppy disk.

Part 2

...

Making the Connection

5

Making Connections: Getting Online, and How to Tap into Hotel Phones, Pay Phones, and Modem-Belligerent Phone Systems

This chapter has a lot of hands-on material, and a lot of useful background information, all devoted to helping you make physical and virtual connections with your portable telecomputing equipment. It first describes what has to take place for your system to call and connect with another computer, and how to dial up and make a connection with another system. It also explains the preparations you'll have to make to accommodate certain situations common to portable telecomputing.

After that, the chapter provides some necessary background on how telephone systems and connections work, then shows you how to deal with the many problems of physically connecting with, dialing up, and communicating through various kinds of phone systems. We'll look at hardware, software, and other ways around communications problems, along with the special problems encountered in cellular and international data communications.

Dialing Up Another System: An Overview

Dialing up and connecting with another computer and modem isn't difficult. Your modem and communications software do most of the work for you, after you tell the modem to dial a number. (Some modem/software combinations do *all* the work, if the software uses autologon script files.) Unless your modem is manual-dial or you're connected to a telephone system that doesn't allow the modem to dial out, all you have to do to dial up an online service or BBS is switch from your communications program's command mode to its terminal mode and send a command string that does the following:

- gets the modem's attention ("wakes it up");
- tells the modem to dial (and, if necessary, whether to use tone or pulse dialing); and
- supplies the number to dial.

The command string usually looks something like this:

ATDT5309019

(This is called a "string" because it's a string of characters.)

This particular string (from the "AT" command set) tells the modem to look for commands with the command **AT**, tells it to dial using tones (DTMF) with the command **DT**, and supplies the number to dial (5309019). An alternate dialing string using pulses to dial (for old phone systems that support rotary dialing only) would be **ATDP** (the "P" is for "pulse").

Most modems require some kind of initialization string to set certain modem parameters. Most communications software packages send the proper initialization string to the modem when they first run. The initialization string is usually something like **AT&S0** or **ATV0X6M0DT**. It is selected by your software when you install it for a particular type of modem, and sometimes includes your preferences (like the "M0" in the second command string, which turns off the speaker). Most programs allow you to edit the initialization string, so as to include your preferences.

If your software doesn't accommodate the particular modem you have, the software uses a "generic" default initialization string. Or, you can type the initialization string that accommodates the modem's requirements and your preferences while you're offline and in terminal mode.

If you can't edit the initialization string to suit your modem or your needs, you can embed initialization commands in the dial string. Anything that follows **AT** and comes before **DT** in the dial string can be an initialization command. For example, the dial string

ATMOS10=20DT5551969

gets the modem's attention with AT, turns the speaker off, sets the S10 register's value to "20", then dials the number 555-1969.

The modem takes over from there. It opens the phone line (also called "going off hook"), dials the number, and waits for an answer. When the other system answers, your modem responds to let it know a computer is calling, and establishes a connection.

(If you have an acoustic or a manual dial modem, you'll probably have to switch to voice/dial mode and dial the number manually, then switch back to data mode when you hear a computer's answering tone. After this, the modem will take over and establish the connection.)

Once the connection is established, you go to work. Type a user ID and password, or issue a command to let the other computer know you're there, and you're online! These steps can be automated by macros and script files, of course.

That's it in a nutshell. Now, let's take a closer look at the preparations and steps involved.

Getting Ready

Before any of the preceding can take place, you have to make certain preparations. The first steps are obvious—turn on your computer and modem, then load and run your communications program. (It's important to have your modem powered up. Some communications programs check to see whether the modem is connected and turned on, and will report an error if they don't find a "live" modem.)

You'll also want to make sure everything's connected properly. The modem/computer cable and the phone line should be plugged in. If you have an acoustic modem, attach the modem's cups to the appropriate ends of the telephone handset. (Making the phone-to-modem connection isn't always as easy as described. More on that later in this chapter.)

Finally, make sure your telephone is on or off the hook (usually on), as may be required by your modem. Put any extension telephones on the hook, or disconnect them.

Setting Communications Parameters (Software)

Set your program's communications parameters next (unless, of course, you're using a prepared autologon script file and/or the program doesn't allow you to change the parameters).

Hopefully, you've read Chapter 4, and know all about communications parameters. (If not, go back and read it now.) Your program may allow you to set any number of communications parameters, but you need be concerned with only these basic parameters in the beginning:

- bps, or "baud" rate
- data bits
- stop bits
- parity
- duplex

Your computer and the remote system *must* agree on these parameters. Otherwise, you'll get no response, garbled data, or be disconnected. (Check Appendix D for more information on dealing with mismatched parameters.) Many systems match your system's parameters automatically when you call, but don't count on this.

The remote system may let you set up a user "profile" to adapt it to the parameters *you* want to use. But you'll have to play by the other system's rules the first time you call.

Ideally, you will know the parameters required by any system you might call, but this isn't always possible. If you're not sure about the parameters, set your system to the "Default" value supplied with the description of each parameter on the following pages.

By the way, you set communications parameters in the "command mode" (see Chapter 4). This is the mode in which you give commands to the software or your computer (as opposed to the "terminal mode," in which all commands and input go directly to the modem). Your program should have some means of toggling to the command mode. (This usually involves pressing a defined key or control-key combination, such as Esc or Control-K or Alt-A.)

You can set a variety of parameters from a program's command mode, but most settings are a matter of personal preference. Or they're set by an autologon script file. We'll concern ourselves here only with the five basic parameter settings:

Bps or "Baud" Rate (Default: 1200 bps.) Most systems that use multiple bps rates automatically adjust to the speed of a calling modem. However, even today not all multiple-bps systems communicate at 2400 bps. 1200 bps is a logical choice, since almost all systems have 1200-bps capability. If, once you're online, you find that the system can communicate at 2400 bps, use that speed next time you call.

NOTE: Some modems, like U.S. Robotics Courier modems, can adjust automatically to the highest baud rate the remote system can handle. This feature is usually set with direct commands to the modem.

Data bits (Default: 7 bits.) Virtually all systems communicate using characters composed of either 7 or 8 bits. The vast majority of online systems can handle both 7- and 8-bit communication, mainly because 7-bit systems usually ignore the 8th bit, or remove it from incoming data. So, try this setting first. Alternatively, try 8 bits.

NOTE: If you are set up to communicate at 7 bits and decide to transfer an 8-bit file such as a program or data file, you won't have to change the parameter to use a binary file-transfer protocol like Xmodem. Your communications program should automatically switch to 8-bit communication while transferring a file using a binary file-transfer protocol.

Parity (Default: Even or E with 7 bits; None or N with 8 bits.) Parity indicates whether each system checks for the sum of the data bits in each character received to be odd or even. This setting is also used by each system to determine whether the parity bit in each character sent is a binary 0 or 1. Seven bits is the most likely setting.

Stop bits (Default: 1.) The stop bit is the bit in a data character used to signify the end of the character. A few systems use zero stop bits and even fewer use 2 stop bits, so 1 is the most likely selection.

A Note On Jargon

The settings for data bits, parity, and stop bits are often referred to collectively like this:

7/E/1

In this example, 7 refers to a setting of 7 data bits per character, E refers to even parity, and 1 refers to 1 stop bit.

7/E/1 happens to be one of the two most common parameter combinations. This is why I listed those settings as a default value in the preceding paragraphs. The other is 8/N/1. (That's 8 data bits, No parity, and 1 stop bit.)

Echo or Duplex (Default: Full.) This setting (sometimes called "Mode") determines whether your computer or the remote system is responsible for echoing the characters you type to your screen.

One computer should be set to communicate at half duplex, or "echo." This means it will display input from its end *and* echo characters received back to the other computer. The other computer should be set to full duplex, or "no echo." This means it doesn't display its keyboard input, but relies on the remote system to echo what is typed to its screen.

If both your system and the remote computer are set to half duplex or echo, you will see double characters, lliikkee tthhiiss. This is because your computer displays what you type, while the remote system echoes what you type.

With both systems set to full duplex or no echo, you'll see nothing on your screen when you type. This is because your computer is set to *not* display what you type, and the remote computer does not echo what you type.

Most dialup systems communicate at half duplex, which means your duplex should be set to "full" or "no echo." Again, in this mode your computer does not directly display what you type. Instead, it displays what you type as an echo sent back by the remote system. (Notable exceptions to this "rule" are the GEnie online service and Telex systems.)

In any event, you should be able to change the duplex or echo setting.

If you dial up a system and see double characters or nothing at all when you type, try changing the duplex setting.

■ ■ ■

If your communications software and/or modem do not allow you to change parameters (a rarity), their built-in defaults are probably those noted above. But, again, you should avoid the problem entirely with a software package and modem that allow you to change these basic parameters.

Setting Modem Parameters

You have the option of setting the communications speed and many other parameters within the modem, using switch settings and command strings.

The parameters you use most frequently can be set with switches. On external modems, these are called dip switches, small "rocker"-type switches on the bottom or side of the modem. (A few external modems have their dip switches inside, in which case you have to open the modem to get at them.)

With internal modems, dip switches are often not available, and you must set the dip-switch parameters via software commands. The commands can usually be incorporated in the modem initialization string used by the software. See your modem's manual for information on the commands you need to add to change the equivalent of dip-switch settings. (For the purposes of this discussion, I'll allude to both physical dip-switch and modem command settings as "dip-switch settings.")

You will have to consult your modem and software manuals for information on required settings and the commands to implement them. But the important dip-switch settings are Carrier Detect, Data Terminal Ready, and Auto Answer.

Carrier Detect (CD) This determines whether the modem should wait for a carrier signal from another modem before it communicates. The normal or default setting for this is "override." This makes the software assume it's connected; the software, in turn, allows the modem to proceed with its activities. A few programs won't tolerate the carrier detect override being on, so you may have to change this setting.

(This setting is also useful when you want to do null-modem transfers using conventional communications software. However, you can substitute changing the modem's dip-switch setting with a software command for null-modem transfers.)

Data Terminal Ready (DTR) This determines whether the modem waits for a "ready" signal from your system before it proceeds to go off hook and dial a number, and to transmit data to and from your system. It's required for the modem to be able to accept commands. Here again, some programs require that this be set to "on," while others require it to be "off."

(Check your software's manual to see which CD and DTR settings it requires. If your modem is among those supported by your software, the software installation program or the manual will advise you as to which settings you should use.)

Auto Answer Whether the modem automatically answers an incoming call can be important if you leave your modem connected to a telephone line, and expect voice calls. Some modems have a default for this dip-switch setting that makes the modem always answer calls. Other modems don't. Whether you change the Auto-Answer switch depends on your modem's default and your needs.

Timing: Preparing for Carrier Loss

A carrier loss is the absence of the carrier signal from the remote system's modem. This happens when there is a disconnect, but can also happen if there's line noise or static, an incoming call on a phone with call-waiting, or a switch in cells with cellular phones. All modems disconnect a set period of time after carrier loss (usually within a second or less).

The time a modem waits after a carrier loss before it disconnects is set with an "S-register" value in most modems, and there will be times when you will want to change this value.

S-Registers An S-register is most easily explained as a setting within the modem that you can alter. A modem may have 20, 30, or more S-registers, numbered 1 through xx. Each has a value that determines one of the modem's operational characteristics.

S-register 10 (S10) determines how long the modem waits after loss of a carrier before hanging up. If you expect momentary carrier losses (as with call-waiting or "noisy" phone lines) you should set the value of S10 higher. The default varies from modem to modem, but is usually a second or so. The value can be set in tenths of a second, usually anywhere from zero to 255. Thus, you can set the modem to tolerate fairly lengthy carrier losses.

To set the value for S10, you'll probably use this command:

ATS10=xx

where xx is the number of tenths of a second the modem should wait after carrier loss before disconnecting. This command can be incorporated in an initialization string, or, if necessary, in a dial string.

Automating Complex Pauses in the Dial String with a Pause Command

Another important S-register for many laptop users is the S-register that allows you to set the length of time a modem pauses for the pause command in a dial string. (The pause command is usually a comma, but may be ~ or any of a number of other characters.) Putting a pause in a dial string is necessary when you have to dial a number or numbers to get an outside line, as with many hotel telephones, before you can dial the phone number you wish to call. It's also useful when making international calls. An example of a pause command in a dial string might be:

ATDT9,555-5567

Here, the modem would wait the requisite amount of time after dialing "9" before dialing 555-5567.

The S-register that determines the time for the pause command is usually S8, and it's usually settable in increments of one second. Thus, if you send the command

ATS8=2

the modem will wait two seconds after the pause command before it dials the remaining numbers.

If you extend the duration of the pause, you may have to extend the length of time the modem waits before dialing, after it gets a dial tone. The S-register that governs how long the modem waits before dialing is usually S7, and it is settable in increments of 1 second. Thus, **ATS7=60** forces the modem to wait a full minute before dialing, rather than dialing as soon as it detects a dial tone.

■ ■ ■

Again, check your modem's manual for specific information on which S-registers do what, and their possible settings. And remember that these settings can be input manually (offline, in terminal mode), or incorporated in an initialization or dial string.

Dialing Up and Making Connection

If your software is installed properly, and you've made all the hardware and software preparations described above, you're ready to dial up another computer.

Using an Auto Dial Modem

Dialing with an auto dial modem is simplicity in itself. All you have to do is tell the modem to dial and give it a number, then wait for connection.

Your communications program must be set to "terminal mode," which is the mode in which anything you type is sent directly to the modem. In terminal mode, the modem acts on what it accepts as a command, or passes what you type on to the remote system, depending on the nature of your input and if it's connected to another system.

Most programs display what you type when in terminal mode but not connected, as shown in Figure 5.1. Some programs, however, will not echo what you type with the duplex parameter set at half, unless the modem echoes input. (Use the command ATE1 to turn on a Hayes or Hayes-compatible modem's character echo feature.)

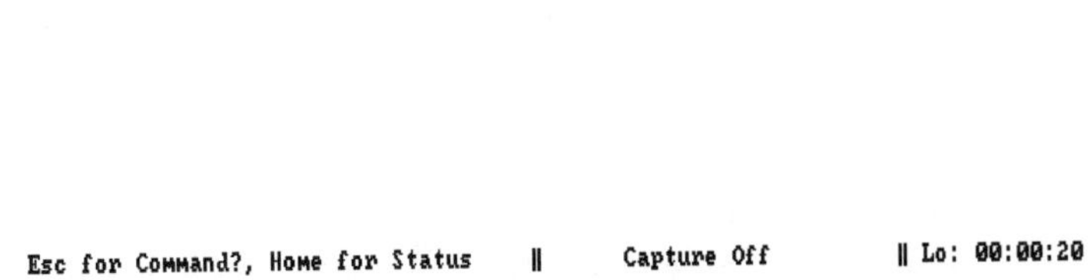

ATDT5309021

Esc for Command?, Home for Status || Capture Off || Lo: 00:00:20

Figure 5.1 Terminal mode screen

Type the commands necessary to tell the modem to dial a number, and the modem goes to work. (Refer to your software and modem manuals for details on what to type.) In the example in Figure 5.1, I've typed the command string ATDT5309019. As described earlier, this string uses the "AT" command to wake up the modem, then tells it which type of dialing to use (tone), and the number to call.

The line at the bottom of the screen in Figure 5.1 is a "command line" or "status line." This line displays various messages from the communications software. It also displays typed commands when the program is toggled to the command mode. This isn't provided by all communications programs; some switch to another screen or use windows to display commands.

When the remote computer answers, your modem establishes the connection.

Using a Manual Dial Modem

With a manual dial modem—acoustic or direct-connect—you must dial the number, wait for the tone (a high-pitched squeal) sent by the answering computer, then quickly switch the modem from voice/dial to data mode to enable the communications program or the modem to answer in kind.

If you have an acoustic modem, you may not have to switch anything. Just slip the acoustic cups over the phone set before you dial. Or, if you need to hear the tones as you dial a number, slip the cups on as soon as you hear the answering tone. Then, as with an auto dial modem, the modem takes over and makes the connection.

Signing On

Your software or modem may display "CONNECT" or a similar message on your computer's screen when a connection is initiated. (This is another parameter you can set with commands to the modem.) When this message is displayed, the remote system will be awaiting input from your system. This can be from you or from your communications software.

If you dial up an "open" system that doesn't require a user ID and/or password, all you have to do is wait for a sign-on recognition from the remote system (sometimes called an "answerback") and/or a menu or prompt. Then you can begin typing, make a selection, or type a command, as you wish.

Making Connections   109

If you've dialed a commercial online service or other system that requires an ID and/or password, here's where you (or an autologon script file) take over. The majority of systems will immediately ask you to identify yourself by user ID and password, as shown in Figure 5.2.

```
^C
User ID: 70007,5110
Password:




CompuServe Information Service
15:12 EDT Sunday 09-Jun-91

Last access: 15:53 08-Jun-91

       Copyright (c) 1991
     CompuServe Incorporated
       All Rights Reserved
```

Figure 5.2 Sign-on Identification Request

If you have no ID, try typing NEW or NEWUSER when the system requests an ID. This may initiate a process whereby you can obtain a user ID online. (Note: Several of the online services covered in this book provide special IDs you can use to sign up online.)

Some systems require you to press ENTER several times at connection. This allows the system to match your bps rate, and/or signals that you accept the system's defaults. So, if you call a system that is new to you and don't get any response after the initial connection, try pressing ENTER two or three times in succession.

A few systems wait for a special character, control-character, or character string before prompting you for a user ID. If you dial up CompuServe via its network, for example, you must enter a Control-C before you start the sign-on process. Similarly, you must type "HHH" to initiate GEnie's sign-on procedure.

When you dial the Tymnet packet-switching network, you must type the letter "A" at some point.

Public Packet-Switching Networks

A number of services can be accessed via public packet-switching networks. These are networks of computers or communications hardware located in hundreds of cities. Each location is called a "node." A node has one or more telephone numbers, each of which can handle more than one call at a time.

To use a packet-switching network to dial up an online service, first dial a local telephone number to connect with the packet-switching network. After you connect with the packet-switching network, you enter an online service's "address" and it connects with the service.

The advantage of using a packet-switching network rather than dialing an online service direct is that the packet network rates are far lower than standard long-distance telephone rates. (The cost of using a packet-switching network is usually built into an online service's rates, incidentally, but can be as low as 25 cents per hour.) Packet-switching networks typically offer some sort of internal or external error-checking protocol (MNP, for example). This is why they are called "packet-switching networks." The networks handle data as "packets," or blocks of characters that are carefully checked before, during and after routing from your system to the online service.

There are two major packet-switching networks in the U.S.: SprintNet and Tymnet. (You may know SprintNet by its former name, "Telenet." The name change is taking place gradually, and you may still find SprintNet nodes that identify themselves as Telenet. However, the prompts and procedures required for SprintNet sign on are the same, whether it is called Telenet or SprintNet.)

Each of these networks requires a slightly different identification at sign on.

SprintNet Sign On SprintNet requires you to press ENTER three times to accept system defaults at 300 or 1200 bps. At 2400 bps, you have to enter @, then press ENTER. In either case, after you press ENTER you'll see this prompt: @. If you don't, press ENTER until @ is displayed.

Enter the address of the online service with which you wish to connect at the @ prompt, and SprintNet will make the connection.

Tymnet Sign On To sign on to Tymnet, enter the letter A when you see a random string of characters marching across your screen (you don't have to press ENTER). Alternately (as with Windows' Terminal program), the cursor will flash fast, then slow; press A when the flashing slows down. You'll then see the prompt, "please log in." Type the address of the service with which you wish to connect.

After the packet network connects with the online service, you'll be asked to enter your ID and password, as described a few paragraphs back.

Once you've properly identified yourself to the remote system, the system's main menu or a command prompt appears.

Telephone Line Basics

Before you can dial up and connect with another system, you must of course have your modem connected to a telephone line.

Most telephone lines can be used for modem communications, whether they're pay phones, hotel phones, or phones in businesses or residences. As a rule, you don't have to look for anything special in terms of the line itself. (There are exceptions to that rule, which we'll get to later.) Any problems you'll encounter will have to do with physically connecting your modem with the telephone line.

First, a few simple basics on telephone lines—things you'll need to know to help you make a connection.

To use a direct-connect modem without adaptors, the telephone line from the wall outlet must have a standard RJ-11 type plug. This type of plug is used in most modern telephone systems in North America. It has four connectors. (Figure 5.3 shows a typical RJ-11 jack in a telephone wall outlet.)

Virtually all direct-connect modems are equipped with jacks that accept the RJ-11 plug. This is true of internal and external

112   Portable Communications

Figure 5.3 RJ-11 Jack in Modem

modems. RJ-11 jacks and plugs are also known as *modular* jacks and plugs.

If you are using a telephone that doesn't have RJ-11 jacks (perhaps a pay telephone or a hotel room phone), there are a number of alternatives to making the modem/telephone connection. These include temporarily "hardwiring" the phone set itself or using any of several gadgets designed to connect a modem to a phone that doesn't have modular connectors. These options are discussed later in this chapter.

Additional elements of your telephone system that may affect telecomputing are discussed below.

Acoustic Modems and Nonstandard Telephones

An acoustic modem or adaptor can often be used to connect with a telephone that doesn't have RJ-11 connectors. However, you may find it impossible to connect the modem to a decorator-style telephone or other nonstandard telephone set. Acoustic modem cups are designed to accommodate the handset of a standard desk telephone, as described in Chapter 3. There are, as you will learn, some alternative acoustic adaptors that will fit almost any telephone handset.

Cordless Telephones

Routing your modem signals through a cordless phone—even if it has a standard handset—is not a good idea; in doing so you introduce a potential weak link into the communications chain.

Also, a cordless telephone may not use the same frequencies that your modem uses. This can result in data being "dropped."

Which Wires Do What?

It's important to know what the wires inside a standard, single-line cable for residential, business, or public telephones do. This information will be useful when you need to tap into a line within a telephone, or at a telephone wall outlet.

If you were to cut open a telephone cable, you would see four wires: one red, one green, one yellow, and one black. A single-line phone uses only the red and green wires. These are the wires to which it is your ultimate goal to connect your modem, be it via a modular RJ-11 jack and plug, or by one of the means of direct connection we'll cover in a bit.

Types of Connectors

As noted, there are other types of connectors than RJ-11 in use in North America. These include RJ-12 and RJ-13, which are for multiple-line telephones (they have six connectors). There are also RJ-41 and RJ-45S plugs. All of these are safe to use with modems. (Even RJ-11 plugs that have provision for powering a "Trimline" or other telephone with a lighted dial are safe to use—with this exception: Do not use an RJ-11 plug that provides power for a lighted dial with a modem that uses an RJ-12 or RJ-14 plug. This can result in damaging voltage being applied to the wrong modem components.)

If, by the way, you want to use a multiple-line or "key" telephone system, you must use a modem that accommodates RJ-12 or RJ-14 plugs; the modem must also be software switchable from RJ-11 to RJ-12/RJ-14 operation. Check your modem's documentation for more information on this.

In sum, the overwhelming majority of single-line business, residential, and public telephones that use modular connectors have standard RJ-11 plugs. So, you shouldn't have much trouble in plugging a phone line into your modem. As for those phones that don't use modular connectors, see the next section.

Making a Single Line Serve Your Phone and Modem with a Y-Jack Connector Many hotel phone sets offer an extra RJ-11 jack into which you can plug a line from your modem. (This is usually on the front or side of the phone set.) If your hotel phone doesn't have one of these, but does have an RJ-11 jack, you will find it convenient to use what is called a "Y-jack" connector, also called a two-way coupler. Shown in Figure 5.4, a Y-jack lets you run two devices from one phone line.

Simply plug the Y-jack's plug into the back of the phone, then plug the incoming phone line into one of the jacks, and the line from the modem into the other jack. Then, you won't have to plug and unplug the phone and the modem line when you want to switch between voice and data communications.

Figure 5.4 Y-Jack Telephone Line Connector

Working Around Connection Problems with Support Hardware

Even though hundreds of thousands of travelers in the U.S. and Canada use modem or portable FAX communications for personal or business reasons, telecomputing isn't universally accommodated by hotel and public telephones. Software considerations aren't that big a deal (although I'll discuss them later). The real challenge in successful portable telecomputing via most hotel or motel room telephones is physically connecting your modem with the telephone.

The connection problems usually involve a hardwired telephone set—basically, a telephone set with a line that you can't unplug. The idea behind hardwired phone sets is to discourage thieves. You'll find them in hotel rooms and business lounges, where the telephone line goes from the wall directly to the telephone set. Pay or public telephones of any kind are also hardwired, and the phone set itself usually conceals the incoming wire.

At first glance, it would seem that nothing short of cutting into the incoming telephone line will let you connect your modem to the telephone line. That tends to be a tricky business, and makes whoever owns the telephone unhappy. Fortunately, you don't have to do that. There are a number of ingenious bits of hardware that you can use to hook up your modem and leave the phone and telephone line intact.

Phone Set Connectors

There are several kinds of devices on the market to connect with hardwired telephone sets. These include acoustic adaptors and devices that connect with telephone handsets. Each makes use of the telephone set, rather than connecting directly with a telephone line.

The devices described below can be used for portable FAX communications as well as dialup modem communications. (At least one portable FAX device, the Worldport 2496 external FAX/modem, comes with an acoustic adaptor.)

Acoustic Adaptors

As described in Chapter 3, acoustic adaptors (also known as acoustic couplers) let you connect with a telephone by providing an interface that converts data signals to audio tones. Figure 5.5 illustrates how an acoustic adaptor is used.

The standard acoustic adaptor is designed for a standard telephone set, and works quite well. It is, however, susceptible to loud noises in its immediate vicinity, which can be picked up and disrupt data signals. Vibrations can also disrupt data signals; if, for example, you place a telephone handset on a hard-surfaced table next to your laptop, chances are the modem will pick up your typing at the keyboard. So, a couple of tips when using an acoustic adaptor:

1. Don't use an acoustic adaptor where there is loud conversation, music, or other sources of noise. If this isn't practical for you, cover the telephone handset and

Figure 5.5 Acoustic Adaptor

acoustic adaptor with a blanket, jacket, or something similar to muffle outside noises.

2. Place the telephone handset and adaptor on a soft surface, such as a carpet or bed, so vibrations are dampened.

Acoustic Adaptors for Nonstandard Telephones

As you know, not all telephones have the standard handset. At the same time, circular acoustic adaptors of the type already discussed cannot connect to anything that is much different from the round, 2-3/16" diameter ear- and mouthpieces on standard telephone handsets.

A number of manufacturers have developed acoustic couplers that can fit almost any telephone handset. These typically use a set of "mini" acoustic cups that press against the center of a mouthpiece and earpiece, rather than surrounding it. Among the best of these is the CP+ Telecoupler, shown in Figure 5.6.

Figure 5.6 Telecoupler Universal Acoustic Adaptor

The distance between the Telecoupler's endpieces can be extended or shortened to fit the telephone. A flexible strap with Velcro fasteners holds the adaptor tightly to the telephone handset—important for a good "connection."

Note that noise and vibration can affect this kind of adaptor more than the cup-type adaptor. This is because the adaptors don't surround the mouth- and earpieces, and don't always cover them completely. So, be sure to muffle noise and vibration when using these.

Note that you can use the Telecoupler and similar connectors with virtually any telephone. So, you may prefer to buy this kind of adaptor before you buy others.

"Direct-Connect" Handset Adaptors

Another kind of acoustic adaptor doesn't rely on an acoustic interface. I call this a "direct-connect" handset adaptor, and there are two varieties. One connects to the handset mouthpiece of standard telephone sets. The other connects between the handset and the telephone set, and can be used with any telephone set that has a plug/jack connection on the coil cord

Making Connections   119

between the handset and phone set. (The plug on this connection looks like a miniature RJ-11 plug.)

Called a *handset coupler* (or *inline connector*), this has quite a few applications. I've see many hotel telephones that have modular connectors on the handset coil cord. I'm not sure why a hardwired phone would have a removable handset, unless it's because the coil cord tends to need replacement, and few people bother to steal only a handset. In any event, inline connectors don't have to be removed when you want to change from data to voice communications, and vice versa. As shown in Figure 5.7, inline connectors are equipped with a voice/data switch.

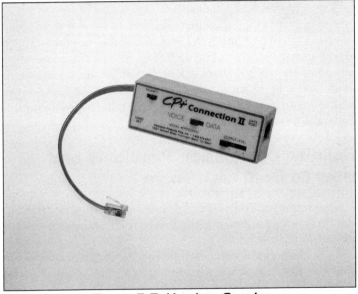

Figure 5.7 Handset Coupler

Handset couplers are also useful if you have to use a phone that won't accept tone or pulse dialing from your modem. (These do exist, and I'll describe in detail how to circumvent them later.) Handset couplers are better to use in this situation because you can listen to a call's progress.

The most prodigious manufacturers of handset couplers are CP+, with their CP+ Connection II, and Unlimited Systems, with their Konexx handset coupler. Note that Unlimited Systems provides an adaptor for use with hardwired handsets, *and* a separate model of the Konexx handset coupler for use with portable FAXes.

Mouthpiece Connection This kind of adaptor connects directly to two connectors beneath the removable microphone in a standard telephone set's mouthpiece. The standard telephone set's mouthpiece can be unscrewed, and contains a small disk that you can safely remove, as it is not attached to the connectors between it.

Marketed under various names, these connectors are great for use with standard phones.

You may find the mouthpiece difficult to remove from some standard telephone handsets. Sometimes the mouthpieces are locked down by virtue of being tightly fitted during assembly. But adaptors like the Blackjack are reliable, not vulnerable to noise, and they're not overly expensive. (You can also use the phone line/modem jumper described in a few pages to connect to the connectors beneath the mouthpiece's microphone.)

Cellular Connection Problems and How to Deal with Them

Telecomputing via cellular phone presents a few problems. You can't connect a modem directly to a cellular phone—but adaptors are available.

You cannot dial a number directly with a cellular telephone, so you'll have to set your modem up to think it has dialed a number. Do this by setting the modem to go "off-hook" (open the phone line) either through software commands or modem dip-switch and S-register settings. This will make the modem think it's already connected.

After you send this command to the modem, dial the number with the telephone's keypad, and your modem should make the connection okay.

See your software and modem manuals for the commands to use for "off-hook" settings. Typically, you must set the dip-switch for carrier detect to make your software assume the modem is connected. Set S7 (the S-register that determines how long the modem waits for a carrier) to a higher number. And, be sure to set S8 to tolerate a lengthy carrier loss, to compensate for cell switching.

The ultimate solution for cellular phones is to buy a cellular modem. Figure 5.8 shows an internal cellular modem, for use with Toshiba laptops.

Figure 5.8 Toshiba T24D/X Cellular Modem

Cellular, of course, operate with conventional "land-line" phone systems. So, a cellular telephone modem, while it is more costly than a conventional modem, can do double duty.

Note that there are some limitations in using a cellular telephone for telecomputing. The quality of the radio links used by cellular telephones usually limit communications to about 1200 bps. A weak signal (as when you're near the maximum range of your cellular system) can further limit communications speed.

Working Around Connection Problems with Direct Phone-Line Connection

Until 1987 or so, I found the overwhelming majority of telephones in North American hotels and motels to be hardwired (that is, connected to old-style phone lines that don't use RJ-11 plugs and jacks). Hard-wired telephones use lines that go directly from a phone wall outlet into the telephone, and which are connected inside the wall and inside the phone set by screw terminals—no plugs or jacks are involved.

These same phones often sport bizarre handset shapes, such as square or ovaloid (my term), which discourage the use of standard round acoustic couplers.

Fortunately, portable telecomputing is on the road to being "legitimized." In 1988, I noticed that several hotel/motel chains started accommodating modem communications. It looks as if this is a trend (perhaps an accidental trend, maybe sparked by manufacturers of hotel telephone equipment, but a trend). I'm not referring to the "business lounges" that some chains offer. (You know, the cramped rooms with five-dollars-per-page FAX machines and maybe the occasional RJ-11 jack, available for a price.) This kind of accommodation is better: A special RJ-11 jack for a modem on every room phone, and unlimited free local phone calls.

But not every hotel or pay phone is so-equipped; indeed, fewer than half the phones you'll encounter outside your home or office have RJ-11 jacks. (I'm reminded of a recent visit to a $300 per-night hotel in New Orleans, where I had to hardwire a line into a phone. At that price, they really should have provided loaner laptops and modems! But, what do I know about the hotel business? I just took care of my online business, then left the phone as I found it.)

Eventually, hotel management-types everywhere will catch on to the fact that the odd-shaped luggage many guests bring with them are laptop computers with modems and FAXes, and we'll see an RJ-11 jack in every room. For now, though, if you want to telecompute on the road, you will often have to cope with modem-belligerent phones, using the previously described hardware, or special techniques I'll discuss here.

If you don't want to buy any of the various adaptors discussed in the previous section, or are in a situation where none work, you can resort to direct-connection. This will let you use any phone line in North America to telecompute. (Cellular phones are an exception, of course.)

I don't guarantee that hardwiring into a phone set or phone line will work, nor do I make any claims as to the safety of doing so. So, you're on your own if you try it. If you do hardwire a line for your modem into a phone set or line, be sure to remove it when you're done using it, and reassemble everything as it was before you got into it.

Temporary Hardwiring

When faced with clever anti-theft and/or low-budget telephone systems, your options often do not extend to using hardware adaptors. When this is the case, you have to connect your modem directly to the telephone line, one way or another.

Hardwiring isn't as difficult as it may seem. With North American telephone systems, all you have to do is connect the green and red wires in the incoming phone cable to their counterparts on a piece of telephone cable that has an RJ-11 jack at one end. (You'll use the RJ-11 jack to plug into your modem.)

To make the connection, you will need to put together a special telephone/modem jumper cable, based on a telephone extension cable of the type available from any store that sells telephones. This extension line has an RJ-11 plug on each end. To make a telephone/modem jumper cable, cut the plug off one end, separate the wires, and attach "alligator clips" to the green and red wires, as shown in Figure 5.9.

When you encounter a hardwired telephone, you can use this in either of two ways: Open the phone set and connect inside, or remove the cover on the telephone wall outlet and connect to the wires on a terminal block. You'll need a small, slot-blade screwdriver, and maybe a Phillips-head screwdriver, to work with either end of the phone line.

In each case, you will be connecting the line to your modem in parallel with the phone, which means you can use either the

124   Portable Communications

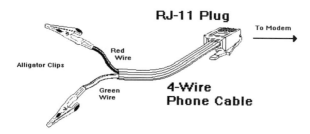

Figure 5.9 Telephone/Modem Jumper Cable

phone or the modem, as you wish. You can dial out (assuming the telephone line will accept your modem's tone or pulse dialing) with the phone set hung up.

CAUTION: With either technique, you'll be working with live wires. The current is low, and the nominal voltage is 45 to 90 volts, DC. But you can still get a good shock if you touch any two wires at once, or are touching metal or an electrical appliance while working with the wires. So, be careful what you're touching.

Alternately, you can connect the two clips to the connectors you'll find inside a telephone set's mouthpiece.

Hardwiring Inside a Telephone Opening a telephone set normally requires removing a couple of screws from the base and lifting the plastic cover from the phone. (Some phone sets don't have screws; you need only pry loose the cover's base to remove it.)

Once you have the cover off, find where the green and red wires from the incoming cable are connected inside the phone. Connect your cable's alligator clips to the terminals or screws to which the incoming wires are connected. Connect only to the wires from the cable that enters the phone, and be sure you connect green to green and red to red. Then, plug the RJ-11 plug at the other end of your cable into your modem's RJ-11 jack.

Tapping into the Wall Outlet Sometimes, the line from the telephone set to the wall connects to a terminal block. To find out whether this is true, follow the phone line from the phone set to where it enters the wall. There should be a plastic plate with a circular hole where the phone line enters.

Remove the cover (there should be two screws). It will be obvious when you remove the cover whether there's a terminal block. If there is, connect the alligator clips to the red and green wires' screws or terminals—red to red and green to green, as described for the internal telephone set connection.

If you remove the cover plate and there's no terminal block, go back to connecting with the phone set. Don't pull on the line. Also, if you see an electrical line when you remove the cover plate, forget making a connection; unless you work with such things routinely, you can get into a lot of trouble when there's an electrical line present.

The benefit of connecting at the wall is that it can be more convenient than connecting to the phone set, in terms of the length of phone line, and where you want to use your laptop.

Traveling in Style

Being somewhat thrifty and hardheaded, I've opened a lot of telephone sets and telephone wall outlets. But I once worked for a telephone company, and I like challenges—most of the time.

However, I suspect many of you reading this book prefer to forego such "challenges." Not everyone likes fooling around with telephone hardware—most modem users prefer to spend their time using their modems, rather than conceiving, designing, and implementing one-shot "fixes" for adverse situations. Fortunately, you can always seek out a pay phone and use an acoustic coupler if you can't do hardwiring.

On the other hand, there are some good kits for doing your own hardwiring. If you don't have a lot of tools, I recommend that you buy one of these. Telecoupler's manufacturer, CP+, offers a tool kit with cables, jumpers, clips, other items, and detailed instructions on connecting your modem with a telephone. The CP+ "Tele-Toolkit," shown in Figure 5.10, is a more sophisticated alternative to merely carrying a telephone/modem jumper cable of the type just described.

Figure 5.10 CP+ Tele-Toolkit

Dialup Problems

Assuming you can connect your modem with a hotel phone's line, you'll usually have to worry about nothing more than adding appropriate dial-out digits and pauses to a dialup sequence in a script file.

In operation, dialing out by modem from a hotel phone is no different than dialing out by voice. You'll have to add the digit required for an outside line (typically, 8 or 9), and insert a pause in the dial string between the outside line digit and the number you want to dial. (A pause is usually added by inserting a "pause character"—a tilde, comma, or apostrophe, depending on your software and modem—between the numbers, as described earlier.)

You may have to specify pulse rather than tone dialing in your dial string or software setup. The dial string will be the same whether you enter it manually or in a script file.

Hotel phone systems that require a human operator's intervention to get an "outside line" invariably disconnect about the time you get a carrier. Where such human-driven phone systems are involved, you may have to use a pay phone. Or, you might have some luck experimenting with pauses and extra digits in the dial string you send to your modem. Or, you can try the techniques described below.

Modem-Belligerent Telephone Systems

As noted, once you've connected your modem with a telephone line, dialing up another computer is fairly simple—provided you have access to a phone that lets you dial out in a reasonably normal fashion. Some phones won't do this. There are hotel phone systems with operators who are relentlessly slow in giving you an outside line for multiple calls. And there are phones that don't "understand" your modem's tone or pulse dialing.

In either of these instances, a handset coupler can be invaluable.

Operators and Outside Lines Dealing with operators running hotel phones is fairly simple, in the beginning. You dial the operator, and ask for an outside line. So far, so good. However, you need to have your modem connected and ready to roll. Thus, you need to be able to use the phone for voice and data communications almost simultaneously.

The easiest approach to this will sound rather unsophisticated, but I use it all the time. First, set up your communications software's parameters, then set it to dial a single digit—any digit will do, as it will be ignored—but don't let it dial. You can do this by typing **ATDT1** or ATDT whatever while your computer is in terminal mode, and *not* pressing Enter. Or, you can create a dialing directory or script file entry whose phone number is a single digit.

Put a handset coupler between the handset and the phone set, switch it to "voice," and get the outside line from the operator. Dial the number you wish to connect with, and listen for a ring. Immediately switch the handset coupler to "data," press Enter or start your script file to dial the desired number, and gently hang up the phone. The modem will keep the line open, and you'll get a connection every time.

A few of these phones are completely hardwired. In this case, you'll have to use an acoustic coupler. Follow the software setup procedures, then get the outside line and dial your number. When you hear a ring, very quickly but gently place the acoustic modem's cups over the phone set.

Dial-Belligerent Phone Systems I can think of no other way to describe phone systems that don't recognize standard DTMF tone dialing or pulses than "dial-belligerent." These systems require that a specific phone set that uses somewhat different tones to dial out be used. I've seen these in use in a number of hotels and motels, and the only justifications for their existence seem to be to make it really undesirable to steal one. (I suspect, though, that the phone system is using nonstandard tones for other reasons.)

Obviously, this kind of phone won't let you dial out using conventional methods, even when you can connect with it. Here again, the handset coupler is a lifesaver. Follow the same procedures described for setting things up to dial out with an operator-assisted hotel phone. (If all you have to do to get an outside line is dial 8 or 9, leave out the step involving the operator, of course.) The key here is that you use the hotel room phone set to dial. It works.

Long-Distance Service Codes

Whether you're dialing out from a hotel phone, a pay phone, or a home or business telephone, long-distance modem dialing can be a drag. There are lots of numbers and several pauses to enter, and sometimes problems such as momentary carrier losses and tones that your modem may mistake as a modem's carrier wave.

You can get around these problems through experimenting with the number sequences and timing, and inserting pauses at appropriate places in the dial string, and/or changing S-register settings to wait before dialing numbers.

There are too many variables involved in this kind of operation for me to give you any guidelines. But, there's an easy way around all this: Use the techniques I described for dialing out via operator-assisted phones.

If you have a direct-connect modem and a friendly extra jack on the phone—or a Y-jack connector—you can forget switching a voice/data switch or rushing to put an acoustic coupler on the phone set. Follow the procedures described, dial all your line-access and long-distance code numbers, and when you get a ring on the final number you dial, initiate the software dialup (again, using a single digit).

The Digital Dilemma

Many large hotels have digital PBXs, and some garble a modem's analog signals in translating them from analog to digital and back to analog again. The only way to overcome this problem is to use an intermediary device that translates data from your modem into a format that will be properly conducted by a digital telephone system. (One such device is the CP+ handset coupler.) To be completely safe, you should avoid binary file transfers, and transferring large files of any kind, when communicating through a digital PBX.

Tools and Supplies for Portable Telecomputing

As you've doubtless surmised from reading this chapter and Chapter 4, you should carry more than your laptop, modem, and their respective power supplies with you when you travel.

On the "required" list I recommend that you get a device like the CP+ Telecoupler; as explained, this will enable you to link with just about any phone. A handset coupler isn't a bad idea, either, unless you're certain you won't be dealing with operator-assisted calls, phone systems with oddball dialing tones, or long-distance service codes.

You'll also need a goodly length of four-wire telephone line—basically, the same line that connects your home phone to the wall outlet. A 10- or 25-ft. length of phone line will remove any limitations as to where in a room you have to place your laptop to telecompute.

To complement the phone line, get a Y-jack so you won't have to swap plugs with the phone set. And, be sure to pick up an inline coupler. This is different from the aforementioned handset coupler; an inline coupler lets you plug two RJ-11 jacks together, letting you extend one phone line with another.

Keep regular (slotted) and Phillips-head screwdrivers in your briefcase or laptop carrying case, too. These are handy for hardwiring, and lots of other tasks.

In addition to those items, you'll probably want most of the following:

- Extra batteries for your modem, if it's an external.
- An extra, charged power supply for your computer.
- A small flashlight, so you can see what you're doing when trying to make a direct connection.
- A pair of needle-nosed pliers, handy for attaching small wires to small terminals. (Be sure the pliers have insulated handles.)

Commercial Telecom Toolkits

As noted earlier, there are commercial traveling telecom toolkits on the market. The best one is the CP+ Deluxe Tele-Toolkit, which has all the tools and connectors you'll need, along with a lighted magnifying glass, a premade phone/modem jumper like the one I described earlier, and detailed instructions. If you want to cover all bets, get the CP+ Toolkit, pictured earlier; this includes all the tools and parts mentioned, plus the Telecoupler and the CP+ Connection II handset coupler.

6

Desktop-to-Laptop Communication: Null-Modeming and Remote Control

Sooner or later, you will have a reason to transfer files between your laptop computer and a desktop computer. This may be via a null-modem cable, or via modem.

There are special considerations for each type of direct, computer-to-computer file transfer. Null-modeming requires special software, or at least special settings for your communications software. The same is true of transferring files between your laptop and a remote desktop computer via modem; you'll be pleased to know that many communications programs are set up to handle this kind of access, and that specialized programs exist to let you use your desktop computer via your laptop computer and a modem.

I'll show you the ins and outs of all this, and more, in this chapter, beginning with some file-transfer basics.

Basic File-Transfer Tips, and Some Applications

I've covered most of what you need to know about file transfers in previous chapters. However, I should remind you of the potential of some binary transfer protocols for "padding" binary (program and data) files, and recommend that you use an archiving program to compress any such files you intend to transfer via null-modem using a regular communications program.

You should also archive any files you will be uploading to online services or to a remote desktop computer. You'll save time, and you'll save money in terms of access-time and storage fees.

Why would you be uploading files? You might want to send reports or other data you've created to someone else while you're on the road. Or, you might want to use an online service or your desktop computer as an "extra disk drive" (as described below).

"Expanding" Your Disk Space: Online File Storage If your disk space is limited, you can use an online service or your desktop computer as a virtual "disk drive." By this, I mean uploading work and program files from your desktop computer to an online service before you leave for a trip, then accessing the files by dialing up the service. Of course, this is practical only on services that provide a personal file-storage area online, like CompuServe or DELPHI. (In a pinch, you can E-mail files to yourself on some systems that don't have personal file areas, like GEnie, but this gets a bit cumbersome.) If the files are on your desktop computer, no problem.

The advantages of this are several: You don't have to lug around lots of program and data disks; you don't have to worry about how to transfer files from your laptop to your desktop computer (and vice versa); and if you have a hard disk, you don't have to worry about running out of space. There are some trade-offs, though: It takes longer to get at your data and programs than if you had them along on disk, and you may incur online storage charges.

Now, let's take a look at exactly how you go about transferring files, beginning with null-modeming.

Side-by-Side Communication: Null-Modeming

As noted in Chapter 4, there are several ways to transfer data from your laptop's hard disk to your desktop computer's hard disk, or vice versa, when they're side-by-side. The best way to do it is to link the computers' serial ports with a null-modem cable and send the data direct.

What You Need: Hardware

The major element in a null-modem connection is the null-modem connector. This is either a cable, like those shown in Figure 6.1, or a connector that connects an RS-232 cable and a serial port, or between two cables.

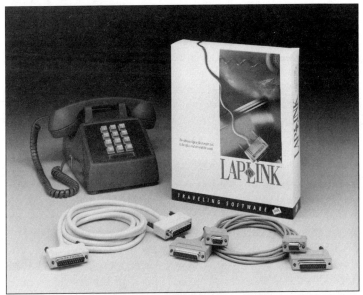

Figure 6.1 Null-Modem Cable

The null-modem cable or connector does one important job: It reverses the serial ports' data send and receive connections. Data transmitted from one computer are sent to the "receive" line on the other computer, and vice-versa. The diagram in Figure 6.2 illustrates how this is done.

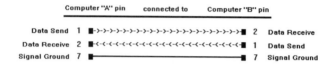

Figure 6.2 Null-Modem Cable Diagram

As you can see, only three lines are connected: the data lines and a signal ground. This is what ready-made null-modem connectors and cables connect. (As noted in a previous chapter, you can make your own null-modem cable, using off-the-shelf parts. See Appendix E.)

A null-modem connector can be placed anywhere in a data link: at either computer's serial port, or at the junction of two RS-232 cables. A null-modem cable simply runs between the two computers, but may be extended with a standard RS-232 cable. Being able to extend a null-modem cable or connector is convenient, but the data signal strength tends to fall off when the cable exceeds 50 feet (thus increasing the potential for lost data).

What You Need: Software

You can use standard communications software to transfer files via null modem, or you can use a program designed for file transfers, like LapLink Pro. The advantages of using a specialized file-transfer program to transfer files between two computers include increased speed, special conveniences that let you find and mark files faster, and more. (It's a good idea to have a specialized file-transfer program like LapLink if you transfer more than the occasional file between two computers.)

Using Conventional Communications Programs to Transfer Files Via Null-Modem

Transferring files via a null-modem connection using a conventional communications program is similar to transferring files via modem. Things go better if you use the same program on each computer, but you can use two different programs.

To set things up for null-modeming, set each program to its maximum speed (19,200 bps is the usual). Use the following setup parameters:

- Communications parameters: 8 data bits, no parity, and 1 stop bit.
- Echo or no echo, whichever is the default.
- No terminal emulation. (Set this by selecting "None" or "TTY" as the terminal emulation.)
- Handshaking off.
- Flow control should be set to use ^S/^Q.
- If the software offers a "Connection Type" setting, set it to "Direct" or "Null-Modem" (as the case may be) rather than to "Modem." (PROCOMM PLUS, among other programs, offers this option.)

Don't use a script file, unless it's necessary to make the computer go online immediately. (Depending on your software, you may have to include or issue a command to tell the software it's already connected.)

If you're going to do null-modem transfers frequently, it might be a good idea to set up a command file or dialing directory entry with these parameters for each program. (When I used Mirror III to transfer files, I created the same command file for each computer, and named it NULL.XTK.)

With the parameters set, go into terminal mode with each system, and type the command to go online (unless, again, your program lets you set things up to assume it is already online).

You can verify the connection by typing a few characters on one computer's keyboard. If what you type appears on the other computer's screen (the characters may be ddiissppllaayyeedd ddoouubbllee, but that's okay), you're connected.

To transfer files, follow these steps (change them as necessary to suit your software):

1. Switch to the command mode on the sending computer.
2. Set up to transmit the file(s) of your choice. This will include selecting a file-transfer protocol (Xmodem or Zmodem will work best), and designating the file(s) you wish to transfer. Set up everything you can, but stop the process just before the actual file-transfer is initiated.
3. Switch to the command mode on the receiving computer.
4. Set up to receive the file(s). This will include selecting a file-transfer protocol, and designating name(s) for the file(s) you'll be receiving. Again, stop one step before the file transfer is initiated.
5. When everything is set up, press the keys or issue the commands to initiate the file transfer on each computer. Begin the transmission on the sending computer an instant before you begin the receive.

As implied, the process will vary with different software packages. And, if you're using Zmodem, you may not have to set up or initiate the transfer on the receiving computer. Many programs that use Zmodem will sense a Zmodem transmission and automatically initiate a file transfer. The same may be true of a proprietary file-transfer protocol, if you're using the same program on each end of the link.

Again, when you use Xmodem (and sometimes other binary file-transfer protocols) to transfer binary data and program files, the files may be corrupted unless you use an archiving program to compress them first.

Using a Null-Modem Program to Transfer Files

Null-modeming is much easier if you use a program designed for computer-to-computer data transfer. One of the best programs of this type is Traveling Software's LapLink Pro. It not only provides a communications link and file-transfer protocol that compresses files as it transfers them (resulting in transfer speeds up to three megabytes per minute), but also a ready-to-use, four-connector null-modem cable that will connect just about any two computers.

Among LapLink's other features:

- The ability to install itself on a remote computer, via serial cable or modem.

- Side-by-side directory displays of source and destination disks.

- Fast file selection via mouse or arrow keys.

- File viewing.

- Multiple file transfer, via batch transfers or directory copying.

- Transfer via parallel port or modem.

There are many other features, but those are the highlights. Figure 6.3 will give you an idea of what it's like to use LapLink, viewing directories and selecting files to copy.

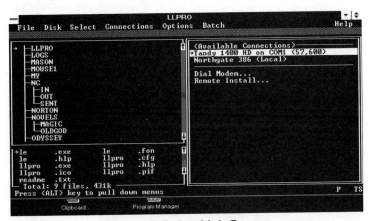

Figure 6.3 LapLink Screen

I also like using a program called Hotwire (from DATASTORM). Hotwire works in pretty much the same way, but is simpler.

I find programs of this type particularly useful in setting up a new laptop's hard disk. I "clone" the contents of each application and data file directory by copying the entire directory, which results in a laptop working environment that is the same as that of my main desktop machine. (Some programs have to be reconfigured, or installed from floppy disk to run properly on the laptop, but the majority of my directories can be cloned.) I'm not the only computer user who does this; LapLink has an option that will clone a disk—hard or floppy—for you.

Otherwise, I copy quite a few data files between computers before and after traveling with a laptop—and when I want to use a laptop outside or somewhere away from my desk.

These programs are also handy for hard disk maintenance, if they offer what is called a "local" operating mode. Rather than designating another computer's disk as the "remote" disk, you designate another directory on the same disk as the remote disk. Then, you can compare the contents of various directories, and quickly view any file. This gives you a clear view of your disk directories, and helps you know which files need to be transferred between directories, and which files are old or redundant and should be deleted. Hotwire is more oriented to this kind of use, and in addition to viewing files, it lets you edit, rename, and move (copy and delete) them. It also lets you rename, create, and delete directories. (LapLink offers these same features.)

Dialing Up and Controlling Your Desktop Computer Via Modem

You've done this, I'm sure: In the rush of making preparations for travel, you forget something important, even vital, to the purpose of your trip. Or, you find yourself 2500 miles from your home or office, and need to check some important records.

Usually in such situations, you're out of luck. If the forgotten or needed item is a file on your desktop computer's hard disk, however, you don't have to worry. If both computers have modems and you've made the proper preparations, the forgotten program or data files you need are almost as easy to access as if they were on your laptop's hard disk.

With the right software running on both computers, you can dial up your desktop machine from anywhere, and transfer files either way. In this case, the "right" software can be as simple as a conventional communications program that has what is called a "host mode." Or, you can set up a very elaborate program that will allow you to dial up your desktop computer and not only transfer files, but also delete files, create directories, and generally do just about anything you could do at that computer's keyboard—all with your laptop and a modem.

Access for file transfer or full remote control offers additional applications for portable telecomputing. You can upload work files from your laptop to your desktop machine to save space on your laptop's disk. Or, if you're security-conscious, upload work files to your desktop machine so you'll have copies of your work in case something happens to your laptop.

Some communications software and remote-access programs offer features similar to those of BBSs. Many have E-mail messaging systems of varying complexity; these are ideal for situations in which someone who has access to your desktop computer needs to leave messages or data for you to retrieve. (Some of these programs also work with LANs.) Finally, a few remote-access programs, as well as communications programs running in host mode, accommodate real-time conferencing.

You may wonder why I don't suggest running a BBS program for remote access. The answer is simple, or should I say "simplicity"—communications and remote-access programs are far simpler to set up and operate (from either end) than BBS programs. And, they take up less space than BBS software.

Remote Access with a Communications Program in Host Mode

As noted, many communications programs offer a host mode. The features vary, but the idea is the same: to allow a caller to connect with a modem-equipped computer.

The features a communications program should offer for remote access include:

- *Password protection.* This is a simple feature that requires the caller to type a password before he or she can access your computer. This is necessary to prevent just anyone from gaining modem access to your computer. The password should be settable, and the option of assigning an ID and password may be included. Some programs with a host mode let you switch between password protection and an "open" system that requires no ID or password. PROCOMM PLUS is one such.

- *Limiting directory access.* This feature lets you set up one directory (or, sometimes, several directories) that a caller can access. Or, you may be able to specify where uploads go, and a directory from which files can be downloaded. This is another security measure, useful if you want to grant others access to your computer. It also helps you by keeping your uploads organized in specific directories.

- *Menus for callers.*

Beyond these vital features, options that some programs' host modes provide include:

- *A proprietary file-transfer protocol.* This can normally be used only when you have the same program running on both computers. (A very few programs use other programs' proprietary file-transfer protocols, but the protocols work best when the same program is running at each end of a connection.) The main advantage of a proprietary protocol is usually speed, as most offer some form of data compression. Error checking may also be a part of a proprietary protocol, as well as automated file transfers.

- Caller-selectable file-transfer protocols.

- A DOS shell that lets you do common DOS tasks, such as copying and deleting files, changing directories, etc.

- Variable user access levels, in systems that let you establish ID/password combos.

- A message base—either private E-mail or public-access.

- A customized sign-on message (provided by you, to let callers know they've reached the right computer).

- Online help for callers, with commands and menu selection.

You'll find a few other host mode features out there, but these are the most common ones.

If this is beginning to look like a list of basic BBS software features and options, that's because many programs' host mode turns your system into a small, personal BBS. I think programs add so many features sometimes for the sake of competitiveness, and sometimes just because it can be done.

Settings and Setup

Before you set your software to host mode, read what the software's manual has to say about required preparations. Many programs, for instance, will require that you set up the modem to *not* ignore the DTR "drop" (hangup) command the software sends (PROCOMM PLUS is one).

Set the speed to your laptop modem's maximum speed, and communications parameters to 8/N/1. Your communications program may let you use terminal emulation in host mode, but it's best to just use "TTY" or "None."

Set the echo (or duplex, if your program calls it that) to "Echo" (or "Half Duplex"). The program will be echoing what you type back to you on your laptop.

You'll also want to set options for host mode. These may include a welcome message, ID/password protection, drive and directory access, etc.

Host-Mode Operation

Once you've set all the options, switch to host mode. This may require a specific command, or just telling the computer to "go online," or to go into terminal mode, depending on the software.

When you switch to host mode, you will see the program's empty terminal screen. There may or may not be a message at the top of the screen or on the status line stating the program is waiting for a call.

You should, of course, test host-mode operation by calling the computer. (With some programs, you won't be able to see what the host mode—menus, prompts, etc.—looks like unless you call it from another computer.)

Match your laptop's parameters to those of the desktop program's host mode: Your laptop modem's maximum communication speed, parameters of 8/N/1, and no terminal emulation. For echo, set to "No Echo" or "Full Duplex." (Remember: The desktop computer will be echoing what you type back to you.)

If you have two phone lines, calling in will be easy enough. Otherwise, take a trip down the street to visit someone who will let you use their phone, or to a pay telephone.

If you experience problems calling your desktop computer with your laptop, try again. Sometimes a bad line will mess up the connection. If you fail twice in a row to make the connection, double-check your software and modem settings, and those of the desktop computer. If the settings don't match, make any necessary corrections, and try again. And, make sure you're typing the proper password, if you've set a password.

If you continue to experience problems getting connection, or after making connection, check the troubleshooting guide in Appendix D. If all else fails, exit the communications programs on both computers, and turn the modems off and back on. Then, restart the communications programs and reset everything.

When you do achieve a successful connection, remember that you won't have full access to your computer, although you will be able to transfer files and, if the appropriate features are available, read and leave messages, execute DOS commands permitted by the DOS shell, and perhaps do other tasks. If you want more complete access to your system, you will have to move up to a specialized remote-access program.

Figure 6.4 shows a communications program in host mode as it appears to a caller.

Using a Specialized Remote-Access Program

Dialing up a computer that is running a specialized remote-access program is somewhat different from calling a conventional communications program in host mode. A communications

```
Welcome to Mike's Place!

First name: Mike
 Last name: Banks
MIKE BANKS
Is this correct (Y/N)? Y
Enter a password: ******
   Please verify: ******


F)iles      U)pload     D)ownload
H)elp       T)ime       C)hat
R)ead mail  L)eave mail G)oodbye
Your choice?
 Esc for Command?, Home for Status    Capture Off    On: 00:00:18
```

Figure 6.4 Calling a Communications Program in Host Mode

program running in host mode provides rather limited access to a computer's files and, sometimes, DOS commands. A remote-access program does more than this; it treats input from the calling computer as if it were input from its own computer's keyboard.

In other words, when your desktop computer and laptop are running remote-access software, the laptop becomes an extension of the desktop computer.

A remote-access program running on a desktop computer—which is called the *host*—lets you do most or all of the following:

- Transfer files to and from a laptop.

- Run programs that are on the host machine's hard disk.

- Access DOS commands for copying, moving, and deleting files on the host.

- Post and read messages.

- Chat (type and read) in real-time with someone at the keyboard of the host computer.

- Access peripherals, such as printers.

These features are typical to remote-access programs, and offered by Softklone's Takeover, one of the better remote-access programs. As you might imagine, the features lend themselves to all sorts of applications. In addition to file transfers and communication with others at the host's location, you can:

- Do almost any work with the desktop computer that you would do if you were there. This includes hard-disk maintenance.

- Run programs that you could not run on your laptop, due to processor, hard disk, or other limitations.

- Start a program and a task that will take some time for the host to perform, sign off, and dial up again later when the task is done.

Figure 6.5 is an example of accessing a desktop computer from a remote laptop system.

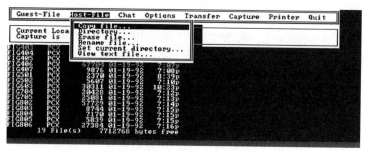

Figure 6.5 Accessing a Computer Using Softklone's Takeover

Obviously, a remote-access program is the next best thing to being at your desktop computer. If your work is computer-intensive, and/or you frequently use programs on your desktop computer that you can't run on your laptop, a remote-access program is the way to go. (If, on the other hand, all you need is file access, a communications program running in host mode—or a specialized file-transfer program like LapLink, which you can use via modem connection as well as null-modem connection—will fill your needs.)

Some remote-access programs require that you use the same program on each end of a connection, or that you use a special access program. (Softklone conveniently includes their Mirror communications program with Takeover, so you have a ready-to-use program with a similar user interface to use from your laptop.) When practical, you should use a communications program that is provided with a remote-access program.

Part 3

...

Applications

7
FAXing on the Road

This chapter will focus on using your laptop computer to send and receive FAX messages. To do this, you will need to add a portable PC FAX—an internal FAX card or an external portable PC FAX.

How FAX Works

I explained how FAX works, in brief, in Chapter 3. To review and elaborate: A FAX machine converts an image on paper into an electronic representation of the image. The conversion is accomplished by scanning. The scanner "sees" anything on paper as the same, whether it's text, graphics, or both. The scanned data are in digital format, and these are converted to analog signals and transmitted via telephone line by a FAX modem. At the receiving end, a FAX modem converts the incoming analog data back to digital data. The data are either stored or printed on paper in a "mirror image" of the electronic data.

The transmission portion of the FAX process (conversion of digital data to analog, transmission, reception, and conversion of analog data to digital) is similar to dialup modem data transmission. However, a FAX modem operates in a manner different from that of a dialup modem. FAX modems operate per a separate standard established by the CCITT, and use different frequencies and modulation techniques to transmit data than those used by dialup modems. This is why you cannot use a dialup modem to send or receive FAXes.

The Computer FAX Connection

Given the fact that a FAX modem converts and transmits digital data, it's easy to see how a computer can be used as a source and reception point for FAX data. It doesn't matter where the data in a FAX transmission originate as long as they are in the proper format—an analog transmission from a FAX modem. The modem that sends the data requires binary data, and computer data are binary data.

The binary data a FAX modem requires must be in a certain format. A portable PC FAX and its attendant software convert data from a computer's native format to a format recognized by its FAX modem. From this point, the data conversion and transmission are handled in the same manner as a FAX machine would handle it.

On the receiving end, the FAX modem built into a portable PC FAX handles incoming data from a FAX machine or from another computer/FAX combination the same as a FAX machine would handle them. Once received, the data are converted (by the modem and software) into a format the host computer can use.

That, in a nutshell, is how FAX works, and why you can send and receive FAXes with your computer.

Making the FAX Connection

What You Need

To send and receive FAX messages with your laptop computer, you will need a portable PC FAX. This will be either an internal FAX card, or an external, portable PC FAX. Which you buy is not entirely up to you. This is because the internal connections that accommodate modem cards used by some laptops are not quite standard. The same slot that accommodates a modem card also accommodates a FAX card. Thus, some laptops require a FAX card made especially for them.

There are some laptops for which there is no FAX card made. If you can't find a FAX card for your laptop, or if you don't have room for another card inside your laptop, you can use an external PC FAX, like the Worldport 2496 FAX/modem shown in

Figure 7.1. The Complete Fax/Portable, from The Complete PC, is another popular external PC FAX.

Figure 7.1 Worldport 2496 FAX/Modem

Dialup and FAX Modem Combinations Most external portable PC FAXes provide a dialup modem, in addition to the FAX modem. This makes using a FAX easy, as you don't have to unplug it to plug a dialup modem into your serial port.

The majority of internal FAX cards also include a dialup modem. This is a convenience because it not only provides both modems, but also frees up your computer's serial port for a mouse or other device.

NOTE: If you install an internal FAX card with a modem in your computer, remember to set your communications and FAX programs to COM2. The external serial port is COM1.)

What to Look for When Buying a Portable FAX/Modem I recommend that you buy only a FAX card or external PC FAX that includes a dialup modem, for the reasons just mentioned. Also, be certain that the PC FAX receives as well as sends; there are several send-only portable PC FAX units on the market, and these will likely be a disappointment to most buyers—although they are less expensive than send/receive portable PC FAXes.

In addition to the aforementioned, you may wish these features in a portable FAX/modem:

- For external PC FAXes only, a plug-in power supply, in addition to battery power. Like external portable dialup modems, external FAX/modems require a lot of power, and batteries do not last long. Therefore, it will be to your advantage to use a plug-in power supply when possible.
- Background operation (this is partially a function of the software), so you can use your computer for other purposes while it is sending or receiving a FAX. You will of course need a certain minimum quantity of RAM to do this; the FAX unit's specifications will tell you how much is needed.
- Autodial capability.

Software Features As I previously advised, it is better to buy a FAX card or external portable FAX that comes with software. Software features and options vary tremendously. Here are a few key features:

- Printer output, to allow you to direct an incoming FAX to a printer rather than to a file. The software should also let you print out a FAX that has been stored on disk.
- On-screen message display. Without this, you won't be able to view an incoming FAX unless you print it out.
- Support for background operation, as previously described.
- A phone directory, which will store names and numbers that you can specify as destinations for FAX messages.
- A text editor to create FAX messages. The software should also be able to convert ASCII text files you've created with your favorite editor to send as FAX messages.
- Cover sheet. A cover sheet is a page that contains the same information, sent as the beginning of the FAX

message. This usually contains the sender's name and phone number. You should be able to include or exclude the cover sheet, as you wish.

- Graphics format conversion, to enable you to convert existing graphics to send via FAX, or to convert received images to any of several popular PC graphics formats (PCX, TIF, GIF, etc.). PC FAX software often uses a proprietary format to store graphics on disk, so conversion is a must.

- Onscreen help.

- OCR (Optical Character Recognition) software, to convert the text in a FAX message on disk into an ASCII text file. This is convenient if you want to resend a text FAX message via E-mail, or edit the message content. (You may have to purchase a separate software package to do this.)

Other Hardware All you need in addition to the PC FAX itself are items to help you connect with a telephone line or telephone. The same hardware discussed in Chapter 5 for use with dialup modems will work with PC FAXes. Your needs will vary according to your situation, but you should have the following on hand:

- A length of telephone extension cord, with RJ-11 plugs on each end, and an inline coupler, to extend the range of your connection.

- An acoustic adaptor, for connecting with pay telephones or other phones that don't have RJ-11 jacks.

You may also wish to carry along a voice/data switch, like that shown in Figure 7.2, if you intend to receive FAXes.

A voice/data switch has one jack for an incoming phone line, and two jacks going out—one for a voice telephone set, and one for a FAX machine (which will go to your PC FAX). When a call comes in, the voice/data switch answers, and determines whether the call is from a FAX. If a carrier wave is detected, the call goes to the PC FAX; if not, the phone rings.

152 Portable Communications

Figure 7.2 Voice/Data Switch

A few PC FAX units can handle voice/data switching themselves.

Connecting with Phone Systems

Just as you will use the same hardware to connect your portable PC FAX to a telephone line as you would to connect a portable modem, you will use the same techniques. Here again, I refer you to Chapter 5.

I'll also remind you that some portable PC FAXes (among them the Worldport 2496 external unit) come with acoustic adaptors.

Sending and Receiving Faxes

Sending and receiving a FAX with your laptop is not very different from sending and receiving a FAX from a desktop computer with a FAX card. To send a FAX, enter the number of the recipient (or select it from the software's phone directory), and specify the name of the file to send. Then, issue the command to send the FAX (or, if the software supports it, set up the day and time the FAX is to be sent). How this is done will vary, depending on the PC FAX and software you're using, but that's the basic idea.

Receiving a FAX is simpler. Assuming your computer is turned on, connect the PC FAX to a phone line. Then, either run the FAX software and wait for a call, or, if your hardware and software enable background operation, just hook everything up and wait.

Where the send and receive processes differ is in terms of the source and destination of the data. The data source for a FAX machine is the scanner, picking up images. The data source for a PC FAX is a disk file. The file may be a text file created with an editor, or a graphics file—which may or may not contain text. The source of the file may be a piece of paper gone over by a hand scanner, but as far as the software is concerned, the source is still a file.

Viewing and Printing Incoming FAXes

Viewing a FAX message you've received should require nothing more than issuing some commands to display it onscreen.

Printing a FAX, of course, requires a printer. Portable printers are usually ink-jet or dot-matrix. A portable printer connects with your printer the same way that any printer does—it plugs into your laptop's serial port.

The portable printer market is rather limited. Perhaps the best portable printers on the market are "The World's Smallest Printer" from CP+, and the Kodak Diconix printer, shown in Figure 7.3.

Like a portable modem, a portable printer should have both battery and plug-in power. A portable printer has to move paper and drive a print head, so it requires quite a bit of power, and uses up batteries quickly.

Beyond these elements, other printer features that may be of concern include:

- Weight.
- Size.

154 Portable Communications

Figure 7.3 Portable Printer

- Speed.

- The ability to use regular (bond) paper, rather than requiring a special paper.

- Compatibility with a common set of commands—the Epson command set is best because almost any program can issue Epson commands.

- Varying type sizes and printing effects (printing effects being boldfacing, underlining, italics, etc.).

- Availability of a sheet or tractor paper feeder.

- Availability of extra and/or rechargeable battery packs.

A typical portable printer weighs less than five pounds, and is approximately the length and width of a piece of typing paper, and perhaps three inches thick at most. Portable printer speeds vary, of course, but should at least match low-end dot-matrix printers with a speed of 60 to 80 characters per minute.

Storing FAXes

For the sake of hard disk space, it is best to print out a FAX as soon as possible after receiving it. A 10- or 12-page text FAX message can take a megabyte or more of disk space; graphic-intensive FAX messages can take even more space.

If you wish to keep a FAX on disk, it might be a good idea to store it on a floppy disk, as either a backup or the only copy. If your FAX software can convert a FAX message to another graphics format, you might convert it if the alternate format requires less disk space. (You can determine this by experimenting, converting a message to several formats.)

Cellular FAX

If you use a cellular phone, you will be pleased to know that it's reasonably easy to integrate your cellular phone with a portable FAX machine or FAX board-equipped laptop. You'll need a coupling device to connect the FAX between the cellular phone's handset and base unit. There are several of these on the market, among them Motorola's CellularConnection.

Or, if you'd just as soon forget connections and adapters, several manufacturers have combined FAX machines or computers with a cellular phone.

The Modem Alternative to PC FAX: FAX Via Online Services

There are very, very few people on the earth who are beyond the range of your modem. Those who have modems are a definite minority, but E-mail can go beyond E-mail boxes—straight to any FAX machine.

How do you reach FAXes via E-mail? In brief: Use outgoing FAX transmission offered by online services, which link your modem to every FAX machine in the world. You can send text messages to any FAX machine, anywhere, using the modem/FAX services offered by commercial online services. It's as simple as sending E-mail.

The E-Mail/FAX Connection

When FAX exploded onto the business and personal communications scene in 1987, the development of modem/FAX services was almost inevitable. There were hundreds of thousands of personal computer users accessing commercial online services via modem at that time. Personal computer- *and* communications-literate individuals who were a potential market for FAX service via the electronics communication medium with which they were most familiar: online services.

Various online services recognized the potential for modem/FAX service, and developed software that translated from 7-bit ASCII to FAX formats, much in the way that PC FAX boards perform computer-to-FAX data translation. Additional software, working with special hardware, handles dialing up and transmitting data to designated FAX machines, along with such chores as interpreting FAX "addresses" (telephone numbers), generating cover sheets, and providing verification of delivery.

As complex as this sounds, using the end product is not that different from using E-mail. As illustrated in Figures 7.4 and 7.5, addressing a FAX message via E-mail requires pretty much the same steps as sending a conventional E-mail message; the major difference is how the message is addressed. (Figures 7.4 and 7.5 illustrate addressing an E-mail message and a FAX message, respectively, on MCI Mail.)

Being able to send FAX messages in the same manner as E-mail offers a number of attractions and advantages for modem users. Modem users can send FAX messages without having to invest in expensive specialized equipment. What's more, they can send computer-generated documents without having to print them out. Messages and documents can be transmitted at any time of the day or night, and the cost is reasonable. In short, sending FAX messages via E-mail offers all of the advantages of E-mail *and* FAX, with few disadvantages.

The only major disadvantage of E-mail/FAX services is the fact that most of them allow you to send only text messages.

Most of the major online services offer at least outgoing FAX service (the ability to *send* text messages and documents to designated FAX machines). These include AT&T Mail, Compu-

```
create

TO:     Jerry Pournelle
        281-4144 Jerry Pournelle                          Studio City, CA
TO:

CC:

Subject: Final Chapters

Text: (Enter text or transmit file. Type / on a line by itself to end.)

Jerry,
        The final chapters are in first draft, and




Esc for Command?, Home for Status   ||    Capture Off      || Lo: 00:07:11
```

Figure 7.4 Addressing an E-mail Message on MCI Mail

```
TO:     Martin Caidin (FAX)

Enter country of recipient. Press RETURN if USA.

Country:
Recipient Fax No: 1-904-555-1212
Options?
Alternate Delivery?

TO:     Martin Caidin
        FAXno: 904-555-1212

Is this address correct (Yes or No)? y

TO:

CC:

Subject: Contracts

Text: (Enter text or transmit file. Type / on a line by itself to e

Martin,
Esc for Command?, Home for Status   ||    Capture Off      || Lo: 00:08:05
```

Figure 7.5 Addressing a FAX Message on MCI Mail

Serve, DELPHI, GEnie, MCI Mail, SprintMail, and others. DASnet, an inter-system E-mail relay service, also offers FAX service.

Several of the services offer enhancements to their FAX services, such as:

- The option of composing a message online.
- The ability to receive FAX messages (this is rare).
- Translation to FAX format and FAX transmission of computer-generated graphics files and documents created with certain word processors.

Various delivery options are also available, including cover sheets.

How It Works

When you create a message online or upload a document to an online service's E-mail system and specify FAX delivery, the message is either translated to FAX format by the service's main computer, or transmitted to a computer that is dedicated to handling FAX messages, which then translates the message.

After translation to the binary format required by FAX machines, the online service's computer calls the number you gave it when you addressed the message as a FAX message. The time between when you "send" the message and when the online service's computer dials up the receiving FAX machine may be a few minutes, or an hour or two, depending on the service you are using and the amount of FAX and other communications traffic it is currently handling.

When contact is made with the receiving FAX machine, the online service's computer transmits your message, then disconnects. If the number you specified is busy, or if there is no answer, the online service's computer will call back. The number and interval of the retries are either system defaults, or specified by you. (This gives you, in effect, store-and-forward capability.)

Some services offer automatic confirmation of delivery. Other services confirm only if a message is *not* delivered. Confirmations of delivery are in the form of E-mail messages to you.

Systems that do not provide automatic confirmation of delivery may offer it as an option, sometimes at an extra cost.

The few systems that receive FAX messages for you deliver them as E-mail messages. The party sending a FAX message to you via an online service must put some kind of identifier (usually on the first line) indicating your ID on the system—the computer handling incoming FAX messages must have this information so it knows to whom to deliver it. The incoming FAX message is converted from FAX format to 7-bit ASCII, after which it is E-mailed to you.

Using E-Mail FAX Services

As illustrated earlier, using an E-mail service to send a FAX message differs little from sending a message as an E-mail message. On some systems you must use a special menu selection to specify FAX delivery, while on others you specify FAX delivery when addressing the message, as shown in Figure 7.5. (The latter option typically moves you to a special FAX subsystem.)

You may also be asked to specify certain delivery options before or after message creation or upload.

After addressing and creating the message, and specifying any options, you issue the E-mail system's **SEND** command (or select it from a menu), and the message will be sent.

Preparing E-Mail FAX Messages Messages or documents intended for FAX delivery via an online service must meet the same requirements as E-mail messages. Depending on how your word processing program stores files, you may have to convert documents to 7-bit ASCII files before the online service will accept them.

PC FAX or E-mail FAX Service?

By now, you may be wondering if you really need a PC FAX board at all, since you can handle text-based FAX traffic via your dialup modem and an accommodating online service. Before you make a decision on whether to let modem/FAX handle all of your FAX traffic, consider its advantages and disadvantages:

E-Mail/FAX Advantages:

- Ease of message creation (online or off).
- Store-and-forward, multiple-recipient, and broadcast FAX capability.
- Time savings (retries and multiple FAXes are handled for you; you only have to go through the sending process once).
- Simultaneous E-mail/FAX/hardcopy delivery.
- Convenience; you can send and receive FAX messages whenever you wish.
- Access to most E-mail features.
- Access to services other than FAX offered by the host online service.

E-Mail/FAX Disadvantages:

- The cost of sending a FAX via an online service may be higher than a direct-dial FAX transmission, when the per-minute charges imposed by some online services are added to the per-page FAX charge.
- Setting up to access some online services via modem may be more complex than using a PC FAX. Once you've learned the ropes, using a specific online service is easy, but you will have to invest some time learning.
- Sending a lengthy document usually requires some kind of preparation—conversion to 7-bit ASCII, modifying margins, etc.

8
Online Services for Traveling Modems

Although this isn't a book about online services as such, you will probably use commercial online services more than any other communications channel—BBSs, direct-dial to your desktop computer, etc. Commercial online services not only provide communications—in the form of E-mail, outgoing text FAX, hardcopy mail, and Telex—but also news, research, entertainment, and even shopping services.

In addition to all that, there are special segments of several commercial online services for laptop users.

This chapter will provide an overview of the services available online, with a concentration on those services of special interest to laptop users. Contact information for each of the online services discussed in this chapter is provided in Appendix C. (For comprehensive information about all the major online services, see *The Modem Reference,* 2nd Edition, by Michael A. Banks, published by Brady Books.)

Online Service Categories

There are three general categories of online services: E-mail specialty services, database and information-retrieval services, and consumer online services. Any may offer some or all of the services offered by the others, and indeed the differences between one type of service or another are sometimes few.

The best way to classify a service is to consider its area of concentration. For example, MCI Mail is primarily an E-mail specialty service, even though it offers bulletin boards and a gateway to Dow Jones News-Retrieval Service. Similarly, DIALOG is an information-retrieval service, even though DIALOG users can send E-mail to one another and share information on bulletin boards.

E-Mail Specialty Services

As you might expect, E-mail specialty services are very good at what they do: transferring text messages and various sorts of files between their subscribers. They offer more features and options with regards to handling E-mail than any other service. Among their more useful features are:

- The option of online message composition or uploading a message.

- E-mail interconnections with other E-mail specialty services, consumer services, etc.

- FAX delivery (as described in Chapter 7).

- Hardcopy delivery (a.k.a. "paper mail"). This E-mail option lets you send a letter to any postal address in the world. The letter is printed out with a laser printer in a city near the destination, then mailed via U.S. Mail. This is particularly convenient if you want to keep in touch with someone via postal mail, but don't have a printer with you—or if you just prefer the convenience of mailing a letter without bothering with printouts, envelopes, and stamps. Suboptions include having your letterhead and signature included on letters.

    Figure 8.1 shows a hardcopy letter from an E-mail service.

- Telex delivery. You can have a text message delivered to any Telex machine in the world.

- Multiple recipients and mailing lists. You can send the same E-mail message to several subscribers on the service, and/or to FAX, hardcopy, and Telex addresses, as

```
September 11, 1991


Michael A. Banks
PR/Online
P.O. Box 312
Milford, OH  45150


     This is an example of a "paper mail" letter sent via MCI
Mail.  The letter is printed out, using a laser printer, in the
city nearest the recipient's address, then mailed in a
distinctive envelope.  This is often faster than sending mail
from your location.
     Options available (but not used in this example) include
letterhead and signature reproduction.

--Michael A. Banks
```

Figure 8.1 MCI Mail Hardcopy Letter

well. Set mailing lists can be maintained, or you can enter addresses manually.

- Message forwarding, with annotations.
- Elaborate online filing systems, with "folders" and other aids to keeping messages together by category.
- Online "return receipts," so you know when an E-mail message has been read.
- Automatic resending of messages at set periods.
- Automatic responses to messages. These are electronic form letters that are sent to anyone who sends you E-mail. This is a useful option to activate when you won't be signing on to a service for a time.

That's an overview of the more common and some of the more elaborate features (especially the last three or four) E-mail specialty services offer. The more elaborate features aren't available on all E-mail services. A few, such as AT&T Mail's system that reads your E-mail to you via voice phone, exist only on one service.

The most popular E-mail specialty services are MCI Mail and AT&T Mail.

MCI Mail is a "general" E-mail service, geared toward the individual modem user as well as the corporate user. Among its features are most of those described on previous pages. It offers many extras, including a gateway to Dow Jones News/Retrieval Service, and public and private bulletin boards. There's also an E-mail gateway to and from CompuServe, so CompuServe and MCI Mail subscribers can exchange mail, and E-mail gateways to other E-mail specialty services.

If you have the right software, you can transfer binary files via MCI Mail. The "right software" includes any of the MCI Mail front ends—Lotus Express or Desktop, or Norton Commander Mail, described in Chapter 4. (If your primary modem application is person-to-person communications and you have to choose one E-mail service, or even one online service, MCI Mail is a good choice. It has more individual subscribers than other E-mail services, and is very economical.)

AT&T Mail is set up for and marketed to corporate users more than to individuals. It serves as AT&T's internal mail system, and provides every imaginable E-mail option (including the aforementioned voice E-mail retrieval system). AT&T offers a front end for AT&T Mail, sold online or with computer/modem/E-mail service packages.

Other popular E-mail systems include SprintMail (operated by SprintNet) and DIALCOM (BT Tymnet). For those who wish to have access to subscribers to a large number of online services of all types, DASnet provides an E-mail transfer service. DASnet's computer maintains E-mail accounts on several dozen online services worldwide, from which it collects specially addressed mail. It sorts out E-mail and sends it directly to the recipient in his or her own private E-mail box. Services that DASnet interconnects include AT&T Mail, BIX, CompuServe, MCI Mail, SprintMail, and many, many more. For many modem users, DASnet is a better alternative to maintaining accounts on several online services.

Database and Information Retrieval Services

Database and information-retrieval services are pretty much what the name says. They provide large specialized and general databases, which you can search in a variety of ways. Like E-mail specialty services, database and information-retrieval services do their job very, very well. They typically provide more extensive search and retrieval services than the average database on other kinds of online services. They also provide very extensive collections of information, most of it specialized, along with current news.

Because consumer services are providing more and more information resources (as you will learn), database and information-retrieval services are having to provide specialized information products to survive. These include industry-specific reference works, newsletters, and databases, as well as archives of special-interest publications.

The top three database and information-retrieval services are DIALOG, Dow Jones News/Retrieval Service, and Newsnet.

DIALOG is perhaps the oldest commercial online service in existence (since the mid-1970s). DIALOG concentrates on industry-specific information—current and archived—and information for professionals. (Researchers are their biggest customers.) More general-interest, consumer products are available, too. Among these are an online encyclopedia, the full text of a number of large city newspapers, and reference works such as *Books in Print* and *Marquis Who's Who*. DIALOG also offers internal E-mail and bulletin boards, and markets a special front-end program called DIALOGLINK.

Dow Jones News/Retrieval Service focuses on news, with a concentration on financial news. It has all the resources of its namesake, along with the contents of numerous esteemed financial publications and well-known newspapers, online. A variety of stock and commodity quote and information services is available, many customized. DJNS, as it's known, also offers consumer services and special-interest services not related to finances, including a college guide, a shopping service, E-mail, and much more. There's also general news from various newswires.

Newsnet provides the content of several hundred newsletters, along with that of large newspapers and near-real-time news from worldwide newswires. The newsletters range from extremely specialized (covering one profession or segment of a business) to industry-wide. It is possible to search any or all of the online resources individually or in groups. It's worth noting here that many of Newsnet's newsletters exist only online. Other newsletters are electronic versions of important hardcopy newsletters. Newsnet also offers internal E-mail.

Unless you do a lot of research, or have need of near-daily updates in areas of special interest, you can probably do without accessing database and information/retrieval services while traveling. They tend to be far more expensive than either E-mail specialty or consumer services. Too, you can obtain much of the information offered (stock quotes and news, for example) on consumer services at lower cost.

Consumer Online Services

Consumer online services offer a combination of the most interesting online products and services. All systems offer a combination of E-mail, databases of one type or another, special interest groups, message bases, and real-time conference.

In addition to the products and services just listed, most consumer services offer any or all of the following:

- News and weather. These services include regional, national, and international news; weather by city, state, or region; and specialized news such as sports and financial news. News is from the same sources as other media use—newswires and syndicates.

- Financial information and services. Stock and commodities market reports and quotes, as well as brokering, are offered online by companies who are in the same business in the real world.

- Entertainment. Online entertainment offerings are heavy on gaming. There are single- and multiplayer games, played real-time or via postings in message bases. Most online games mirror disk-based computer games, so you'll find a lot of role-playing and "adventure"-type games. There are also arcade games (most of which require either special software or terminal emulation).

- Reference and education. Online encyclopedias head the list here, with products like *Grolier's Academic American Encyclopedia* and *Compton's Encyclopedia* available on just about every service.

A variety of other references are online, too, ranging from *Marquis Who's Who* to the Magazine Index.

Education services include reference services like the College Board and Peterson's College Guide, as well as online tutoring, study, and degree programs.

- Special-interest groups. Special-interest groups (or SIGs, to use the common acronym) are the heart of many online services. Known variously as Forums, Round-Tables, and conferences, SIGs may host a variety of services, including message bases, databases, upload/download services, online advertising and sales, and any of a number of other activities.

- Travel services. Travel information, in the form of services sponsored by carriers or destinations, as well as from travel agencies and the Eaasy Sabre and Official Airlines Guide (OAG), is popular online.

- Shopping and online product support. Online shopping is just now coming into its own. Although specialty retailers and computer and software discount operations have enjoyed some success online over the years, it's taken the presence of major national retailers, such as Waldenbooks, Sears, and the like, on a number of online services to legitimize online shopping.

Online product support—almost exclusively for computers and software—has been fairly well-received, although there seems to be some competition among online services to be the only host for some companies' online product support.

- Specialized news and database services. As you might expect, there are a number of computer news services and columns online. Some are "unofficial" products in the form of special-interest newsletters uploaded to public databases, like *PC Review Online*. Others are "official" products, presented in their own areas or as menu selections, like Charles Bowen's "A Networker's Journal" on CompuServe and GEnie. Specialized newsletters that have nothing to do with computing are showing up, too. Among these you'll find newsletters for occupations such as writers, and PR and advertising professionals.

- Full text versions of general- and special-interest magazines and newsletters. Online newsletters have been around for quite some time. Newspapers have been online for several years, too. Selected computer magazine articles and program listings have been popping up within SIGs for some time, but it is only since the very late 1980s that the complete content of computer magazines (articles) have been put online. The same is true of noncomputer magazines, like *National Geographic*, and this is still a very small part of the online world.

- Gateways to specialized services. Gateways that allow you to use one online service through another are becoming more and more popular, to the point where some interconnections might be viewed as "a network of networks." You can "gateway" to Eaasy Sabre or OAG from just about any of the major services, and several consumer services have gateways to Dow Jones News/Retrieval Service, DIALOG, and more esoteric information services.

- E-mail links. Only a few services offer E-mail links to other services, but E-mail communication between services is a trend that's accelerating.

How these are implemented varies from one system to another. But these are the basic product categories of consumer services.

Consumer Online Service "Extras"

Each consumer service has a number of "extras" that make using it easier, faster, or just more interesting. The extras may include membership directories; variable menu and prompt levels; terminal emulation; real-time communication in the form of "one-liners" or "whispers" between any two users online; member-to-member file transfer (usually a part of E-mail); private online file storage areas; an online index of services; and other features.

Most consumer online services are text-based, which means they offer text only, with limited graphics under terminal emulation. BIX, CompuServe, DELPHI, and GEnie are text-based. A few services are graphics-based, using front-end programs that enable a graphic-rich environment. America Online and Prodigy are graphics-based.

Now let's take a closer look at what's online, on the major services just mentioned. (I classify these as major services based on numbers of users, services offered, and nationwide accessibility via packet-switching networks.)

America Online

Introduced in October 1989, America Online (AOL) uses a graphical user interface based on Geoworks Ensemble, complete with icons and pull-down menus. Its services are organized into eight categories: Computing & Software, Entertainment, News & Finance, Lifestyles & Interests, Learning & Reference, Travel & Shopping, and What's News/Online Support. These are illustrated by the service's sign-on screen, shown in Figure 8.2.

Navigation is via menu-selection and mnemonic keywords (the keyword feature is invoked by a simple Ctrl-K). The service also uses several function- and control-key combinations for commands.

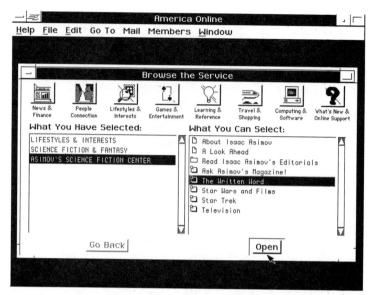

Figure 8.2 America Online

America Online features a sophisticated E-mail system that lets you review messages you've already read, copy them to disk, attach files to messages, and check to see whether a message has been read. FAX and paper mail delivery options are also available.

There are a number of real-time conference venues, referred to as "rooms" and "auditoriums." There's also an "instant message" feature that lets you send messages of several dozen words to anyone online. A systemwide member directory lets you see where a member is from, and, if the member has entered an online profile, read other information about that person.

Special-interest groups, called Forums, provide message bases, and real-time conference areas. Forums are probably AOL's most popular products. As with most services, AOL's special-interest groups cover specific computing, hardware, and software interests, as well as hobby, lifestyle, and personal interest groups and forums ranging from science fiction to veterans' interests.

Forums also have software downloads. Or, you can search for and download software and data or information files in a central area. AOL uses a proprietary binary file-transfer protocol.

The software search setup AOL offers at its central software area makes it easy to find files by letting you specify any combination of categories, a range of time, and/or keywords. The search facilities in the message bases are similarly well-designed.

Among AOL's other highlights are national news, weather, and sports information services; stock quotes; travel services like Eaasy Sabre; shopping with Comp-U-Store online and other vendors; computing and consumer news features and columns; and access to *Grolier's Academic American Encyclopedia*.

Online gaming is fairly popular on AOL. There are numerous "play-by-mail" games and single-player games. Special add-on front-end programs that you download from AOL are used to play several games.

AOL access is through SprintNet and Tymnet, but the network connections are transparent because the America Online software handles all elements of sign-on (with the exception of the user having to enter his or her password, for verification).

AOL software is an integral part of GeoWorks' Ensemble GUI, and a standalone version is provided free. Connect-time rates are $5.00 per hour nonprime time and $8.00 per hour prime time, with a $5.95 per month minimum charge. (The minimum charge includes one hour of connect time.)

BIX (Byte Information eXchange)

BIX is an acronym for **Byte Information eXchange**. Established in 1985, BIX uses the UNIX-based COSY computer conferencing system. (That's "computer conferencing" in the traditional sense of the term—meaning conferencing via message bases, not real-time conferencing.)

A very straightforward system, BIX doesn't attempt to provide every kind of online product; rather, it emphasizes communications—between *Byte* and its readers, between various hardware and software vendors and their customers, and among *Byte* readers—who happen to be some of the most involved and knowledgeable personal computer users anywhere.

With its numerous vendor support areas, the technical acumen of its users, and its link with *Byte* and the magazine's contributors, BIX is probably the single most comprehensive online source of technical information on contemporary personal computing. It's also a community, and a friendly one at that. Most BIX users take pride in being a part of the system (they've created a name for themselves—"BIXen"), and welcome newcomers.

Communication isn't limited to personal computer topics, however; noncomputer conferences cover everything from writing to automobiles to disasters. Anyone can join BIX, no matter what his or her interests.

BIX has four main services: computer conferencing, electronic mail, real-time conference, and software/file databases. (Note: BIX uses lowercase letters for names and commands; I'll follow that convention here.) An area called "options" lets you set up and change how BIX communicates with you (your online profile), and you can create an online "resume" with information about yourself that other users can access from most prompts by typing "show resume <username>".

BIX is primarily command-driven, but provides an optional menu system, as shown in Figure 8.3.

```
BIX Main Menu

1  Electronic Mail
2  Conference Subsystem
3  Listings
4  MicroBytes - Industry News Briefs
5  Subscriber Information
6  Individual Options
7  Quick Download
8  Command Mode (abandon menus)
9  Logoff (bye)

Enter a menu option or ? for help: 2

   Conference Subsystem Menu

1  See conference groups and join conferences
2  Read new messages
3  Join a conference by name
4  Resign from a conference
5  Search conference index
mm Main menu

Enter a menu option or ? for help:
```

Figure 8.3 BIX Main Menu

The heart of BIX is its computer conferencing system. The system is based on a series of message-base subject areas called "conferences," each of which is a part of a "group" of related conferences. BIX currently hosts more than 200 conferences. Individual conferences are further organized into such topics as are appropriate for the conference subject.

The conference system is fairly sophisticated. In addition to letting you read, scan, post, reply to, and search for messages, BIX allows you to locate and follow message threads, and much more. You can participate in (join) as many or as few BIX conferences as you like. And you can select specific topics within a conference to participate in. (A few conferences are "closed," which means you must request or be invited to join them.)

BIX's mail system (referred to as "BIXMAIL") offers most basic E-mail options. You can send messages to more than one person via a multiple addresses or a "carbon copy" option, reply to, forward, and edit and file messages using BIX's online editor. You can also attach a binary file to a message. Messages are retained after reading unless you delete them, in a simple "inbox/outbox" filing system that tags messages that have been read. The system also allows you to cancel an E-mail message after you've sent it—an option that's perhaps too rare.

BIX's "CBix" real-time conferencing system is a fairly easy-to-use multiband, multichannel CB simulator. Features include "whispers," "handles," and more. The system makes interesting use of specific terminal features. If your software can emulate VT-100 or any of a dozen-odd other terminals, you can take advantage of screen-clearing, a chat window, a window for "whispers," and other special features.

Downloads of all types can be found in special BIX areas called "listings." ASCII, Kermit, Xmodem, Xmodem/CRC, Ymodem, and Zmodem protocols are available for file transfer. (Billing is automatically turned off when you upload a file.)

BIX can be accessed in the U.S. by direct-dial, via Tymnet, or through BIX's own packet-switching network at 300, 1200, or 2400 bps. Canadian access is through Tymnet, or a DataPac gateway to Tymnet.

BIX gives users their choice of per-minute billing or a flat rate. The flat rate arrangement is $39.00 per quarter for *unlimited* access to BIX, 24 hours per day. This doesn't include access via packet-switching network. If you dial up BIX through Tymnet, there is an additional charge of $6.00 per hour for prime-time access, or $3.00 per hour for nonprime-time access. If you use BIXnet, there's a $6.00 per hour surcharge for prime-time, and $2.00 per hour for nonprime-time access. Alternatively, you can opt for unlimited nonprime-time access through Tymnet or BIXnet at a cost of $25.00 per month.

BIX's hourly rate is $4.00, 24 hours a day. This doesn't include Tymnet or BIXnet charges, which are the same as described in the preceding paragraph. Hourly rate subscribers are also charged an annual subscription fee of $59.00. Different rates apply for Tymnet access from outside the 48 states and in Australia, Canada, Europe, and US territories.

CompuServe

CompuServe is among the world's largest public online services. It is also one of the first commercial online services to cater to computer hobbyists. Established in 1979, CompuServe today has more than 500,000 subscribers.

As with any online service, providing a detailed listing of CompuServe's offerings here would be impossible. A complete survey of CompuServe would fill a book (and, indeed, several have been written). However, I'll provide at least an overview of CompuServe's plethora of services.

We'll begin at the beginning, with CompuServe's main menu, called the TOP menu (Figure 8.4).

CompuServe's TOP menu is like the tip of an iceberg. While it shows in general what is there, there is much, much more than the TOP menu even implies. Literally hundreds of services exist on CompuServe—among them some extremely useful electronics communications. Beyond this menu lie general and specialized news and information services; special-interest groups for computerists, professionals, hobbyists, and others (called "Forums" on CompuServe); online games and other entertainment; sophisticated research services; a free online tutorial; and much, much more.

CompuServe has the standard newswires, including AP, UPI, and Reuters, as well as some more exotic services. There's

```
CompuServe                    TOP

 1 Member Assistance (FREE)
 2 Find a Topic (FREE)
 3 Communications/Bulletin Bds.
 4 News/Weather/Sports
 5 Travel
 6 The Electronic MALL/Shopping
 7 Money Matters/Markets
 8 Entertainment/Games
 9 Hobbies/Lifestyles/Education
10 Reference
11 Computers/Technology
12 Business/Other Interests

Enter choice number !
```

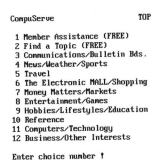

Figure 8.4 CompuServe's TOP Menu

also a clipping service that delivers news stories of interest to your E-mail box, based on keywords you specify.

CompuServe provides more weather information than any of its competitors. In addition to regional, city, and worldwide current weather and forecasts, there are several kinds of weather maps—including a satellite photo—that you can download. The maps are updated several times each day. CompuServe also has a pilots' weather service, with reports on current conditions and forecasts for hundreds of airports, and other useful info.

CompuServe is particularly strong in online research facilities, among them *Grolier's Academic American Encyclopedia,* and gateways to Dow Jones News/Retrieval Service and several specialized services—including IQuest, a collection of more than 700 specialized research databases.

CompuServe's Forums feature sophisticated message bases, a reasonable database system, and real-time conferencing separate from the system's CB Simulator.

Also of interest are CompuServe Mail's two-way gateways to MCI Mail and Internet. CompuServe Mail also handles outgoing FAX and Telex messages, and paper mail, and you can use CompuServe Mail to transfer files to other CompuServe users.

File transfer options in Forum databases, E-mail, and certain product areas include ASCII, Xmodem, Xmodem/CRC, CompuServe's own B and B+ protocols, among others.

CompuServe can be accessed via SprintNet, Tymnet, DataPac (from Canada only), and its own national packet-switching network, the CompuServe network. Access is at 300, 1200, 2400, and 4800 bps, with a number of 9600-bps nodes opening up on the CompuServe network. (Both V.32 and USRobotics HST modems are supported.)

CompuServe's basic rates are $5.00 per hour at 300 bps, and $12.80 per hour at 1200 or 2400 bps, through the CompuServe network, 24 hours per day. Additional charges are incurred for higher speeds, and for access through other networks. Various optional service plans are available, and gateways and certain other services are surcharged.

CompuServe is, as of this writing, testing a plan whereby a set group of monthly services are made available for a small monthly fee. These include various news, weather, and consumer services, as well as access to *Grolier's Academic American Encyclopedia* and several games, among other services. This plan also includes an electronic mail "allowance" of $9.00 per month, which lets you send the equivalent of about 60 three-page E-mail messages per month with no extra charges.

If you subscribe to CompuServe, I strongly urge you to buy one of the CompuServe front-end programs, CompuServe Information Manager or TAPCIS, described in Chapter 4. For laptop use, I prefer CompuServe Information Manager. Either program will help you organize your online sessions, and reduce your online time.

DELPHI

DELPHI is operated by General Videotex Service (GVC). Established in 1982 as an online encyclopedia (the first of its kind), DELPHI has evolved into a full-service network, providing products and services of all types.

An especially friendly system with a real sense of community, DELPHI is a good place to meet others who share your interests in computing and other areas.

As is the case with CompuServe, DELPHI offers enough features to fill a book. We'll begin with DELPHI's Main Menu (Figure 8.5), which will give you an idea of the extent of DELPHI's products and services.

```
MAIN Menu:

Business & Finance    News-Weather-Sports
Conference            People on DELPHI
DELPHI/Regional       Travel
Entertainment         Workspace
Groups and Clubs      Using DELPHI
Library               HELP
Mail                  EXIT
Merchants' Row

MAIN>What do you want to do?
```

Figure 8.5 DELPHI Main Menu

As I said of CompuServe's TOP menu, DELPHI's Main Menu is like the tip of an iceberg. It shows what's available only in a general sense. Like CompuServe, DELPHI sports a variety of general and topical news and information services, online entertainment and games, special-interest groups, two online encyclopedias (Grolier's and the original Kussmaul Encyclopedia), a unique gateway to the DIALOG information service, and more.

DELPHI's special-interest groups are particularly noteworthy, both for the BBS-style communication facilities they provide and for the software and information available for download. The SIG message bases are extremely sophisticated, allowing you to find messages based on almost any criteria imaginable, including content. There's a message filing, forwarding, and copying system, too. The SIG database structure is equally sophisticated, and allows you to use multiple keywords to narrow or widen searches. Each SIG has its own real-time conference area, separate from the main conference area.

Also of note on DELPHI are weekly online real-time "poker" and trivia tournaments, a scrambled word game available in the main real-time conference area, and games that take advantage of VT-100 terminal emulation.

DELPHI also gives you a personal online storage area, called Workspace, which you can use to store files created online or off, transfer files for E-mailing, and other purposes. File-transfer options in Workspace, in SIG databases, and certain other areas include ASCII, Kermit, Xmodem, Xmodem/CRC, Ymodem, Ymodem/Batch, and Zmodem.

DELPHI's E-mail is the most powerful, yet easiest to use (once you learn to use it), E-mail system offered by a consumer service. Also of interest in the area of communications is the fact that all DELPHI members can not only send FAX and Telex, but can also receive incoming Telex messages free of charge (beyond normal connect-time charges).

DELPHI can be accessed via SprintNet, Tymnet, DataPac (from Canada only), or via its direct-dial numbers in Boston. Regional versions of DELPHI in Boston, Kansas City, Miami, and Buenos Aires offer gateways to the national DELPHI service. Access speeds are 300, 1200, and 2400 bps.

DELPHI offers two rate structures. The basic connect fees are $6.00 per hour nonprime time, with a $5.95 per month minimum (this covers your first hour of usage). This is through Tymnet, direct-dial, or PC Pursuit only. (DELPHI's Boston and Kansas City services offer gateway service to DELPHI/national at the same rates. Boston and Kansas City users can also have unlimited access to their regional services for an additional $4.00 per month.) There's a $1.80 per-hour surcharge for SprintNet access during nonprime time.

DELPHI's 20/20 plan is designed for those who are online frequently. Under this plan, members are billed $20.00 per month, for 20 hours' nonprime-time access. Additional time costs only $1.20 per hour. This offer is available for those who access DELPHI through Tymnet only, and includes Tymnet charges. Unlike the flat-rate or alternative plans offered by some services, this plan covers the entire service—real-time conferencing, SIGs, databases, etc.

Prime-time rates under either plan are $9.00 per hour through Tymnet and $12.00 per hour through SprintNet. Access from outside the 48 contiguous states may incur additional network surcharges. There is a $39.00 sign-up charge for a lifetime membership.

A few services, such as DELPHI's link to DIALOG, are surcharged no matter which plan you use.

GEnie

GEnie (General Electric Network for Information Exchange) is a consumer network operated by General Electric Information Services. GEnie offers services for home and business microcomputer users, professionals, and computer hobbyists.

Established in 1985, GEnie is the fastest-growing service of its kind. It enjoys a tremendous growth rate, thanks to its services, an aggressive advertising campaign, and a friendly price structure.

GEnie's TOP menu (Figure 8.6) provides an overview of service categories.

```
GEnie                           TOP                      Page    1
                         GE Information Services

   1.[*]GEnie*Basic                  2.[*]GEnie News, Index & Information
   3.[*]User Settings/Billing Info.  4.   Communications (GE Mail & Chat)
   5.   Computing Services           6.   Travel Services
   7.   Finance/Business Services    8.   Online Shopping Services
   9.   News, Sports & Weather      10.   Multi-Player Games
  11.   Professional Services       12.   Leisure Services
  13.   Educational Services        14.   Leave GEnie (Logoff)

Enter #, <H>elp?
```

Figure 8.6 GEnie's TOP Menu

GEnie offers the same categories of services as CompuServe and DELPHI. News, weather, sports, and travel information are particularly strong areas for GEnie, as are GEnie's versions of special-interest groups, called RoundTables (RT for short).

The RoundTables are fairly simple to use, but their message bases lack sophistication, and you cannot specify more than one search keyword in the RTs' software libraries. This makes using either area more time-consuming—unless you're using a GEnie front end.

Online research facilities include *Grolier's Academic Encyclopedia* and a gateway to Dow Jones News/Retrieval Service. GEnie's news offerings include searchable headline news, and columns by a number of well-known writers in the computer field. There's also a clipping service that delivers news stories of interest to your E-mail box, based on keywords you specify.

GE Mail—GEnie's E-mail service—lets you send and receive letters from other GEnie users, and send paper mail and FAX messages. An Internet gateway may be available by the time you read this. GEnie offers a unique feature in an option by which a GEnie user may have his or her own Telex number, at an extra fee. (Other online services offer incoming Telex service via one Telex number, identifying the user to whom a Telex message is to be sent by the inclusion of the user's online ID in the first line of a message.)

GEnie has no personal file system as such, but you can upload messages to send to other GEnie users via a special utility. Uploads and downloads are via Xmodem.

GE Mail has a command that lets you cancel a message that you've already sent, removing it from the recipient's online mailbox. GEnie's mail address file is located on the GE Mail menu, too. It features a flexible search system that you can use to find both GE Mail addresses and the names of people online. (An online personal profile/resume area contains more detailed information that members enter about themselves.)

GEnie's game offerings are extensive. In addition to trivia, parlor games, sports, role-playing, and single-player games like adventure games, GEnie has some very attractive real-time, multiplayer action games. In particular, "Air Warrior" has attracted a large and extremely devoted following.

GEnie offers 300/1200/2400 baud access, via its own national network of direct-dial, local numbers in several hundred U.S. cities.

NOTE: GEnie differs from the vast majority of online services in that it expects your computer to operate at half duplex, and thus does not echo what you input. This can be changed once you're online, but be sure to set your software or modem to half duplex operation the first time you dial up GEnie.

GEnie also has a number of 9600-bps, V.32 nodes, with more being added. V.42 nodes are coming online, as well.

GEnie offers flat-rate access, currently $4.95 per month for unlimited nonprime time use of E-mail, news, and other selected services. GEnie charges 10 cents per minute during nonprime time for services not included in the flat-rate access (like Round-Table software libraries, and real-time conferencing). The prime-time rate is $18.00 per hour.

There is a $2.00 per hour surcharge for calling from a very few cities, and a surcharge for 9600-bps access. Certain products, such as GEnie's gateway to Dow Jones News/Retrieval Service, cost extra.

GEnie members should get a copy of the Aladdin front end for GEnie (described in Chapter 4). This is especially useful for laptop users, because it reduces the amount of time spent online, and organizes messages and downloads. (One thing Aladdin does that no other online service front end does is give you a list of files you've downloaded when you exit the program.)

Prodigy

Prodigy is very different from other consumer services in both how it's set up and what it offers. If you're a software junkie looking for downloads, or a real-time conference maven, you won't find those things here. But, contrary to opinion among certain of the modem-using public, Prodigy has virtually all the other trappings of a full-service consumer service. And you'll find some unique offerings not available elsewhere among its more than 750 products and services.

Introduced in several cities in 1988, Prodigy is a product of The PRODIGY Services Company, a partnership of IBM and Sears. Intended to be a simple yet powerful online service for the general consumer market, it has done a good job in reaching its intended audience—that being computer users who aren't technically oriented. Indeed, it sometimes seems most of

Prodigy's members have never before used a modem. Some certainly never before used a computer.

Prodigy is a high-resolution graphics-based (and graphics-intensive) service that requires Prodigy software for access. (The graphics format, NAPLPS, is such that *everything* displayed onscreen is graphics—even text.)

Of course, Prodigy software stores much of the graphic information displayed by the service on your hard disk or Prodigy software floppy disk, which means not everything you see on your screen has to be transmitted each time you view it. This speeds up access and response time, but those who use slower computers still complain about access time. (Some of this may be due to the service updating the information stored on your disk with automatic downloads.)

Prodigy software is available for MS-DOS and Macintosh computers and supports a variety of functions.

Prodigy's success can be credited in large part to its format. Indeed, I find the medium to be literally part of the message, especially in interactive graphics areas like Air New Zealand's extended advertisement, where you use a map to key on ANZ destinations you wish to explore. Similar setups have been used to deliver news and other information, as during the early stages of the Middle East war, when a map of the region was used to provide information on the various countries involved.

Graphics are but one ingredient in Prodigy's success formula. Much of the service's success has been due to something Prodigy discovered through extensive market research (later backed up by other services' research and testing): Modem users—especially those new to online services—are more comfortable if there is no billing clock running while they're online. Thus, Prodigy charges a flat rate for access (even Tymnet access is not surcharged). The only way you can spend money beyond the flat-rate fee is to order something online, or to send more than the minimum number of mail messages permitted each month. (More on charges later.)

E-mail, news, weather, and travel services head the list of Prodigy offerings. Most news and travel services are the same as you'll find elsewhere. However, many of Prodigy's information-providers and advertisers are not online anywhere else.

Online Services for Traveling Modems 183

Prodigy's offerings are so numerous that even a book about the service could not cover them all. Here's a list of some of the major product and service categories.

ADVICE	HOME IMPROVEMENT
APPLIANCES	HOROSCOPES
ART	INSURANCE
AUDIO/VIDEO	INVESTMENTS
AUTOMOBILES	JEWELRY
BANKING	LOANS
BOATING	LOTTERIES
BOOKS	LUGGAGE
BROKERAGE	MORTGAGES
BUSINESS	MOVIES
CHINA/GLASS/SILVER	MUSIC
CLOTHING	NEWS
COLUMNISTS	OFFICE PRODUCTS
COMPACT DISCS	OFFICE SERVICES
COMPUTER ACCESSORIES	PETS
COMPUTER HARDWARE	PHOTOGRAPHY
COMPUTER NEWS & TALK	PRODIGY SERVICE
COMPUTER PERIPHERALS	PUBLICATIONS
COMPUTER SOFTWARE	REAL ESTATE
CONSUMER REPORTS	RESTAURANTS
CREDIT CARDS	SCIENCE
CREDIT REPORTS	SHOPPING ONLINE
CURRENT AFFAIRS	SPORTING GOODS
DEPARTMENT STORES	SPORTS, NEWS & INFORMATION
EDUCATION	
ELECTRONICS	STATIONERY
ENTERTAINMENT	TAPES, AUDIO
FACSIMILE	TELEPHONES
FINANCIAL PLANNING	TELEVISION
FLOWERS & PLANTS	TOOLS
FOOD & BEVERAGES	TOYS
FRAGRANCES	TRAVEL, AIRLINES & TICKETS
FURNITURE	TRAVEL, HOTELS & RESORTS
GAMES & QUIZZES	TRAVEL, RENTAL CARS
GARDENING	TRAVEL, TIPS & INFORMATION
GROCERS	
HEALTH & BEAUTY AIDS	TRAVEL ACCESSORIES
HEALTH & FITNESS	TRAVEL AGENTS
HOBBIES	VIDEOTAPES
HOME	WEATHER

Prodigy's E-mail features include mailing lists, printing messages, forwarding messages, and retaining messages in your mailbox. There's an associated online member directory, in which you are included only by choice.

Reading news on Prodigy is a lot like reading a newspaper; you can select news to read by headlines, and jump to other articles whenever you wish. You can print out news stories, too. Like newspapers, Prodigy offers pictures and charts—in the form of color graphics—with some news stories. (The Prodigy software won't print the graphics, however.)

Prodigy supports many other information features with graphics, among them weather reports illustrated by Accu-Weather maps, updated twice daily.

Special-interest news, in the form of columns and—where appropriate—chart listings—covers movies, films, people, and other topics.

Several nationally known magazines are Prodigy service providers. Among them are *National Geographic*, which provides an especially attractive and enlightening excerpt, with graphics, each month. You'll also find *Billboard* music charts, *Changing Times* magazine, and more.

Among the most interesting features for some members are columns by well-known writers and syndicated columnists.

WGBH's "Nova" puts together a monthly feature that is best described as a "program," covering a topic and/or individual in science. The "Nova" features are graphic-rich and interactive.

Prodigy doesn't have SIGs as such. Instead, there are things like the "Computer Club" and "Arts Club," which combine access to features like columns, news, and bulletin boards.

Bulletin boards are the major drawing card for many Prodigy customers. Most are part of a club's offerings. The boards are searchable by subject or member ID. Prodigy screens BBS messages before posting them, because they want to maintain a "family service" image, and they don't want people to post commercial notices.

Online gaming is graphic-intensive, as you might expect. Although you're not likely to spend much time with online games on other services at per-minute rates, Prodigy doesn't charge extra for their games. Thus, you can while away your idle hours with games such as MadMaze (a role-playing/adventure game that surpasses some disk-based games of its type), an online version of Broderbund Software's *Where in the World is Carmen Sandiego?*, and other games.

In addition to almost all the travel services hosted by other online services, Prodigy hosts information and products from British Air, Swissair, United Airlines, and Air France, among others. Airline reservations are available via American Airlines' Eaasy Sabre and several travel agents. Various vacation and cruise information and products are available, too.

Grolier's Academic American Encyclopedia heads the list of reference resources on The PRODIGY service, which also includes columns and clubs on a variety of home, special-interest, and business topics, as well as information from computing and general-interest magazines.

Several banks offer services such as certificates of deposit and online applications for lines of credit and credit cards. Online banking (bill paying in particular) is popular on the service, too. Discover cardholders can check their balances online, and those who don't have Discover cards can apply for them online.

Stock quotes and financial news and columns are also provided. You can even use services provided by Sears Financial Services and Coldwell-Banker to calculate mortgages. You can also apply for mortgage loans online.

Prodigy originally used a private network, gradually adding nodes until it was available in more than two dozen cities. Late in 1990, Prodigy service added national access through Tymnet. Now the service is available from almost anywhere in the U.S.

Prodigy costs $12.95 per month (plus local sales tax, where applicable). This fee covers unlimited access, day or night. (There is no surcharge for Tymnet access.) Prodigy lets you have up to six IDs per household, so you are, in effect, getting six accounts for one price. (As of this writing, Prodigy is beta-testing 9600-bps, V.32 access. Look for Prodigy to offer it in late 1992 or early 1993, with a surcharge.)

There is a 25-cent surcharge for each E-mail message after 30 in one month, per household. (E-mail to advertisers of Prodigy Member Services is free.)

Prodigy start-up kits are sold for $39.95 at Sears and computer stores nationwide. However, Prodigy runs constant promotions in which the software is given away, along with a month's free trial. The Prodigy service start-up kits are also bundled with computers, IBM's PS/1 in particular.

Six, 12, and 24-month memberships are available for $65.70, $119.40, and $199.95, respectively. Prodigy also offers specialized services, called "Custom Choices," for additional fees. Among these are Baseball Manager, a "fantasy league" baseball game that costs $119.95 per member for the entire baseball season, and Strategic Investor, which costs $14.95 per member per month.

If you use Prodigy, you should obtain a copy of PRO-PLUS or Promaster, described in Chapter 4. These add many vital features to the Prodigy software.

Spotlight: Online Resources for Laptop Users

I've already discussed most of the resources offered by online services in depth. I will note, however, that online services provide quite a few specific resources for laptop computer users, in the form of laptop computer special-interest groups.

As previously noted, special-interest groups go by various names on different services. Whatever sobriquet it goes by, a SIG is a meeting place and a general resource for those who share a common interest. You can expect to find pretty much the same features in any SIG. Specifically:

- A public message base, where you can leave questions or comments, or simply "lurk" and take in whatever everyone else is saying.

- A file download/upload area, where you'll find programs, text files on various topics, data files, and the like. (On most services, uploading is free.)

- A real-time conference area, where you can meet and chat with other users of the service informally, or participate in formal discussion groups, often with a "guest speaker."

- An information area, where you can find out who runs the group, what it's all about, how to use it, etc.
- "Gateways" to other services offered by the online service that hosts the SIG (E-mail, for example).

Some SIGs also offer shopping and classified ad services.

You can find useful programs and information in other computer-specific SIGs on each of the major consumer services. However, the laptop SIGs are where you'll find the greatest number of useful files, helpful users, and other resources typically provided by SIGs. Also, you're more likely to find information about older portable computers, such as Epson, Geneva, and Starlet in laptop SIGs.

Laptop SIGs are also the perfect place to post a query about telecomputing accommodations in a specific hotel, chain, or region. Leave an inquiry in a message base, and chances are you'll have four or five answers within a few days, telling you whether or not a specific hotel offers RJ-11 jacks, and/or which hotels in the area you intend to visit do.

You'll find laptop-oriented special-interest groups on BIX, CompuServe, DELPHI, and GEnie.

BIX Laptop Resources

BIX hosts a "laptops" conference that features, among other things, quite a bit of discussion on the problems of telecomputing on the road.

Traveling Software sponsors a conference on BIX, too, and you'll find conferences devoted to products from Tandy, Toshiba, and other companies that manufacture laptops.

Of peripheral interest are the "ibm" and "bbs" conferences.

CompuServe Forums for Laptop Owners

CompuServe offers the Tandy Model 100 Forum, for owners of Tandy's early laptops, as well as Forums for owners of Toshiba, Zenith, and other companies that manufacture laptop computers.

If you use a Poquet or other palmtop computer, visit the Palmtop Forum for files and information from other palmtop users.

The IBM Hardware Forum contains files and information of interest to laptop users, as well.

Communications software publishers, like Crosstalk, sponsor Forums on CompuServe, too. These are operated by people on the publisher's staff, and are the ultimate resource for answers to software-specific questions.

Portable Place on DELPHI

DELPHI's "Portable Place" SIG is information central for laptop owners. Other SIGs on DELPHI offer information and files of use to laptop users, too. (Most types of portable and laptop computers are covered here, but there is extra emphasis on MS-DOS laptops and Tandy Model 100/200 and 600 laptop computers.)

For additional MS-DOS files, check out the PC SIG.

GEnie's Laptops RoundTable

GEnie's "Laptops RT" is a special-interest group that provides resources for all sorts of portable/laptop computers. Most types of portable/laptop computers are covered, but the emphasis is on MS-DOS, Tandy, and some of the older laptop computers.

GEnie's Tandy RT also provides support for both kinds of Tandy laptops—the 100/200/600 series and the newer MS-DOS laptops.

GEnie's Laptops RT is sponsored in part by Traveling Software.

■ ■ ■

Laptop SIGs on all online services are a tremendous resource for any laptop owner. Many of the applications of such a SIG are obvious: the wealth of software to be downloaded, product-specific news and information, shopping bargains, and access to other services (news, financial, E-mail, etc.) offered by the host online service. But, in a word, the most valuable resource in a laptop SIG is people. You, the thousands of other laptop users you'll find online, and the SIG managers are the source of all programs, data, and information. Without people, the channels of information flow—message bases, real-time conferences, and software databases—are nothing more than software.

Which Service?

Beyond considerations of online support for your laptop activities just described, the online service or services you use will be determined by your applications. If you need lots of specialized information, the databases and information-retrieval services should be on your list. Which of these you select will depend on what's offered.

If your major online applications are communications, you should consider an E-mail specialty service—most likely MCI Mail—or CompuServe. Each can handle your FAX, Telex, and hardcopy mail needs, and each gives you access to hundreds of thousands of individuals and companies via internal E-mail and E-mail gateways. With whom you wish to communicate by E-mail may dictate that you use a specific service, too.

If you're seeking news and general information, one of the five consumer online services will fill the bill. Ditto for entertainment and shopping.

In any event, I do recommend that you use more than one online service. Doing so is not an extravagance, and it's often a necessity.

9
Portable Telecomputing Tips, Tricks, and Traps

This chapter is a collection of miscellaneous information that will help you with problems you may have getting online, and with problems you may encounter after you've made the connection. You'll also find some helpful information on using online services, suggestions for making portable telecomputing easier, and information on international telecomputing.

Connection and Communications Problems

The vast majority of connection problems are the result of "operator failure," or improper setup. It's been my experience over the past ten years that a majority of modem users are more likely to blame the problem on anything but their own system. The typical individual who tries to call a system and fails immediately blames the other system—be it a BBS, online service, or personal computer.

It's easy to see why this is: If the trouble isn't on your end, you don't have to fix it. But guess what, folks? The problem is almost always on your end! Granted, packet-switching networks and remote systems' modems occasionally have problems, as do computers you might be trying to call. But, out of hundreds of "trouble calls" I've had from people who can't get online with this or that, 95 percent of the problems were in the caller's system.

"I Can't Call Out!" If you can't get your modem to dial out, it's fairly easy to go through some tests to see if your system is properly set up. Initially, operate under the assumption that you aren't getting a connection. After all, your portable PC communications connections are temporary, and changed frequently. First, make sure your modem, telephone, and computer cables are plugged in (it doesn't hurt to push them in, just in case). Double-check the phone line by connecting a voice telephone set and picking up the handset. If you don't get a dial tone, you know the problem is in the telephone system. If you do get a dial tone, go ahead and dial the number you wish to call with your modem. If you get an answer and hear a high-pitched squeal, you'll know the remote system is answering.

If the phone you're using is in a hotel, or any of a number of other locations with PBXs, listen to the tones when you press the numbers you dial. If you hear odd tones, it may be one of those phones I described in Chapter 5, a phone that uses nonstandard tones to dial.

If you're using an external modem, check to see if it is turned on, and check the batteries and/or power supply. If you're using an internal modem and can easily get to it, open your computer and gently push the modem card into its slot; vibrations may have loosened its connections.

Using an acoustic adaptor? Go through a "dry run" by having the modem dial out without the acoustic adaptor connected to the telephone. Listen for the sound of dialing tones or pulses.

If all the connections and power supplies check out, and you have a dial tone on the phone line, your software may not be set up properly. If you've recently changed modems, you may have to go through your software's setup or installation routine to accommodate the new modem.

Assuming you've gone through all of the above, it may be that your modem has problems. The quickest way to check this is to substitute another modem; if the second modem works, your modem needs repair. If the second modem doesn't work, the odds are in favor of the problem being in the software setup, at the serial port, or—in the case of an external portable modem—in the computer-to-modem hookup.

Portable Telecomputing Tips, Tricks, and Traps 193

If you can't get another modem with which to test your system, you can at least try issuing commands to the modem with your software in terminal mode. Try **ATZ** and **ATH0**. If the modem doesn't respond by sending "OK" to the screen, it probably isn't receiving commands.

If all else fails, call the customer service number of the online service and/or packet-switching network you're using (or the operator of the BBS or personal computer you're trying to call). If there is a system problem, you'll be told about it, and you'll know it's not your system.

Or, just wait and call later. Sometimes even the large multi-user commercial online services "max out" with too many users, and can't handle the load.

"I Get a Connection, The Other System Won't Respond, or Hangs Up on Me" If you get a call through but can't get the other system to respond, see nothing but "garbage" characters, or the system you're dialing hangs up on you, the first items to check are your communications parameters. Make sure the modem speed, data bits, parity, and stop bit are set to match the system you're calling. Change from 8/N/1 to 7/E/1 or vice versa and call back; this often clears the problem up.

If you do make a connection but can't log on or can't make sense of what's happening because random characters appear on your screen, hang up and call back. This is usually the result of a poor phone connection or noisy line. Calling again may get you a better line.

For information on other postconnection problems—how to identify them and how to solve them—see Appendix D. It has tables with detailed information on what the symptoms you may be experiencing mean.

Online Service Shortcuts and Time Savers

Because online services cost money and tend to be more complex than BBSs, I offer the following suggestions for saving time and being efficient mainly with them in mind. However, since BBS time is usually limited, and frustrations on any kind of online system are aggravating, the suggestions can be applied to using BBSs, as well.

Speed

Although it may seem best to always use the highest possible speed in communicating with an online service, this isn't strictly true. Some online services levy a surcharge on 2400-bps access, and all have a surcharge for 9600-bps communications. So, if you zoom online at 2400 or 9600 bps, you're likely to pay two or more times what you would pay at 300 or 1200 bps. Thus, you should consider carefully when a higher speed is beneficial.

Generally 2400- and 9600-bps access speeds are beneficial only when you are downloading files or capturing large amounts of text. If you're reading text online, 1200 bps is about the highest speed at which you can comprehend text streaming by. (Yes, I know—a few of you, like me, *can* read those 2400-bps displays. But most can't.)

If you're in real-time conference, you may well want to use 300 or 1200 bps (unless, like me, you just can't adapt to the crawling characters that 300 bps displays). This is because most people take several seconds to type each line, and you spend a lot of time in real-time conference just *waiting*.

Timing Yourself

Hopefully, your communications software program or modem includes a timer feature, which displays the amount of time you spend online. If not, keep your eye on the clock. Or, get in the habit of typing the command (offered by most BBSs and online services) that displays the amount of time you've been online. The command is usually **TIME**.

Planning Ahead

Whether you dial up another computer for business or pleasure—or both—you'll enjoy your online time more and spend it more effectively if you take a few minutes before each session to plan how you are going to use your time. You don't have to make a major project of it—just jot a few quick notes to guide you through the session.

Portable Telecomputing Tips, Tricks, and Traps   195

If you have a specific set of tasks you'd like to accomplish while online (finding and downloading certain programs, checking on news items, etc.), make a list of those tasks—*and take care of them first*. Most online services are so fascinating that it's easy to enter an area just to "look around," and then forget your original goal.

Plan *how* you are going to accomplish your tasks, too. For instance, if you plan to search a database, make a list of the keywords you're likely to need. And, when you're searching databases that offer file descriptions, you might download the descriptions of all files found during a search for offline perusal. Then you can take your time deciding which files suit your needs.

If you are going to enter a long message, create a "rough draft" so you won't waste time trying to remember what you wanted to say.

If you are after certain types of information but unsure of where to look, check the service's offline reference and list the most likely areas for the information. Once you're online, make use of the service's online index, if one's available, to locate the information you need by category. (Referring to the relevant chapters in this book will help, too.)

After you've accomplished your tasks, *then* explore—this way, you'll not be frustrated because you missed an important conference or forgot a download.

Online Versus Offline Message Creation and Reading

If you use an online service's front end, you will probably create and read all messages offline for E-mail and bulletin boards. This is one of the great advantages of a front end. If you don't use a front end, you can still enjoy the benefits of offline messaging.

Message Creation   Most people find that they can compose a message or other document much faster and easier with their own computer's word processor than with an online editor. You, too, may find it a good idea for you to compose lengthy files (messages, newsletters, reports, etc.) offline. When you compose text files offline, you'll not only save online time (uploading takes less time than composing a message online), but also end up with a document of better quality.

NOTE: Any files intended to be read online should be in pure ASCII format, with no formatting codes. Consult your word processor's manual for information on how to create an ASCII text file, if necessary.

Reading Files If you're a slow reader, or if you will need to refer to a file often, you may prefer to download files rather than read them online. (XMODEM, KERMIT, or even a straight ASCII download will transfer a file to you much faster than you can read it.)

You may also wish to download your mail messages for reading and/or storage offline, after which you should delete the online originals. (Many online services charge for online storage beyond a minimum amount, and your mail messages are usually a part of your online storage.)

Menu/Prompt Levels

Menus are handy, but they can be a waste of time if you don't need them. The default prompt level for most online services displays full menus and prompts for every area that uses them. However, after several sessions on a service, you may notice that you rarely look at the menus in areas that you frequent. When you reach this point, try moving around without menus. This not only removes the distractions of menus, but also saves time in moving from one area to another, as you do not have to sit through menu displays.

You'll be able to set the menu level either via a command or in an online profile area. If you get lost, typing **MENU** or **?** will usually display a menu.

Efficient Use of Online Profile Settings

As soon as you learn how to do so, set up your online profile to reflect the defaults you plan to use. That way, you won't have to make as many menu selections when it comes to things like file transfers.

For example, if Xmodem/CRC is your primary file transfer protocol, make sure you enter this in your profile—that way, you won't have errors when the system tries to transmit without CRC, and your software looks for CRC.

Similarly, set your screen width and length to the appropriate numbers, so that you don't waste time going back over text online because it was improperly displayed.

If you find yourself using a particular area of an online service almost every time you sign on (and this isn't unusual), set that area's menu as your "default menu" (if the option is available). A default menu setting is the means whereby you can direct a service to sign you on at the menu you use most often, rather than at the service's main or top menu. This saves time because you don't have to issue the commands to access the menu of interest and sit through intervening menus and prompts.

Online File Management

As noted earlier, many services charge for online file storage. For this reason, you will want to keep your online storage to a minimum.

You'll also want to keep the number of files in your personal file area low for the simple reason that the more files you have online, the more difficult it is to remember what they are, and to find specific files.

Use these simple guidelines to keep your personal file area clear:

- As suggested previously, download your mail messages, and delete them immediately after.

- Remember that when you upload a file to your personal file area to send or submit, it is *copied,* and the original remains in your personal file area. So, if you upload programs, text, or other files to your personal file area for submission to SIG databases, be sure to delete them after the submission. Once a file has been submitted, you shouldn't need it online again.

    Similarly, files that you upload to send to another user should be deleted after sending.

- On systems that offer a file-compression utility (such as the Compress utility in DELPHI's E-mail area), use it frequently, and delete any backup files generated by the utility.

- In general, check your personal file area's directory often, and make certain that all of the files there are there for a reason. As with any storage area, it's amazing what you can accumulate!

Learning About and Exploring an Online Service

Learn as much as possible about a service *offline* before you sign on. As suggested earlier, you should use this book, plus any manuals and command cards provided by a service to learn about a service. If you have a friend or associate who uses a service you plan to access, you might check with him or her for tips. The service's customer service department can answer any advance questions you might have, too. You can never learn too much about an online service.

Many online services provide an automatic tutorial for first-time users. When this is offered, take it, even if you think you already know everything you need to know (you may be surprised). If it's not offered automatically, check around to see if a tutorial is offered; if so, take the ride. It's not a bad idea to capture such tutorials (and as much as possible of any session on a service new to you) on disk (preferably a RAMdisk).

Once you have the command basics down, you'll want to explore. Again, check offline references first. Then, take on one area at a time; if you jump from area to area, you may find yourself trying selections that were available in the last area you visited, but not in the current area.

Using Type-Ahead

When offered, the option of typing commands and selections ahead can be a real time-saver—if you know what you are doing. Don't try type-ahead until you are familiar with a service's basic commands as well as the major selections on the menus you use often. If you aren't familiar with commands and selections, you may blunder into new areas and may waste more time backing out than you saved by typing ahead.

Using Help

It is true that lessons learned "the hard way" are the best-remembered, but when it comes to online services this maxim should be tempered with the knowledge that you are paying for those lessons in more ways in one. So, make things easy on yourself; keep in mind the fact that HELP is just five keystrokes away on most services:

HELP <ENTER>

When you get stuck, don't waste time experimenting—type **HELP**.

On the other hand, you're better off not using an online help system as a reference; learning about a service offline by reading this book and manuals is far less costly and time-consuming than trying to learn a service by trying out commands and menu selections at random. It's less frustrating, too.

The Complete Traveling Computer: Packing for Portable PC Communications

It's surprising (or maybe not) just how often some of us forget the most vital items when packing for a trip. I'm the first to admit that I don't remember many things that I should take with me; most of the time, when I leave on a trip I have to return home once or twice to get some vital item that I remember two or three miles down the road. And all too often I find that I didn't remember everything when I'm two or three hundred miles away.

I always remember my computer and telecomputing support hardware and software, though. I keep all the support items in an old hard-shell briefcase, and the first thing I do when I return from a trip is replace items I've used or lost. That way, everything's there when I'm ready to go again.

What do I keep in the briefcase? Pretty much what you should carry:

- A small notebook with the customer service numbers for all the online services I use, and for packet-switching networks. I use these numbers to call and obtain online service or packet-switching network dialup numbers for wherever I may be when I wish to use my laptop to communicate. The notebook also has 800 access numbers for several services (such as AT&T Mail and MCI Mail) that provide them, and the online "addresses" for accessing services I use via packet-switching networks.

    You will find all of these numbers in Appendix C, by the way—a good reason to remember to pack this book in your telecomputing traveling kit.

- A list of my online IDs. I've memorized my passwords; hopefully, you will, too.

- Connection-support hardware, in the form of a "Tele-Toolkit" from CP+. Described in Chapter 5, the Tele-Toolkit contains an acoustic adaptor, extra phone line, an inline coupler, a Y-jack, and other items you need to make a physical connection with any phone or phone line. While you don't have to buy this specific product, you should have the items mentioned, along with a telephone-line/modem jumper (like the homemade item described in Chapter 5), a regular and Phillips-head screwdriver, and a handset coupler like the CP+ Connection II or Konexx (also described in Chapter 5).

- An extra, charged battery for my computer.

- At least one set of extra batteries for my external modem or FAX/modem. If you're using rechargeable batteries, take one or two extras, and the charger. (Charge the batteries before you leave.) And don't forget the modem's power supply!

- An extra modem-to-computer cable. (It's surprising how easy it is to misplace a cable.)

- A ten-foot AC extension cord. This lets me use my laptop anywhere in a room, rather than stay within a few feet of a wall outlet.
- A ground plug adaptor for each plug-in power supply. This is an adaptor that lets you plug a three-prong power supply into a two-prong wall outlet that doesn't have a ground.
- A multiplug adaptor that lets you plug more than one power plug into a single outlet. Computer, modem, and FAX/modem power supplies draw little enough power that putting two or three on one outlet won't usually draw more current than the outlet can supply. And, due to the size and shape of some power supply plugs—especially when the transformer is what you plug into an outlet—it may be necessary for you to have a multiplug adaptor to be able to use an outlet for more than one plug. Sometimes a transformer covers both receptacles on a wall outlet.
- Masking tape, for keeping cables and cords in place.
- A small flashlight, so I can see what I'm doing when trying to make a direct connection.
- A pair of needle-nosed pliers, handy for clipping small wires to small terminals. (Be sure the pliers have insulated handles.)
- A DOS startup disk, so I can boot up and use my computer from a floppy disk if the hard disk or ROM setup has a problem. (In some situations, you can access the programs and data on a hard disk after you boot from a floppy, even if the hard disk won't let you boot.)
- Backup copies of vital software (my communications program and word processor, along with the portable PC communications "support" software discussed in Chapter 4) installed to run on a floppy disk. This backup is insurance against anything happening to my laptop's hard disk. (It's wise to copy data files from your hard

disk to a floppy whenever you conclude a work session. That way, you'll have your data as well as your programs should something happen to your hard disk.)

- Extra blank floppy disks.

- A null-modem cable. (I have had need, when traveling, to transfer data to and from a desktop computer that has 5-¼" disks, whereas my laptop uses 3-½" disks.)

These items should enable you to handle just about any connection and communications situations.

Even though my laptop has an internal modem, I also take along an external portable modem, just in case. I've never had to fall back on the external modem, but it's good to know I have it, should my internal modem fail.

Carrying It All

As noted, I pack everything just mentioned in a hard-shell briefcase. There's room for pens, paper, and envelopes in that briefcase, as well as a portable printer and a book or two.

I find the hard-shell briefcase perfect for my needs. It has several folders and compartments built into the lid, and carries literally everything I need for my traveling office except for my laptop computer. That goes into a soft carrying case made for it. You don't have to buy a carrying case designed for your laptop, or to carry laptop accessories, however. In fact, if you find a shoulder bag and briefcase into which your laptop and its accessories fit, these may well be more suited to you than computer carrying cases. They'll certainly cost less.

The Executive Lounge: Using Someone Else's Computer System

It may happen that you have to use someone else's system to telecompute. This may be because your laptop isn't working, or perhaps because you know that a computer is waiting for you to use at your destination point. Or, you may have to find a substitute for your computer for whatever reason.

The computer you use may be a rental you pick up before you leave, a machine owned by a friend or business associate, or a rental through a car rental company or hotel (yes, these are available), or a unit in an airline club or hotel "executive lounge." Whatever the source, you'll need to make certain preparations:

- Copy all data files you intend to work with onto floppy disks. Copy related kinds of data (word processing, database, etc.) to the same disk.

- If you borrow or rent the computer you'll use before you leave, install all the programs you need at home. Then test each program.

- For a computer that will be waiting for you after you leave, take copies of the programs you'll be using most (applications and support software). You'll be more comfortable using your own software, and there's no guarantee that the machine you'll use will come with the software you need. For those programs that require customizing to suit a computer's hardware, you may have to take copies of the original distribution disks. Or, if you can identify the installation program and the data files it requires (screen drivers, etc.), just copy the files from your system's hard disk. Remember that you may well be using a different modem, so be prepared to redo the setup for your communications program to accommodate that program.

- If you don't know for certain that the system you'll be using has a hard disk, make up work copies of your software on floppy disks. (See Chapter 4.)

- Make a list of your user IDs and, if you cannot remember them, passwords for systems you intend to call. (Try to remember the passwords; it's not a good idea to have them on paper.)

- If you have an external portable modem, take it with you. The rental or loaner machine you'll be using may

- not have a modem, or you may find it simpler to use your modem. Be sure to pack the modem's manual, too.

- Take along any connection aids you have, including an acoustic coupler, direct-connect aids, and other support hardware discussed in Chapter 5.

- If you have them, pack a telephone extension line, an inline coupler, and a Y-jack (duplex) RJ-11 connector. Even if a rental computer has an internal modem, it won't come with these often vital items.

Making International Connections

Calling the U.S. with your modem from another country involves overcoming several obstacles, paramount among them making physical connections to power supplies and phone lines. There's also the problem of how to make your call once your modem is connected. I'll address both of those areas here.

Power Supplies

Many European power lines supply 220 volts at 50 cycles per second, as opposed to the U.S. standard of 110 volts at 60 cycles. Separate from the European mainland, the United Kingdom uses 240-volt lines. The only solution is to take along power adapter plugs, and a 220/240-volt transformer. These can often be found at your local Radio Shack, electrical and appliance stores, and stores that sell travel supplies.

Note that lower-wattage transformers are required for laptop computers. The high-power transformers, sold for use with heavier electrical appliances, can burn out your computer's circuitry. Before you go shopping for just any power transformer, check with the manufacturer or supplier of your laptop; there may well be a European transformer/power supply made especially for your laptop.

Some newer laptops come with built-in transformers that can deal with European voltages. But, even if your computer has a 220/240-volt capability, you may have trouble plugging it in. Again, you need to carry a complete plug adapter set. CP+ provides a "Franzus International Adapter Plug Set" with four plugs that enable you to connect with outlets in Australia, Japan, the Middle East, and the U.K. Radio Shack sells a similar set. You'll probably want plug extenders, too: European wall sockets are often set deep in a wall, so a power supply can't be plugged in without an extender.

You also need a U.S. ground plug adapter (three-prong to two-prong); some transformers and adapters don't have a three-hole socket.

Phone Connections

The good news on phone connections is that RJ-11 modular connectors are becoming a standard in many countries. The bad news is that the U.K. and a few other countries use unique connectors. (Interestingly enough, it's the countries that have had telephone service the longest that have their own standard phone connectors. RJ-11 connectors are more common in countries that are "emerging.") And, as in North America, older phone systems don't have RJ-11 connectors. So, don't count on finding an RJ-11 jack to plug into everywhere you travel.

Fortunately, there are RJ-11 adaptors available. These connect with "standard" phone-line connectors in other countries. They're called "PTT to RJ-11 adaptors." In most major European cities you'll find some help in the form of computer stores that sell telephone-connection equipment. If you travel frequently to a country that uses something other than an RJ-11 connector, you might buy a telephone extension cable there and mate it to a short cord with an RJ-11 male connector on the end. That way, you can hook the modem and the telephone into the circuit at once.

(Some seasoned travelers with a knowledge of which wire does what in this country or that can make their own connectors. For instance, I'm told that red and green lines in the telephone line from your modem connect with the two outer lines in the four-wire British telephone plug. Given this knowledge is correct, you might combine it with a British telephone plug and an RJ-11 plug to make a ready-to-use phone adaptor.)

In any event, take along a laptop toolkit, like the "Tele-Toolkit" from CP+, or Travel Tech's "Mo Fone" to ensure you'll be able to connect. If you don't have a complete toolkit, at least take a flexible acoustic coupler, like the Telecoupler.

Line Quality

European and Asian telephone systems are generally noisier and less reliable than the North American telephone system. So, error checking, in the form of MNP 4 or LAP/M (V.42), is almost a must. (Remember that the modem you're calling must have the same error-checking capability.) Likewise, it's important to use an error-checking binary file-transfer protocol, even for small ASCII text files.

Preparations: Direct Dialing and Packet-Switching Networks

Making a dialup connection to the U.S. from overseas can be as difficult as power and phone-line connections. It all depends on whom you want to call (individual or online service) and how you intend to do it—by direct dial or packet-switching network (public or private).

Foreign Service Gateways If you are a member of certain online services, you can take advantage of their overseas numbers to make connections. The presence of Americans in Europe and Japan is strong enough that several of the consumer services have made special accommodations for them. CompuServe has direct-dial nodes in London, England, and Munich, Germany. The London connection is available at normal CompuServe rates, plus a network surcharge of $9.50 per hour. 1200- and 2400-bps communication is available, and the network supports MNP 5. U.K. customers who live outside London can connect through British Telecom's "PSS Dialplus" network, which has nodes in 60-odd U.K. cities.

GEnie, having the advantage of access to an existing worldwide telecom network through its parent company, GEIS, is available in "local" versions in several European countries, from which users can log into the American version of GEnie. In Germany and elsewhere, GEnie is putting together special local language versions of the service that callers dialing into GEnie will see it in their language. CompuServe is planning similar setups.

In Japan, CompuServe access is available via the NIFTY-Serve network (which in many respects is a lot like Compu-Serve, discounting the Kanji characters). Another Japanese service, NEC's PC-VAN, hosts a GEnie gateway.

DELPHI's Latin American counterpart, DELPHI/Argentina, offers South and Central American users a gateway to DELPHI. In the U.S. Japan's ASCII NET also offers a DELPHI gateway.

These interconnections greatly simplify getting to your "home" online service from overseas. All you have to do is dial up and sign on to the local online service, then use its gateway to the American online service. Billing is simplified, too; you don't have to worry about settling a telephone bill immediately, as you might have to do with direct dialing. And, of course, using a service's gateway gives you the benefit of its packet-switching network for error correction and faster response.

Being a member of the American counterpart of an online service in another country, or one to which a native service has a gateway, won't be enough in itself to get you online. You'll have to make arrangements with the host service in the other country, to pay for the service you use. Check the aforementioned gateway areas, and with the management of CompuServe, GEnie, or DELPHI, as appropriate, for more information.

International Direct Dialing You can, of course, dial up any online service's direct-dial number from overseas, placing the call the same way you would place an international voice telephone call. The same is true for dialing up a packet-switching network number for a node in the U.S. However, you may have to go through an operator, and you'll certainly experience delays at one point or another, so it is probably best to make the call and connection manually. Use the techniques described in Chapter 5, and be sure to use error correction.

Using International Packet-Switching Networks Packet-switching networks routinely carry data traffic to and from most countries. Thus, there is already a network of packet-switching networks in place. The resources in this network include Sprint-

Net, Tymnet, private networks (like CompuServe's or GEnie's), and domestic packet-switching networks.

If a call is through a SprintNet or Tymnet node (or via a private network like GE's GEIS) in the other country, it may still be carried at some point by a local network in the country of origin. This has to do with complex regulations within some countries. Typically, a call is made to a local PTT (Postal, Telephone & Telegraph) data network, after which the user can select SprintNet, Tymnet, or another major international data carrier by entering the desired packet-switching network's address.

After you make connection with a U.S. packet-switching network, communications are handled the same as a call from within the U.S. (the user enters an online service's address, then proceeds with the sign-on process). There is an additional charge for using a local PTT data network.

When a call is carried "direct" from its country of origin to the continental U.S. by a network in the country of origin (such as the Venus P network or Tympas network in Japan), the call is usually routed to its final destination via SprintNet or Tymnet. The overseas user pays directly (via having established a SprintNet or Tymnet account) or indirectly (the charges are included in his/her local network bill). The interface between a foreign network and SprintNet or Tymnet is usually transparent to the user, although routing parameters may have to be given to the local network.

Both SprintNet and Tymnet now offer direct packet-switching network service between the U.S. and numerous other counties—among them Japan, the U.K., and Australia. If you have an account with SprintNet or Tymnet, you can dial up the network in another country where it provides packet-switching network operations, then use it to sign on to an online service in the U.S. The connection procedure is pretty much the same as connecting from within the U.S. (Contact SprintNet and Tymnet for full details on costs, how to set up an account, etc.)

10
What's Ahead in Portable PC Communications

In 1991, computer and peripheral manufacturers began to respond to the demand for portable PC communications products in a big way. As with early attempts to respond to the market for portable computers, there were quite a few attempts to fill needs that didn't exist, or to create markets with products that were at least interesting and at best represented good ideas for which there were few applications. And for some products there were more manufacturers than the market could support.

This will continue to occur, as it always has in the personal computer market, but the market for portable PC communications products now is fairly mature. Thus, we can look forward to a plethora of useful hardware, software, and online products.

Hardware

The keywords for the future of portable PC communications hardware are smaller, lighter, and faster. The market-driven nature of the computer market will guarantee this; the demand for portable communications is now large enough to have increased the market for smaller, lighter, and faster laptop computers—not to mention modem and support hardware.

Size, Weight, and Color Look for four-pound 386SX notebook computers, and a few five-pound 486 notebooks, to be common in 1993. The size of these newer notebooks will remain about the same as contemporary notebooks; certain minimum dimensions are dictated by the keyboard and display.

Advancements in gas-plasma and active dot-matrix displays (the result of large-screen TV research in Japan) will bring full-color VGA to laptop computerists who can afford it. Color won't drop in price for a couple of years, at least, due to the relative difficulty and expense of the manufacturing process.

Power Better batteries are on the way. They're already here, to an extent, although they're costly. Lead-acid batteries and new technology will gradually replace the rechargeable nickel-cadmium batteries so popular in laptops now. Throwaway batteries will also see improvements.

At the same time, manufacturers will be working to keep power consumption low with new computers, modems, and portable printers. The upshot will be battery life that's either the same as or better than what we have today, with better equipment.

Disk Drives Laptop hard drives will continue to increase in size as the price decreases. 100-megabyte hard drives will soon be as common as 20-megabyte hard drives were in 1990.

The 3-½" floppy disk will continue to be the disk of choice among laptop users. Consumers, mindful of the last "floppy disk-size war" (not to mention market battles between Beta and VHS, and audio tape formats) will present no little resistance to new, smaller floppy disks.

Modems and FAX/Modems As I noted several times earlier in this book, 9600-bps will become the standard communications speed for dialup modems. At present, 2400-bps is the *de facto* standard among personal computer users, and will remain so for a time.

This isn't due to price considerations; 9600-bps dialup modems cost less than many dot-matrix printers. Before 9600-bps modems can become standard in the sense that a majority of computer users have them, online services and packet-switching networks will have to drop surcharges for 9600-bps access.

What's Ahead in Portable PC Communications 211

We went through the same thing with the change from 1200-bps to 2400-bps as the modem user's standard. What's required is enough subscribers who have 9600-bps modems to create a big demand for 9600-bps access—and enough time to pass for these services to amortize their investment in equipment to accommodate faster access.

People are already buying 9600-bps modems, thanks to the price cuts and the silly (and usual) battles by some manufacturers to force their proprietary standards on the market. Now that things have settled down with V.32, V.42, and V.42bis as the accepted standards for 9600-bps communications, prices are dropping in response to increased demand, which in turn creates more demand. So, it shouldn't be too many months before online services have enough people online at 9600 bps to be able to start dropping surcharges.

FAX (both send and receive) will be standard on many modems bundled with laptop computers in 1993. FAX/modem combinations (both internal and external) will be very common, and far less expensive than they are now. It may well develop that FAX/modems will become as common as dialup modems.

Wireless connection for both dialup modem and FAX communications are on the way. This will be a spinoff of the popularity of cellular telephones. Computer users seeking to access the cellular phone network, and cellular phone users looking for more ways to use their phones, are beginning to create a market for "plug-'n'-go" modem and FAX communications hardware. Look for a lot of specialized, dedicated devices over the next couple of years—in particular, dedicated terminals that either plug into your cellular phone set, or which use the worldwide satellite paging system now being constructed. I suspect the eventual direction for all this will be dedicated terminals, but there will be accommodations for laptop users to tap into the new messaging system.

Phone Systems ISDN and fiber-optics are important elements of the telephone system of tomorrow. ISDN (Integrated Services Digital Network) is set up to be the data pipeline for tomorrow's consumer. ISDN networks will carry data in digital rather than analog form used by today's telephone systems—and they'll do a much better job. But don't worry about having to adapt to ISDN by buying new equipment. As ISDN systems come online this decade, low-cost adaptors for existing portable PC communications equipment will be right behind it.

Fiber optics serve as conductors for communications systems. Rather than conducting electrons, as is the case with conventional wires, fiber-optic conductors carry signals in the form of light. Fiber-optic conductors are already built into some phone systems; you may well have used a long-distance phone connection that incorporated fiber-optics without even knowing it. But you don't have to be concerned over problems with adapting to the growing network of fiber-optic connections—the fiber-optic legs of circuits are adapted to existing technology as they are installed. They provide a virtually noise-free signal, by the way, which is a great improvement over existing conductors.

On a more mundane level, don't be surprised if, as in-room modem jacks become standard in hotels, management figures out a way to charge extra for data communication. Also, I look for some chains (or an enterprising company) to set up telecom accessory sales and rental operations at front desks. The prices will, of course, be exorbitant. (You doubt that? Ever pay $2.00 for a 50-cent candy bar in a hotel gift shop? I rest my case.)

Software

The biggest developments in personal computer communications software have already occurred. All that can be done now is to refine how things work. Some refinements we might see in the near future:

- FAX software that can read and transmit any graphics format, and which can convert the text in any incoming FAX to ASCII file—bundled with FAX/modems. Also, look for more FAX software to be able to handle text from popular word processors (WordPerfect, Word, etc.) in their native formats.

- "Master" front-end programs that either manage multiple online service front ends, or which themselves serve as front ends for several online services.

- Improvements in background operation, especially in low-end computers. Laptop users who want to use their machines for something else while their communications programs send and receive messages, files, and FAXes constitute a big market for this. The programs that can deliver on promises of true background operation will receive a positive reception.

- Along with the preceding, more and better programs that operate with multitasking/task-switching software like Windows, DESQview, and Ensemble are on the way.

A few specialized portable communications programs will hit the market. These will provide functions related to providing online help and creating and addressing messages.

Online Services

It's worth noting that, although online services offer a plethora of services, the services used most often are E-mail and file transfer—the very foundations on which online services are based. This is not surprising; the most valuable commodity in contemporary society happens to be information, and sharing and gaining information is what E-mail and file transfer are all about.

The current expansion of E-mail capabilities by various online services will continue. You'll see more systems interconnected directly (à la the CompuServe-to-MCI Mail link), and indirectly (via DASnet or similar services). Online service management can no longer pretend to their subscribers that their competitors don't exist, and providing an E-mail link with a competing service helps keep subscribers from spending time on other services just to exchange E-mail with subscribers there.

Perhaps, within five years or so, you won't have to join four or five online services to get all the online products and services you want. The major products will be everywhere, and you'll be able to exchange E-mail with people on other services.

The number of data and program files available for download will continue to grow. Most of the major online services have gone through periods where they had to delete many old files, and restrict new uploads, but most have added enough storage to accommodate their needs for some time to come.

Online services will continue to find new ways to market their services, often presenting existing services under new names to match the changing online demographics. New products will evolve, as well—with a particular concentration on tie-ins with well-known publishers and consumer product manufacturers.

A majority of new online service products will have nothing to do with computers—at least not directly. Continuing an existing trend, online service providers will present information and entertainment products in all imaginable categories. Where one formerly found news and features about computing in preponderance, there will be news and features covering the range of topics you find covered by the magazines in a well-stocked newsstand. In fact, the contents of many of those magazines will be online.

Along with current information, online research and information resources will continue to grow. Encyclopedias are already a mainstay of consumer online services, and the reference works formerly common only to expensive database services are going online everywhere.

There's more—much more—but perhaps you can see the trend: Online services will be marketing to *people,* as opposed to computer users as such, over the next ten years. The new products they'll be marketing will in large part consist of online versions of books, magazines, and television and radio offerings.

■ ■ ■

All of the preceding indicates that portable PC communications will be faster and easier. There will also be more applications. As more people go online, you will have more reason to be online yourself—both because there will be more people with whom to communicate, and because there will be more online products and services to accommodate them.

Part 4

...

Reference

Appendix A
Manufacturers

This appendix contains contact info for computer, modem, PC FAX, and laptop and PC communications peripherals manufacturers and vendors. Each entry is accompanied by a brief description of the company's portable products.

This by no means represents all hardware manufacturers; nor is it intended to do so. Rather than provide interminable listings of material that you can obtain by looking through a couple of computer magazines, I've opted to provide contacts for those manufacturers whose products are mentioned in this book, and those who offer products of particular interest to laptop users, whether or not I covered the products in this book. Consider this to be a "sampler" of manufacturers and vendors of some of the more interesting and useful products. For more information on portable PC communication products, contact the manufacturers listed herein, and watch for reviews and roundup articles in computer magazines.

Laptop and Notebook Computer Manufacturers and Vendors

Atari Corporation
1196 Borregas Avenue
Sunnyvale, CA 94088
(800) 443-8020, (408) 745-2000
Atari Portfolio palmtop computer.

Compaq Computer Corporation
P.O. Box 692000
Houston, TX 77269
(800) 231-0900, (713) 370-0670

Compaq's product line includes several popular laptop and notebook computers, among them its SLT 286 and 386 systems.

NEC America, Inc.
383 Omni Drive
Richardson, TX 75080
(800) 225-5664, (214) 233-5021

Full line of laptop and notebook computers, including the popular NEC UltraLite.

Northgate Computer Systems, Inc.
P.O. Box 59080
Minneapolis, MN 54549
(800) 548-1993; (612) 943-8181

Laptop and notebook computers, including the Slim*Lite* notebook.

Poqet Computer Corporation
650 N. Mary Ave.
Sunnyvale, CA 94086
(800) 624-8999, (408) 737-8100

Sharp Electronics Corporation
Sharp Plaza
Mahwah, NJ 07430
(201) 529-8731

Sharp manufactures a number of laptop and notebook computers, often innovative products that remain on the market for only a short time.

Tandy Corporation
300 One Tandy Center
Fort Worth, TX 76102
(817) 390-3100

Full line of laptop and notebook computers, including the 1800 HD and 2180 HD notebooks.

Texas Instruments, Inc.
P.O. Box 2022230
Austin, TX 78720
(800) 527-3500

TravelMate 2000 LT286 laptop computer and other laptop and notebook computers.

Toshiba America Information Systems
9750 Irvine Blvd.
Irvine, CA 92718
(800) 334-3445, (714) 583-3000

Full line of laptop and notebook computers, including the popular T1000.

Zenith Data Systems Corporation
1501 Feehanville Drive
Mt. Prospect, IL 60056
(800) 553-0331, (708) 699-4800

SuperSport and MasterSport and other 286, 386, and 486 laptop and notebook computers.

ZEOS International
530 5th Ave., NW
St. Paul, MN 55112
(800) 423-5891, (612) 633-4591

Varied line of laptop and notebook computers.

Modem Manufacturers and Vendors

CompuCom Corporation
1180-J Miraloma Way
Sunnyvale, CA 94086
(408) 732-4500

CompuCom SpeedModem Champ proprietary protocol 9600-bps modem, and several CCITT-compatible internal and external V.32 and 2400-bps modems.

GVC-Chenel Corporation
99 Demarest Road
Sparta, NJ 07871
(800) 243-6352, (201) 579-3630

SM-96M and SM-96 PCM V.32 9600-bps modems, and 2400-bps V.22/V.22bis and V.42 modems, all CCITT-compatible.

Hayes Microcomputer Products, Inc.
P.O. Box 105203
Atlanta, GA 30348
(404) 449-8791

Full line of CCITT-compatible internal and external modems (including Smartmodem and ULTRA series). Perhaps the world's largest manufacturer of internal, external, and specialized modems for personal computers.

Tandy Corporation
300 One Tandy Center
Fort Worth, TX 76102
(817) 390-3100

Wide variety of modems, 300 through 9600 bps, all CCITT-compatible. Product line includes modems made especially for Tandy laptop and notebook computers.

Touchbase Systems, Inc.
160 Laurel Avenue
Northport, NY 11768
(516) 251-0423

Manufacturer of high-quality portable, battery-powered, CCITT-compatible modems and modem/FAX units, including the WorldPort 2400 portable modem (with MNP), and the 2496 portable modem/FAX.

USRobotics
8100 McCormick Blvd.
Skokie, IL 60076
(800) 343-5877, (708) 982-5010

Manufacturer of a full line of internal and external modems for all types of personal computers. Offers Courier HST (proprietary), CCITT-compatible, and dual-standard modems.

PC FAX and FAX/Modem Manufacturers and Vendors

Fremont Communications Company
46309 Warm Springs Boulevard
Fremont, CA 94539
(415) 438-5001
FAX: (415) 490-2315

Fax96 FAX/modem.

Hayes Microcomputer Products, Inc.
P.O. Box 105203
Atlanta, GA 30348
(404) 449-8791

JT FAX.

Tandy Corporation
300 One Tandy Center
Fort Worth, TX 76102
(817) 390-3100

2400-bps modem and send-only FAX combination, with software, among others. FAX/modems are designed to work with Tandy laptop and notebook computers.

Touchbase Systems, Inc.
160 Laurel Avenue
Northport, NY 11768
(800) 541-0345, (516) 261-0423

WorldPort 2496 portable external FAX/modem.

Laptop and Communications Peripherals Manufacturers and Vendors

Computer Products Plus, Inc. (C+)
16341 Gothard St.
Huntington Beach, CA 92647
800-274-4277, (714) 847-1799

Manufacturer and/or distributor of several products for portable computing, including the "Telecoupler," "Tele-Toolkit," and other aids to telecomputing on the road. Also a distributor for Toshiba replacement and expansion peripherals.

Eastman Kodak Company
343 State St.
Rochester, NY 14650
(800) 242-2424, 716-724-4000

Kodak is the manufacturer of the popular Diconix portable printer.

Radio Shack
700 One Tandy Center
Fort Worth, TX 76102
(817) 390-3300

Manufactures a full line of telephone and modem lines, cables, and connectors, including acoustic couplers, telephone hardware and tools, international plug adaptors, and supplies.

Samsonite Corporation
(800) 443-5500

Hardshell computer carrying case.

Targus
P.O. Box 5039
Cerritos, CA 90703
(714) 523-5429

Portable computer carrying cases.

Traveling Software, Inc.
18702 North Creek Parkway
Bothell, WA 98011
(800) 343-8080, (206) 483-8088

Manufacturer of a wide variety of portable computing products, including LapLink Pro, LapLink Mac III, DeskLink (permits two computers to share a printer or files through a simple connection), and WinConnect (for linking a laptop to Windows on your desktop computer). All come with ready-to-use connectors and cables.

Travel Tech
18702 N. Creek Parkway
Suite 116
Bothell, WA 98011
(800) 343-8080

Manufacturer of the Mo Fone and Mo Fone II acoustic couplers. (Mo Fone is sold under several brand names.)

Unlimited Systems
5555 Magnatron Blvd., Suite J
San Diego, CA 92111
(800) 275-6354, (619) 277-3300

Manufacturer of the Konnex handset connector/voice-data switch, the Konexx Coupler acoustic coupler, and other portable PC communications aids.

Appendix B
Software and Books

This appendix lists contact information for the software publishers whose products are mentioned in this book. The software is listed in three categories: communications programs, online service front ends, and utilities and operating systems.

Following the software listings is information on several books you will find useful in expanding your knowledge of telecomputing.

Communications Programs

Crosstalk Communications
1000 Alderman Drive
Alpharetta, GA 30202
(404) 442-4000

COMMUNICATIONS (a self-guiding basic communications program), Crosstalk Mk.4, and Crosstalk XVI.

DATASTORM Technologies, Inc.
P.O. Box 1471
Columbia, MO 65205
(314) 443-3282

PROCOMM and Procomm Plus (shareware and commercial software, respectively), and Hotwire.

Don Milne/Micropak, Ltd.
Shareware Publishing
3a Queen Street
Seaton
Devon EX12 2NY
ENGLAND

Odyssey shareware communications program.

Softklone
Suite 100
300 Office Plaza Drive
Tallahassee, FL 32301
(904) 877-9763
BBS: (904) 8778-9884

Mirror III and Takeover.

Online Service Front Ends

America Online
8619 Westwood Center Drive
Vienna, VA 22182
(800) 525-5938, (703) 448-8700

Front-end software for America Online, PC-Link, and Promenade.

AT&T Mail
AT&T
P.O. Box 3505
New Brunswick, NJ 08903
(800) 367-7225, (800) 624-5672

AT&T Mail Access II.

CompuServe Inc.
P.O. Box 20212
Columbus, OH 43220
(800) 848-8199, (614) 457-0802

CompuServe Information Manager (CIM).

Appendix B: Software and Books 227

Dialog Information Services
   3460 Hillview Avenue
   Palo Alto, CA 94304
   (800) 334-2564, (415) 858-3810
DIALOGLINK front-end software for DIALOG and Knowledge Index.

Gateway Software, Inc.
   61 East 8th Street, Suite 128
   New York, NY 10003
   CompuServe: 73567,2755
   GEnie: P.RABERGEAU
   Prodigy: WNWB44A
Developer of Proplus and Promaster add-on utilities for the Prodigy front end and EVA front end for GEnie.

GEnie
   401 N. Washington Street
   Rockville, MD 20850
   (800) 433-3683, (301) 340-4000
Aladdin front-end software for GEnie.

MCI Mail
   111 19th Street, NW
   Washington, DC 20036
   (800) 444-6245, (202) 416-5600
Lotus Express front-end software for MCI Mail.

The PAN Network
   P.O. Box 162
   Skippack, PA 19474
   (215) 584-0300
PAN Messenger front-end software for DELPHI and MCI Mail.

Prodigy
   445 Hamilton Avenue
   White Plains, NY 10601
   (800) 284-5933, (800) 822-6922
Prodigy software.

SprintMail
12490 Sunrise Valley Drive
Reston, VA 22096
(800) 835-3638, (800) 336-0437

PC SprintMail front-end software for SprintMail.

Support Group, Inc.
Lake Technology Park
McHenry, MD 21541
(800) USA-GROUP, (301) 387-4500
CompuServe: 74020,10

TAPCIS front end for CompuServe.

Symantec Corporation
10201 Torre Avenue
Cupertino, CA 95014-2132
(213) 391-2000

The Norton Commander, with MCI Mail front end.

Utilities and Operating Systems

DynaCorp, Incorporated
4828 Loop Central Drive, Suite 520
Houston, TX 77081
(713) 664-1492

DynaCorp publishes REDline, a cursor highlighting program that highlights the entire line in an application.

GeoWorks
2150 Shattuck Avenue
Berkeley, CA 94704
(510) 644-0883

GeoWorks Ensemble with GeoComm.

Microsoft Corporation
16011 NE 36th Way
Box 97017
Redmond, WA 98073
(800) 426-9400

MS-DOS and Windows.

PKware, Inc.
9025 N. Deerfield Drive
Brown Deer, WI 53223
(414) 354-8599
(414) 354-8670
PKZIP file-compression software.

Quarterdeck Office Systems
150 Pico Boulevard
Santa Monica, CA 90405
(213) 392-9851
DESQview 386 and QEMM.

SkiSoft Publishing Corporation
1644 Massachusetts Avenue, Suite 79
Lexington, MA 02173
(617) 863-1876, (800) 662-3622
No-Squint II cursor enhancement and Eye Relief word processor.

System Enhancement Associates
21 New Street
Wayne, NJ 07470
ARC file-compression utility.

Traveling Software, Inc.
18702 North Creek Pkwy.
Bothell, WA 98011
(800) 343-8080, (206) 483-8088
Manufacturer of a wide variety of portable computing products, including Battery Watch II, LapLink Pro, and LapLink Mac.

Reference Books

The Modem Reference, 2nd Edition, by Michael A. Banks (Brady Books, 1991).

CompuServe A to Z, by Charles Bowen (Bantam Books, 1991).

Appendix C
■ ■ ■
Online Services

Online Services: Overview and Contacts

If you are wondering whether to sign up for a commercial online service (or join a second or a third), this brief guide may help you decide which service may be best for you.

I've put together a quick-reference description of the services most likely to be of interest, with descriptions keyed to the needs of laptop owners. Special-interest groups of interest to laptop owners are listed, as well as SIGs for those whose work is on the road, at home, or anywhere else telecomputing can come into play. (See Chapter 8 for more detailed descriptions of these services' offerings.)

AT&T Mail
AT&T
P.O. Box 3505
New Brunswick, NJ 08903
(800) 367-7225, (800) 624-5672

Business-oriented E-mail system, set up to handle large-scale corporate communciations requirements. Many extra features typical of an E-mail specialty service.

America Online
America Online, Inc.
8619 Westwood Center Drive
Vienna, VA 22182
(800) 227-6364, (703) 448-8700

A complete consumer service, America Online has a number of areas of interest to portable computer users, including MS-DOS hardware, software, and communications forums, as well as online vendors.

BIX
1030 Massachusetts Avenue
Cambridge, MA 02138
(800) 227-2983, (603) 924-7681, (800) 544-4005

BIX's "laptops," "bbs," and "tandy" conferences are vital sources of technical information and help for laptop computer users. Vendor and product-specific conferences, like those covering Toshiba and Zenith products, provide additional help.

CompuServe, Inc.
P.O. Box 20212
Columbus, OH 43220
(800) 848-8199, (614) 457-0802

CompuServe has a Laptop Forum, as well as numerous Forums sponsored by hardware and software vendors, or dedicated to specific products. To get a handle on all that's available for laptop users in CompuServe's many Forums, start with the IBM File Finder. This invaluable feature is accessible by typing GO IBMFF. Once you're in the IBM File Finder area, select "keyword search" (item 1 on the menu) and use the keywords "portables," "laptop," and "communications." Then, narrow your search with additional keywords.

DASnet
DA Systems, Inc.
Marketing Department
1503 E. Campbell Avenue
Campbell, CA 95008
(408) 559-7434

E-mail relay system. Transfers E-mail for its subscribers among several dozen online services worldwide.

DELPHI
1030 Massachusetts Avenue
Cambridge, MA 02138
(800) 544-4005, (617) 491-3393

Appendix C: Online Services

DELPHI's Portable Place SIG is the starting point for laptop computer users. Here you'll find many useful program and data files, and lots of helpful laptop users to share information. After checking out Portable Place, expand your software horizons with a visit to the PC SIG.

Dialog Information Services
3460 Hillview Avenue
Palo Alto, CA 94304
(800) 334-2564, (415) 858-3810

A massive database and information-retrieval service, DIALOG was the first commercial online information product. Excellent for researchers seeking both specialized and general knowledge.

Dow Jones News/Retrieval Service
P.O. Box 300
Princeton, NJ 08543
(609) 452-5211

Primarily a financial news, information, and service network, DJNS has extended its services to provide general and special-interest news, online shopping, and other services.

GEnie
401 N. Washington Street
Rockville, MD 20850
(800) 433-3683, (301) 340-4000

GEnie's Laptops RoundTable is the place to go for information and files pertaining to just about any portable computer. To find other online products of interest, use GEnie's online Index. Type Index and select item 5 on the menu, or type M15 5 and enter a keyword ("laptop," "communications," "portable," etc.).

MCI Mail
1111 19th Street, NW
Washington, DC 20036
(800) 424-6677, (201) 833-8484

The first consumer and business E-mail service. Lots of features and options. Gateway to Dow Jones News/Retrieval Service, and E-mail link with CompuServe.

NewsNet
945 Havorford Rd.
Bryn Mawr, PA 19010
(800) 345-1301, (215) 527-8020

Online news and information service, featuring hundreds of special-interest business and industry newsletters. Also offers national and international newswires.

PC-Link
America Online, Inc.
8619 Westwood Center Drive
Vienna, VA
(800) 458-8532, (703) 448-8700

PC-Link offers the same features as America Online, but is tailored for owners of Tandy's MS-DOS computers.

Prodigy
445 Hamilton Avenue
White Plains, NY 10601
(800) 284-5933, (800) 822-6922

An information- and graphics-intensive consumer online service, featuring online advertising. No software downloads or uploads, but offers E-mail and public messaging with its plethora of information products and services.

SprintMail (formerly Telemail)
12490 Sunrise Valley Drive
Reston, VA 22096
(800) 835-3638, (800) 336-0437

E-mail specialty service, offering a full line of domestic and international E-mail services for corporations and other organizations.

Packet-Switching Network Customer Service Numbers

Use the voice numbers listed below to report network trouble, or to obtain local access numbers when you're traveling.

Appendix C: Online Services

Network	Customer Service Numbers		Information Numbers
Alascom, Inc.	800-544-2233		907-264-7391
CompuServe Network	800-848-8990		614-457-8650
DataPac	800-222-9734	Ottawa	
	800-267-9502	New Brunswick	
	902-894-7313	Prince Edward Island	
	514-282-8611	Montreal	
	416-581-4455	Toronto	
	403-265-6703	Calgary	
	604-688-0801	British Columbia	
DIALNET	800-334-2564	or	416-387-2689
			800-387-2689 (in Canada)
DRInet	800-227-2983		603-924-2983 (In New Hampshire and outside the U.S.)
SprintNet	800-336-0437		703-589-5700 (Outside continental United States)
			907-264-7391 (in Alaska)
Tymnet	800-872-7654		408-922-6051 (Outside continental United States)

Getting Online Information from the Networks

If you have a local SprintNet or Tymnet number, you can get listings of numbers nationwide, and other information, direct from the network. Follow the procedures described below.

SprintNet

At SprintNet's @ prompt, type **MAIL**. At the ensuing username and password prompts, type **PHONES**. You will enter SprintNet's information system, which contains a listing of all local dial-up numbers, among other information.

For international access information, type **MAIL** at the @ prompt, type **INTL/ASSOCIATES** at the username prompt and **INTL** at the password prompt.

Tymnet

At Tymnet's please log in or username prompt, type **INFORMATION**. You will enter Tymnet's information system, which contains a listing of all local dialup numbers, information on all services accessible via Tymnet, etc.

DATAPAC

For more information on DATAPAC, dial your local DATAPAC number. Enter . for 300 or .. for 1200 baud access. Enter **2:1, 3:126** <cr> for full duplex. If you would like help in English, type **9210 0086** <cr>, then type the letter **A**. For help in French, type **9210 0086** <cr>, and then the letter **B**.

Online Service Network "Addresses" and Direct-Dial Access Numbers

This list provides the network "addresses" of the major services discussed in this book. The addresses are what you enter at a network's sign-on prompt to direct the network to connect you with the service in question. Where appropriate, direct-dial access numbers are also included.

Service	SprintNet	Tymnet	Direct-Dial
America Online	(SprintNet/Tymnet access; automatic signon)		
AT&T Mail	n/a	n/a	800-624-5123
BIX	n/a	BIX	617-861-9667
CompuServe or	C 202202 C 614227	COMPUSERVE	(CompuServe network)
DELPHI	C DELPHI	DELPHI	615-576-0802
DIALOG	C 41548D	DIALOG (also accessible via DIALNET)	415-858-2575
Dow Jones News/Retrieval	C DOW	DOW1;;	n/a

Appendix C: Online Services

Service	SprintNet	Tymnet	Direct-Dial
GEnie	(private network access; various local numbers)		
MCI Mail	n/a	MCIMAIL	800-234-MAIL
NewsNet	C NET	NET	215-668-2035 at 300 bps 215-668-2645 at 1200 bps
PC-Link	(SprintNet/Tymnet access; automatic signon)		
The PRODIGY service	(various local and Tymnet numbers)		
SprintMail	MAIL	n/a	n/a

Appendix D
...
Troubleshooting and Tips

Unless you like challenges and frustration, I think you'll find this appendix extremely useful. It contains advice to help you avoid and deal with online problems, and important tips on using online services. Read it before you sign on to a new system and refer to it frequently; it will save you time, frustration, and money.

How to Avoid Online Problems and What to Do If You Have a Problem

If you experience a problem during sign on or while online, *don't panic*. As with anything else, if you jump in and type commands at random, you'll end up confused and no further toward resolving the problem than when you started.

Being Prepared

Most online "problems" are not problems at all, but the result of not understanding how to use a particular system. Like any other computer system, BBSs and online services normally do exactly what you tell them to do; thus, you need to understand what you are telling a system to do with each command. If possible, familiarize yourself with the service by studying its manual or command reference card. Keep these materials handy during your online sessions, too.

You need to understand your end of the connection, too. Before you try to dial up a BBS or online service, you should, of course, be familiar with your communications hardware and software. Spend some time with their respective manuals. (You will find it useful to keep this book handy during your online sessions, as well.)

Preventing Problems

The best solution for any problem is to solve it *before* you sign on. To save time you should go over the following checklist—at least mentally—before dialing. The items to check are basic and very simple, but are the most frequent source of problems.

— *Check your computer.* Make sure the computer's power supply and any peripherals are properly connected.

— *Check your modem.* Make sure your modem is properly connected to its power supply, to the computer, and to the telephone line. Read the manual accompanying your modem completely, so that you understand exactly how it operates, and know what to expect. If you are confused about or have any problems with its operations, contact the dealer from whom you purchased the modem, or the modem manufacturer.
And, if the modem has a power switch, turn it on.

— *Check your software parameter settings.* Make sure that all communications parameters are set properly for the system you are calling (you may have changed them to accommodate another system). Are you using the proper dialup procedure? Are the telephone number, your system ID, and password properly entered in the autologon file (if any) you intend to use?

Common Problems and Solutions

The following sections list commonly encountered problems and their remedies. (Take a few minutes to look them over now, so you'll have an idea of what's going on if you do encounter these problems.)

Sign-On Troubleshooting Guide

Trouble/Symptoms:
You issue the commands to dial, but nothing happens.
Remedies:
- Check the power supply to your modem; make sure it is on.

Appendix D: Troubleshooting and Tips 241

- Check the cable between the computer and modem, and make sure the connectors are firmly in place.
- Check to see that the telephone cable is plugged into the modem, or, if you are using an acoustic modem, make sure the modem is connected to the telephone.
- Try to dial the phone manually (call a friend) to make sure it is not out of order.
- Check your software to make sure it is issuing pulse or tone dialing commands, as necessary.
- If you need to dial an extra digit (such as a 9 to "get an outside line" from your office) make sure you are doing that, or that your software knows to do that.
- Make sure your modem switches are properly set for dialing out (see your modem's manual).
- Is there more than one serial port on your computer? If so, make sure that you have told your software to address the right one (usually COM1).
- If you have call-waiting, make sure that it is disabled (if this is possible in your area).
- If you have extensions, make sure that nobody has picked one up.

Trouble/Symptoms:
Your autodial modem dials a number, but the sound of the tones is extra loud, and no connection is made.

Remedies:
The sound is extra loud because the telephone line to the modem is unplugged; plug the telephone line into the phone jack on the back of the modem or into the wall jack, as necessary.

Trouble/Symptoms:
You dial up a packet-switching network number, but you hear a slow busy signal.

Remedies:
The network node is temporarily busy; all available ports are in use. Hang up and try again.

Trouble/Symptoms:
You or your software dial a packet-switching network number, but you hear a fast busy signal.
Remedies:
This indicates a temporary overload in local telephone circuits. Hang up and try again.

Trouble/Symptoms:
The telephone rings, but there is no answer.
Remedies:
Check to see if you've dialed a wrong number. If you've dialed the correct number and the problem persists, call the network help or information number.

Trouble/Symptoms:
You hear the answering tone from the other system, but your computer makes no response. (The connect tone may change after a few seconds.)
Remedies:
Check your modem's connections. If this does not remedy the problem, turn off the power to the modem and computer and reboot your computer. If this does not remedy the problem, have your modem tested by qualified repair personnel. (If possible, substitute another modem to verify that your modem is at fault.)

Trouble/Symptoms:
The system you are calling doesn't recognize your ID and password.
Remedies:
The ID and password entry system may be case-sensitive. Try re-entering your password in all caps or all lowercase letters.

Trouble/Symptoms:
The other system answers and yours responds, but lines of garbage characters scroll up your screen nonstop.
Remedies:
You have dialed up at a speed that the other system can't handle. (Example: You are dialing a system that has a 300-bps modem at 1200 bps.)

Appendix D: Troubleshooting and Tips   243

Online Troubleshooting Guide

Trouble/Symptoms:
The characters you type aren't displayed on your screen.

Remedies:
- Change the duplex or mode setting on your terminal software to half or full (the opposite of its current setting). The current combination of your software's duplex setting and the other system's handling of duplex is, in effect, telling the other system not to echo.
- Go to the "Setup" or "Parameters" section of the BBS or online service you are using and change the duplex setting in your online profile to half or full (the opposite of the current setting). Select the setting that you use most often with other services.

Trouble/Symptoms:
Each character you enter is displayed twice on your screen.

Remedies:
- Again, change the duplex or mode setting on your terminal software, or tell the system that you are using the opposite duplex or mode setting. The current combination of your software's duplex setting and the other system's handling of duplex is, in effect, telling the other system to echo what you type at the same time your system is displaying what you type.

Trouble/Symptoms:
Your screen displays "garbage" text with no pattern (Example: xxxx~xxx@xx~@xxx).

Remedies:
- Check your terminal software's or modem's speed setting to make sure that it is what you intended it to be.
- If you are on an online service, check the number you dialed; you may have dialed a 2400-bps access number rather than a 1200-bps number, or vice versa.
- If you have to tell the system you are calling (or the packet network you are using) your modem speed at sign on with an identifier code, make sure you've done that.

- Make sure that the system you are calling is set up to handle the bps rate you are using.

If all of these factors are eliminated, hang up and try again; you probably have a bad telephone connection.

Trouble/Symptoms:

Your screen displays partially garbled text (Example: Welc"@~nm@e).

Remedies:

- Check your parity setting; experiment with different parity (your choices are Even, Odd, or None).

Trouble/Symptoms:

The screen displays garbled text consisting of oddly-spaced characters, like this:

Remedies:

Your data bits setting is wrong; experiment with different settings (your choices are 7 or 8 data bits).

Trouble/Symptoms:

The system you are on disconnects.

Remedies:

- Someone has lifted an extension phone, and the line noise has made the modem disconnect.
- Your call waiting has beeped.
- Has it been several minutes since you typed a command? Most systems will hang up after a preset time if there is no input from your keyboard.

Trouble/Symptoms:

You type commands and control characters, but absolutely nothing happens—the other system does not respond, and what you type is not echoed on your screen.

Remedies:

- Have you entered a Control-S? This is an almost universal "pause" signal, and it will cause the other system to stop sending to and receiving from your system. Enter Control-Q to get things moving again.

Appendix E

How to Make Modem and Null-Modem Cables

You learned something about RS-232 cables earlier in this book, but we'll take things a few steps farther here. I'll show you exactly how RS-232 cables are put together and how they work. Specifically, I'll show you how to make RS-232 cables and null-modem cables, and how to tie a DB-25 connector to a DB-9 connector. I'll also show you how to set up to transfer data between different brands of computers (Macintosh to PC, for example).

(If you haven't done so already, I strongly recommend that you read Chapter 3 before trying to make your own RS-232 cable. It explains the whys and hows of RS-232 communications.)

Sooner or later, you're going to need a new or extra cable. If you want to transfer data directly between two computers with serial ports, you'll need what is called a null-modem cable. If you buy a modem that has a male connector rather than the standard female connector, or a computer with a male rather than a female connector, you will need a cable with the same gender connector on each end. Or, you might acquire a desktop or laptop computer with a DB-9 connector on its serial port, requiring a cable with a DB-9 connector at the computer end, and a DB-25 connector at the modem end.

Now, you *can* go out and buy one, but you may find it expedient to make what you need yourself. Before you start shaking your head, let me point out that it is not difficult to make an RS-232 cable. All you have to do is attach two connectors to a length of cable; if you can solder or use a mini-wire wrap tool, you can make a cable. Don't want to fool around with that stuff? You can use solderless connectors, if you prefer.

Okay, you're thinking, maybe I can—but why? I can give you several answers to that question:

- Making your own cable costs much less than buying one. (Often by a factor of 8, not counting the cost of a consultant.)

- You save time—there's no waiting for "out-of-stock" items. Making an RS-232 cable takes about half an hour.

- Finally, making your own cable will add to your intuitive knowledge of how telecomputing works.

RS-232 Cable Components

The components of an RS-232 cable are a length of 24-conductor cable and two connectors.

Cable

RS-232 cable comes in two varieties: round and flat, the latter more commonly known as ribbon cable. Ribbon cable (Figure E.1) is used in RS-232 applications more often than round cable.

Figure E.1 Ribbon Cable
(Photo courtesy of Radio Shack, a division of Tandy Corporation)

Appendix E: Modem and Null-Modem Cables

RS-232 cables are usually between three and six feet in length. They can, however, be up to 50 feet long (any longer than that, and there's a chance you'll lose data).

Connectors

As explained in Chapter 3, connectors are classified by "gender," based on whether they have plugs or sockets. Connectors with plugs are "male," while connectors with sockets are "female." (Both plugs and sockets are referred to as "pins.")

Connectors are available in two varieties: solder-type and solderless. Wires from the ribbon cable are soldered (or attached using a "wire wrap" tool) to metal pins that extend to the rear of their plugs or sockets on solder-type connectors (Figure E.2).

Figure E.2 Solder-Type Connectors
(Photo courtesy of Radio Shack, a division of Tandy Corporation)

Solderless connectors (Figure E.3) are set up to accept ribbon cable in a slot. Pressing two halves of the connector closed causes a tiny spike to be driven into each wire.

Connections

The vast majority of asynchronous communications applications use only eight or nine pins out of the 25 pins in the RS-232C

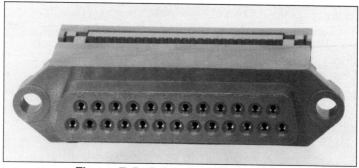

Figure E.3 Solderless Connectors
(Photo courtesy of Radio Shack, a division of Tandy Corporation)

standard (connecting pin 1 is optional in many applications, leaving eight pins in use):

Pin	Assignment
1	Equipment ground
2	Transmit data
3	Receive data
4	Request to send
5	Clear to send
6	Data set ready
7	Signal ground
8	Carrier detect
20	Data terminal ready

This results in a connection like that illustrated in the diagram in Figure E.4.

Making a Standard RS-232 Cable

Making a standard RS-232 cable is fairly uncomplicated. All that is required is that pins 1 through 8 and pin 20 on each connector be directly connected to their counterpart on the other connector. In other words, a wire should connect pin 1 on Connector A with pin 1 on Connector B, pin 2 on Connector A with pin 2 on Connector B, etc., as in Figure E.4.

Some systems also require that pin 22 (Ring indicator) on the connectors be connected, mainly because of software operating

Appendix E: Modem and Null-Modem Cables

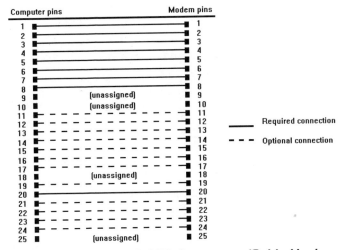

Figure E.4 Typical RS-232 Connector/Cable Hookup

parameters. If pin 22 is connected, pin 1 may not be used. (Consult your system's software and hardware manuals for details on pin-connection requirements.)

Making a Null-Modem Cable

If you have two computers (say, an Apple IIe and an IBM PC), and need to transfer data between them, there are several ways to do it. If both have serial ports, you might use your modem to upload the data from one computer to an online service or BBS, then download it with the other computer. Or, you might pay to have the data converted from one format to another. To transfer data between a laptop and a desktop computer, you can use the modem route, or copy to and from floppy disks.

However, this is time-consuming, and—where an online service or data-conversion service is involved—costly. Both machines already have what it takes to communicate with one another: serial ports. All you need to do is link them directly, substituting a null-modem cable for modems and telephone lines, as detailed in Chapter 6. (The term "null-modem" derives from the fact that there is no modem involved, by the way... "null" implying "none.")

A minimal null-modem connection (as illustrated in Figure E.5) uses only three pins: 2, 3, and 7 (Transmit data, Receive data, and Signal ground, respectively).

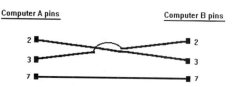

Figure E.5 Minimal Null-Modem Connection

The connections between pins 2 and 3 are reversed—i.e., pin 2 on Connector A is connected to pin 3 on Connector B, while pin 3 is connected to pin 2. This is so that each computer's Transmit data pin is hooked directly to the other's Receive data pin—the logic is (I hope) obvious.

Pin 7 on Connector A is connected directly to Connector B's pin 7. Its function is to provide an electrical ground for the signals.

Because of the operational requirements of many RS-232 ports and communications programs, the typical null-modem cable uses the nine basic pins mentioned earlier (either 1 through 8, and 20; or 2 through 8, 20, and 22).

These pins are not connected in exactly the same manner as they are in a normal RS-232 computer-to-modem cable, however. For openers, only two pins are connected to their counterparts: 1 and 7. The other pins are reversed and/or jumped, as shown in Figure E.6.

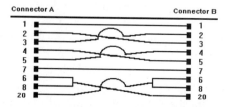

Figure E.6 Typical Null-Modem Connection

Appendix E: Modem and Null-Modem Cables 251

The connections between pins 2 and 3 are reversed (i.e., Connector A's pin 2 is connected to Connector B's pin 3, while Connector A's pin 3 is connected to Connector B's pin 2). This way, each computer's data send and data receive lines are always open.

Pins 4 and 5 are likewise reversed, resulting in each computer seeing a constant "ready" signal from the other when checking whether it's okay to send data.

Pins 6 and 20 are reversed to "fool" the computer into thinking it is properly connected to a modem that has established a telephone connection with another computer. Pin 8 on each computer is jumped to pin 6 to simulate a carrier signal. (Without it, the computer's software would think that the carrier had been lost, and disconnect.) The voltage from pin 20 sets pins 6 and 8 to a level that appears to the host system to indicate a proper connection. (See Chapter 3 for more detailed information on what each of these pins does.)

Some systems may use the configuration shown in Figure E.7, in which pins 4, 5, and 8 are "jumped" to one another on their respective connectors to provide the appropriate signal levels to fool the serial port and software into thinking a modem is at work.

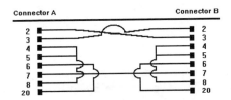

Figure E.7 Alternate Null-Modem Hookup

Cross-Connecting a DB-9 and DB-25 Connector

If you have a newer PC (or any of a number of aftermarket serial cards), you will find that your serial port has a DB-9 connector, rather than a DB-25 connector. This can be quite a surprise—and more than a little frustrating—when you unpack an external modem to find a DB-25 connector on the modem, and a cable with a DB-25 connector at each end.

Equally frustrating is the prospect of exchanging data between an IBM PC/compatible with a DB-25 connector and another with a DB-9 connector.

Why DB-9?

I'm uncertain as to *why* certain serial ports use a DB-9 connector. The DB-9's existence appears to be the result of some arbitrary decisions; there aren't really any advantages or disadvantages to using a DB-9 connector that are worth mentioning.

The DB-9 plug is possible because, as I mentioned earlier, only 8 or 9 of the 25 available pins on an RS-232 port are used during asynchronous modem communication. Its pin assignments are as shown below:

Pin	Assignment/function
1	Carrier detect
2	Receive data
3	Transmit data
4	Data terminal ready
5	Signal ground
6	Data set ready
7	Request to send
8	Clear to send
9	Ring indicator

You may have noticed that the numbers of DB-9 pin assignments are different from those for DB-25 pin assignments. This is another unfathomable occurrence, because most of the numbers could certainly be matched. In any event, here's a list of the DB-9 pin assignments and their DB-25 counterparts:

DB-9 Pin	DB-25 Pin	Assignment/function
1	8	Carrier detect
2	3	Receive data
3	2	Transmit data
4	20	Data terminal ready
5	7	Signal ground
6	6	Data set ready
7	4	Request to send
8	5	Clear to send
9	22	Ring indicator

Appendix E: Modem and Null-Modem Cables

On IBM AT-type serial cards, Equipment ground (DB-25 pin 1) isn't used. However, the IBM serial port does require that Carrier detect (DB-25 pin 8, DB-9 pin 1) be used. And, Ring indicator (DB-25 pin 22) is sometimes used by MS-DOS communications software, so it is used in the DB-9 connector (designated pin 9).

Making the Connection

To properly connect a DB-9 with a DB-25 connector, wire the pins as shown in Figure E.8 (DB-9 pin 1 to DB-25 pin 8, etc.).

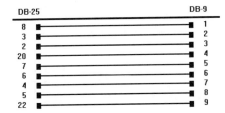

Figure E.8 DB-25 to DB-9 Connection

The basic idea is to connect the pins per their assignments, rather than going by their numbers, although you will use the numbers imprinted on the connectors to identify the pins.

DB-9 Null-Modem Cables

Both DB-9 to DB-25 and DB-9 to DB-9 null-modem cables can be constructed, following the pin-assignment requirements I discussed for DB-25 null modem cables. Again, go by pin assignments in determining which pins are directly connected to their counterparts, which are reversed, and which are jumped.

A DB-9 to DB-25 null-modem cable would be wired in the configuration shown in Figure E.9.

A DB-9 to DB-9 null-modem cable would be wired in one of the configurations shown in Figure E.10.

254 Portable Communications

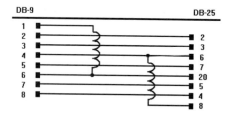

Figure E.9 DB-9 to DB-25 Null-Modem Cable Wiring Configuration

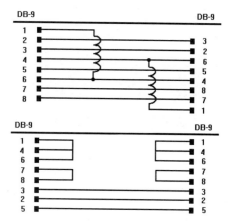

Figure E.10 DB-9 to DB-9 Null-Modem Cable Wiring Configurations

Special Notes on Variations in Pin Assignments

A possible reason for making your own cable that I didn't mention earlier is to connect two computers that aren't designed to interface—say, a Radio Shack Model 100 (which uses a DB-25 connector at its serial port) with a Radio Shack Color Computer (which uses a "DIN" connector—see below). Cables aren't manufactured for many such esoteric link-ups.

Appendix E: Modem and Null-Modem Cables 255

Extreme caution should be exercised when attempting a connection of this type, simply because connector pin assignments (and sometimes the connectors themselves) can vary quite a bit.

Other Configurations

While the RS-232C pin assignments for DB-25 connectors discussed here prevail with the majority of systems, you will encounter systems that differ in which pins are used. For example, while Apple's Super Serial Card uses a DB-25 connector, ten pins are used:

Pin	Assignment
1	Equipment ground
2	Transmit data
3	Receive data
4	Request to send
5	Clear to send
6	Data set ready
7	Signal ground
8	Carrier detect
19	Secondary clear to send
20	Data terminal ready

That configuration isn't too strange, as it makes use of RS-232C pin assignments for a DB-25 connector. But the 300/1200 bps Apple Modem, on the other hand, uses a DB-9 connector, with these pin assignments:

Pin	Assignment
2	Data set ready
3	Signal ground
5	Receive data
6	Data terminal ready
7	Carrier detect
8	Equipment ground
9	Transmit data

I'll leave it as an exercise for you to work out how you might wire a cable and connectors to connect the Apple Super Serial Card to output a null-modem connection. It should be simple enough; as I've stressed previously, the important thing is to get the pins connected based on their assignments.

Other Connectors

A few machines don't use a DB connector at all. For example, the Apple IIc, Radio Shack's Color Computer, the Macintosh Plus, and certain other computers (and modems) use what is called a DIN plug—a round connector with four, five, or eight pins—to connect with the serial port.

This may seem confusing at first, but it's not, once you understand the pin assignments. For example, the five-pin DIN connector used with the Apple IIc serial ports has these assignments:

Pin	Assignment
1	Data terminal ready
2	Transmit data
3	Signal ground
4	Receive data
5	Data set ready

Wiring this kind of connector to a DB-25 connector should be fairly straightforward—again, if you understand the pin assignments at both ends of the connection.

Other Standards

On some newer machines, you will find connectors that look familiar, but which do not use the RS-232C standard. For example, serial ports on the original Macintosh 128 and 512K machines use a DB-9 connector—but the pin assignments are based on the RS-422 standard:

Pin	Assignment
1	Equipment ground
2	+5V
3	Signal ground
4	Transmit data
5	Transmit data
6	+12V
7	Handshake
8	Receive data
9	Receive data

These are clearly different from the pin assignments used by the DB-9 connector.

Cautions

Obviously, you should know the pin assignments for the computer and the peripheral (or other computer) that you intend to connect before you try to make a connecting cable. If you connect the wrong pins, you will at the very least experience a failure, and may well damage the equipment.

You'll also want to make certain that the voltage levels used by each system are the same. (You'll normally run into this problem only when differing standards—such as RS-232C versus RS-422—are in effect in the computers and/or peripherals in question.)

Providing information on all the serial communications standards and variants in use is certainly beyond the scope of this book—or any single book, for that matter. You will find hardware and software documentation, as well as books such as those listed in Appendix C, of tremendous help in running down the information you need to connect the serial ports of "alien" devices. It doesn't hurt to ask someone who knows, either. If you can't find the pin assignments for your computer(s) and/or peripheral in their documentation, by all means contact the equipment manufacturer or a knowledgeable computer technician.

Notes on Null-Modem Transfers

There are certain software considerations to keep in mind when conducting a null-modem transfer between two computers. At the top of the list is the fact that you should use the same software package with each machine (assuming the computers use the same operating system). Whether or not you use the same program on both computers, be sure that both computers' parameters match, and select the same file-transfer protocol when you transfer files.

You won't use dial commands to initiate a connection between two computers connected by a null-modem cable. Most programs should be set to what is called the "Direct Connect" mode; this is usually a menu selection designed to accommodate situations when your modem has already initiated a connection with another system (which is the net effect of using a null-modem cable). If the null-modem connection is established before the programs are booted, some of the more "intelligent" programs will sense a connection and move immediately into direct-connect mode.

Some programs require you to set up one machine as the "host" (in the answer mode), and the other as the caller. If the software package you buy has a good manual, it will tell you exactly how to set the software up for a null-modem transfer. If not, experiment with direct-connect, answer, and call modes.

Finally, as has been noted before, the precaution of using an archiving program to pack binary data or program files to safeguard against Xmodem or other "padding" should be observed for null-modem transfers.

About the Author

Michael A. Banks is a full-time freelance writer, consultant, and "explorer." The author of more than two dozen nonfiction books on topics ranging from model rocketry to personal computer applications, Banks has also published four science fiction novels, more than 1,500 magazine articles and short stories, "... and a few catchy advertising slogans." Among his best-selling books are *The Modem Reference* and *Getting the Most Out of DeskMate 3*, both in second editions from Brady Books.

Banks is a popular speaker at writers' conferences and science fiction conventions, and frequently serves as a consultant to businesses on written communications, computer applications, and telecommunications. He has also been involved in the management of online databases and special interest groups.

In his spare time, Banks enjoys travel (with his laptop and an assortment of communications support gear), model building, playing R&B music, and *shorin ryu*. He currently lives in an incredibly small town near Cincinnati, Ohio, with his wife, two children, and two stubborn Siberian Huskies. He can be contacted at: P.O. Box 312, Milford, OH 45150.

Shopper's Guide

Although I've mentioned many products by name, my intent in this book has not been to promote specific products as superior to others in their category (although there have been a few clear exceptions). Rather, my purpose has been to show you how to make the most of portable PC communications. Along the way, I've tried to give you an idea of what's available in the way of hardware and software tools to help you achieve your communications goals.

For your convenience, I've arranged for several manufacturers and publishers to provide additional information on specific products in the following pages. (You'll find some money-saving offers here, too.)

Consider this brief shopping trip a bonus—and, perhaps, an enhancement to your modem activities.

 **Communications Software Designed for *Simplicity* and Programmed for *Power***

Whatever your information requirements are, you need communications software that strikes a balance between simple operation and the power to connect your PC to a wide range of remote computer systems. MIRROR III delivers that balance.

Simplicity.
- Easy-to-use Dialing Directory interface with pull-down menus and mouse support
- On-line menus for easy access to MIRROR III's online features
- "Learn" mode that automatically writes your auto-logon scripts
- Extensive on-line Help system
- Automated installation procedures, and easy-to-understand instruction manuals

Power.
- Error-free file transfer protocols, such as CompuServe B, KERMIT, XMODEM, YMODEM, YMODEM-G, and ZMODEM
- Multiple terminal emulations, including ANSI, DEC VT-100 / 220, and Wyse-50
- PRISM™ and Script communications programming languages with 300 commands
- 16550 UART support for reliable high-speed communications

List Price - $149, You Pay $59
(Includes U.S. and Canada shipping. Limit one copy, offer expires 12/31/93)

 "This combined communications and remote control package offers users speed and simplicity."

TAKEOVER allows you to remotely control another PC, provide remote customer support, work from home or while you travel, print files at a remote location, transfer files, and provide remote LAN access. TAKEOVER also includes a complete copy of MIRROR III.

TAKEOVER Provides:
- SENTRY™ Host security feature provides control over Guest access to the Host PC
- Automatic call back, and voice-to-data switching
- Supports Monochrome, CGA, EGA, VGA or Hercules video modes
- Background file transfers on the Host PC
- PRISM and Script communications programming languages with 300 commands
- Allows the Host keyboard and/or screen to be disabled
- Includes software for both the Guest and Host PCs on 5.25" and 3.5" diskettes

List Price - $295, You Pay $118
(Includes U.S. and Canada shipping. Limit one copy, offer expires 12/31/93)

Other products available from SoftKlone include MIRROR III-FAX™ for Class 1 and Sierra SendFax™ compatible data/fax modems, and MIRROR™ for Windows™.

To Order Call 1-800-634-8670
60-Day Moneyback Guarantee

MIRROR III-FAX, MIRROR, PRISM, and SENTRY are trademarks of SoftKlone. MIRROR III and TAKEOVER are registered trademarks of SoftKlone. Other trademarks appearing herein are the property of their respective companies.

Get more from your PC with PRODIGY

Connect to the PRODIGY® service and you'll become part of a vast network full of computer information and services. All you need is a PC, a modem and an ordinary phone line to discover... Advice from other computer enthusiasts all over the country...Expert advice on personal computing from Larry Magid...Daily news bytes on the hottest computer industry news and reviews of new software and hardware products...*PC Catalog* for comparing prices on computer products available by mail order...Articles from *Computer Gaming World*...An online software guide.

And PRODIGY is much more than an incredible resource for computer information. You can also play games...check stock and mutual fund quotes...pay bills online from your existing checking account (bank fees apply)...follow sports scores as games are being played... reference an encyclopedia that never goes out-of-date, and much more.

Call 1 800 776-0836, ext. 136 today to receive a FREE Membership Kit.

Yours Free with this offer!

You — and up to six members of your family — can enjoy PRODIGY Service Membership for a low $12.95†a month. That's less than 44¢ a day, an incredible value made better by this offer:

Call 1 800 776-0836, ext. 136 to join the PRODIGY service. To get you started, we'll send you a FREE Membership Kit including the PRODIGY® software you need. You'll be billed a one-time New Member Initiation Fee of just $9.95.

To run the PRODIGY service, you'll need:

COMPUTER	SYSTEM SOFTWARE	MEMORY	DISK DRIVE	GRAPHICS	MODEM
IBM* PC, XT™, AT*, PS/2* or compatible	DOS version 2.0 or higher	At least 512K	One (3.5" or 5.25")	VGA/MCGA/EGA/ CGA/Hercules™ or compatible	1200 or 2400 bps Hayes* or compatible

If you are unsure of your computer's compatibility with the PRODIGY service, feel free to call our 800 #.

Offer Terms and Guarantee: Try Membership in the PRODIGY service for one month. If after your trial month you'd like to continue as a Member, simply pay $12.95 (plus tax) for each month's Membership* fee, beginning with your trial month. If at any time you're not completely satisfied, you can cancel your Membership and receive a refund of the unused portion of any prepaid Membership fees; and if you act within 30 days of receipt of your Membership Kit, you'll also get a full refund of your prepaid Initiation Fee. There's never an obligation to continue.

*Membership includes 30 personal messages per month. Additional messages in any month, including your trial month, will be billed at only 25¢ each, due even if you cancel your Membership. †Prices guaranteed through 9/1/92, subject to change thereafter without notice. Usage limits may apply to certain features. Current pricing is available on the service prior to enrollment or call our 800#. This offer is for new Members only and is limited to one per household. Offer expires 6/30/93 and is subject to change; orders subject to acceptance. PRODIGY service content is as of 5/92 and is subject to change. Additional options or features are available and charged for separately. Phone Company charges may apply. Major credit card may be required to pay fees due Prodigy Services Company. The PRODIGY service is available in the continental U.S.A. and Hawaii only. PRODIGY is a registered service mark and trademark of Prodigy Services Company. IBM, AT and PS/2 are registered trademarks, and XT is a trademark, of IBM Corp. Hayes is a registered trademark of Hayes Microcomputer Products, Inc. Other product and service names are trademarks and service marks of their respective owners. © 1992 Prodigy Services Company. All Rights Reserved.

PC592

What Your Computer Was Really Meant For.

EXPANDING HORIZONS

There's a vast world of information and services out there. A world that's current, vital, and constantly updated. DELPHI, your complete online personal resource, brings that world a little closer. With your modem, you can join special interest groups, download software, meet new friends or tap into the world's most comprehensive databases to expand the horizons of your computer.

EXTENSIVE SERVICES

With a simple phone call from your home or office, you get the latest *news* from the major wire services, discounts on *travel reservations*, complete business and financial services, *stock quotes*, online *shopping*, sophisticated *electronic mail, telex, fax*, conferencing, interactive games, special interest groups and even a complete encyclopedia.

PARTICIPATE

Chat with other members and computer experts in Conference, and post or respond to messages in Forum. Win great prizes when you jump into a worldwide trivia tournament and play computer games!

WALLET-FRIENDLY

You can reach DELPHI with a local phone call from almost anywhere. There is NO premium for access at 1200 or 2400 bps, and standard connect rates are only $6/hour. The basic fee of $5.95 per month includes your first hour of usage. For even lower rates, join DELPHI's new 20/20 Advantage Plan and enjoy 20 hours of usage per month for only $20!

FREE MEMBERSHIP

For a limited time you can join DELPHI for free!

NO RISK

With DELPHI there is no risk. If for any reason you aren't satisfied, cancel your membership and request a refund of your first monthly fee.

Join now online for FREE:

Dial **1-800-695-4002** (by modem)
At *Username:* enter **JOINDELPHI**
At *Password:* enter **MB55**

Questions? Call **1-800-695-4005** (voice)

DELPHI
The World's Premier Online Service

Where Do You Go for Help When <u>You're</u> the Expert?

BIX — the Online Service for People Who Know Computers!

- Get quick answers to tough coding questions
- Interact with other developers
- Download source code, utilities, and other programs
- Keep up with the latest developments
- Send and receive private e-mail with binary attachments
- Chat with other users in real time

BIX has libraries packed with the latest high-quality tools, programs, and code to help you do a better job. Whether you're looking for a special utility, TSR, highly-qualified advice, or just stimulating conversation, you'll find it on BIX.

Here are just a few of the Conferences currently offered on BIX: Windows Programming, Borland International official technical support, C++ programming, OS/2, Utility software for PCs, Microsoft product support, and Amiga support from Commodore.

You can become a BIX subscriber today for only $13 per month! Choose from 2 affordable usage plans, and enjoy local access from over 600 locations throughout the continental U.S.

Join BIX Today!

1. Via modem, dial 1-800-225-4129
2. At the "login:" prompt, enter "bix"
3. At the "Name?" prompt, enter "bix.banks"

Questions? Call 1-800-695-4775

BIX is a service of General Videotex Corporation, 1030 Massachusetts Avenue, Cambridge, MA 02138, 1-800-695-4775, 617-354-4137

Index

A

AC extension cord, 201
acoustic adaptors (acoustic couplers), 56-57, 116-17, 128
   for FAX devices, 151
   for nonstandard telephones, 113, 117-18
Aladdin, 72, 76-78, 181
Alascom, Inc., 235
America Online (AOL), 79, 169-71, 226
   addresses" and direct-dial numbers, 236
   overview and telephone numbers, 231-32
ARC.EXE program, 88-89
archiving programs, 88
ARJ, 89
ASCII files
   conversion programs and, 91
   FAX software and, 61
aspect ratio, 31
AT&T Mail, 164, 226, 231
   "addresses" and direct-dial numbers, 236
Atari Corporation, 217
AT command set, 53, 98
Auto Answer setting, 104-5
autologon capability, 68

B

backup copies of vital software, 201-2
banking, online, 19
   on Prodigy, 185
batteries, 9-10, 200
   future of, 210
battery life, 9-10
   modems and, 51
   monitoring, 41
   saving, 40-41
Battery Watch II, 41
baud rate, 101
BBSs (bulletin board systems), xxvi, 21-22

bulletin boards in, 15
definition of, 14
operating speed of, 47-48
Bell 103 and Bell 212A
standards, 44
BIX, 15, 171-74
"addresses" and direct-
dial numbers, 236
laptop computer special
interest groups on, 187
overview and telephone
numbers, 232
Blackjack, 120
bps (baud rate), 101
briefcase, 202
bulletin boards
definition of, 14
Prodigy, 84
bulletin board systems. *See*
BBSs
Byte magazine, 171

C

cables
null-modem, 249-57
RS-232, 245-49
variations in pin assign-
ments, 254-57
CALLWAIT.BAS, 92
call-waiting, 92
Carrier Detect (CD) setting,
104
carrier loss, 105
CCITT standards, 44
FAX devices and, 58, 61
cellular modems, 121
cellular telephones
connection problems, 120-
21
FAX devices and, 62-63,
155
CGA displays, 30-31
CHANGE CURSOR utility,
36
chatting, 14
color displays, 32-34
Comander Mail, 78-79
command files, 69
command mode, 66-67
commands
conventions used in this
book, xxviii-xxix
definition of, xxvii
communications software,
65-66
command mode, 66-67
disk space and, 92-93
front-end programs, 71-72
future of, 212
publishers of, 226-28
future of, 212-13
graphic-based, 66
multitasking operating

Index 273

environments and, 80
null-modeming with, 86-87, 134-36
options of, 67-70
publishers of, 225-26
remote access with, 139-42
setting parameters in, 100-3
shareware, 70
terminal mode, 67, 107
text-based, 66
communications support software, 87-92
archiving and file-compression programs, 88-89
macro programs, 90-91
RAMdisk software, 90
text-file converters, 91
TSR programs, 89-90
utilities, 92
Compaq Computer Corporation, 218
COM ports, 50-51. *See also* serial ports
CompuCom Corporation, 219
CompuServe, 174-76, 226
"addresses" and direct-dial numbers, 236
front-end programs for, 73-75
international connections, 206, 207
laptop computer special interest groups on, 187-88
overview and telephone numbers, 232
rates, 176
CompuServe Information Manager (CIM), 73-75, 176
CompuServe Network, 235
Computer Products Plus (C+), 221-22
computers, portable. *See* portable computers
conferences, definition of, 14
conferencing
BIX, 173
real-time, 16, 173
connections, making
celullar telephone connection problems, 120-21
command string, 98
connection problems, 115-20
dialing, 107-8
dialup problems, 126-29
floppy disks, 148-52
initialization string, 98-99
international, 204-8
direct dialing, 207
line quality, 206
packet-switching

networks, 207-8
phone connections, 205-6
power supplies, 204-5
overview of, 98-99
with packet-switching networks, 110-11
preparations for, 99-106
  setting modem parameters, 103-6
software parameters, 100-3
problems with, 191-93
signing on, 108-10
telephone line connectors, 111-15
  direct connections, 122-26
telephone set connectors, 116-20
  acoustic adaptors, 116-18
  direct-connect handset adaptors, 118-20
tools and supplies for, 129-30
connectors
null-modem, 133-34
RJ-11 jacks and plugs, 111-14
telephone line, 111-16
CP+ Connection II, 119-20, 130

CP+ Deluxe Tele-Toolkit, 130
CP+ Telecoupler, 117-18, 129, 130
CP+ Tele-Toolkit, 125-26, 130
CPUs (central processing units), 27-28
Crosstalk Communications, 225
Crosstalk Mk.4, 83
cursor, programs for improving visibility of, 35-36
CVC-Chenel Corporation, 219

D

DASnet, 164-65, 232
database and information-retrieval services, 165-66, 168
  CompuServe, 175
data bits, 101-2
DataPac, 173, 178
  customer service numbers, 235
  getting online information from, 236
DATASTORM Technologies, Inc., 225
Data Terminal Ready (DTR) setting, 104

DB-9 and DB-25 connectors, 55, 251-56
DELPHI, 176-79
　"addresses" and direct-dial numbers, 236
　front-end programs for, 75-76
　international connections, 207
　laptop computer special interest groups on, 188
　overview and telephone numbers, 232-33
DeskMate, 79, 80
DESQview, 27, 80, 85
DIALCOM, 164
dialing directories, 70
dialing string, 98-99
　pause command in, 106
DIALNET, 235
DIALOG, 90, 165, 177, 227
　"addresses" and direct-dial numbers, 236
　overview and telephone numbers, 233
DIALOG Information Service, 18
dialup problems, 126-29
digital PBXs, 129
dip switches of external modems, 103-4
direct connect data transfer, 20-21
direct-connect handset adaptors, 118-20, 127-28, 200
displays, 29-37
　future of, 210
　programs for improving clarity of, 35-36
　resolution of, 30-31
　size and aspect ratio of, 31
　types of, 31-35
　　color, 32-34
　　gas-plasma, 34-35
　　LCD (liquid-crystal), 31-34
DKEY, 91 Don Milne/Micropak, Ltd., 226
DOS. *See* MS-DOS
Dow Jones News-Retrieval Service, 165-66
　"addresses" and direct-dial numbers, 236
　overview and telephone numbers, 233
DRInet, 235
duplex setting, 102-3
DynaCorp, Inc., 228

E

Eastman Kodak Company,

222
echo setting, 102-3
editor, pop-up, 68
education services, 167
EGA displays, 30
E-mail, 15-16, 168
  America Online, 170
  BIX, 173
  CompuServe, 175, 176
  DELPHI, 178
  FAXes via, 155-60
  future of, 213
  GEnie, 180
  Prodigy, 184, 185
  specialty online services, 162-65
telephone numbers of services, 231-34
EMS (Expanded Memory Specification), 29
encyclopedias, online, 18, 167
ENTER key, xxviii
entertainment services, 167
entry, definition of, xxvii
error-checking protocols, 48-49, 54. *See also* protocols, file transfer
EVA, 77-78
expanded memory, 29
extended memory, 28-29
Eye Relief, 36-37

F

FAX cards, 58-62
  features and options, 61-62
  Group 3, 58-59
FAX devices, 147-55. *See also* FAX cards; FAX/modems
  cellular telephones and, 155
  connecting w telephone systems, 152
  E-mail FAX services versus, 159
  Group 3, 58-59
  hardware accessories for, 151-52
  manufacturers and vendors, 221
FAX'EM, 60
FAXes, 147-60
  via online services, 155-60
  sending and receiving, 152-53
  storing, 155
  viewing and printing, 153-54
FAX/modems, 58-62, 147-50
  features and options, 61-

62
   future of, 210-11
   Group 3, 58-59
   serial port for, 149
FAX software, 59, 61
   features of, 150-51
   future of, 212
fiber-optics, 211-12
file-compression programs, 88
file transfers, 17-18, 131-32. *See also* null-modeming
financial information and services, 166
   Prodigy, 185
floppy disks, 37
   features of, 149-50
foreign countries. *See* international connections
Franzus International Adapter Plug Set, 204-5
Fremont Communications Company, 221
front-end programs, 71-72
   future of, 212
   publishers of, 226-28
full duplex, 102-3
FUNCREDO, 91
function-key assignments, online services and, 85
future of portable PC communications, 209-14
   batteries, 210
   disk drives, 210
   displays, 210
   future of, 210
   modems and FAX/modems, 210-11
   notebook computers, 209-10
   online services, 213-14
   phone systems, 211-12
   software, 212-13

G

games, online, 171
   DELPHI, 178
   GEnie, 180
   Prodigy, 184-85
GASGAUGE, 41
gas-plasma displays, 34-35
Gateway Software, 79, 227
gateways to online services, 168
   foreign, 206-7
GE Mail, 180
gender changers, 55
General Videotex Service (GVC), 176
GEnie, 25, 179-81, 227
   front-end programs for,

72, 76-78
international connections, 206-7
laptop computer special interest groups on, 188
overview and telephone numbers, 233
GeoWorks, 228
GeoWorks Ensemble, 79, 80, 90, 169
graphic files, FAX devices and, 62 ground plug adapter, 201, 205

H

half duplex, 102-3
handset adaptors, direct-connect, 118-20, 127-28, 200
handset couplers, 119-20
hard disks, 37
future of, 210
power-down feature for, 40
hardware, required, xxv-xxvi
hardwiring into phone sets or lines, 122-25
Hayes command set, 53
Hayes Microcomputer Products, Inc., 220, 221
hotels and motels
dialup problems in, 126-29
direct telephone line connections in, 122-23
Hotwire, 137, 225

I

information-retrieval services, 165-66
initialization string, 98-99
inline connectors, 119-20
input, definition of, xxvii
international connections, 204-8
direct dialing, 207
line quality, 206
packet-switching net works, 207-8
phone connections, 205-6
power supplies, 204-5
Internet, 175
IQuest, 175
ISDN (Integrated Services Digital Network), 211

J

jumper cable, telephone/

modem, 123-24

K

Konexx handset coupler, 120

L

LANs (local area networks), 20-21, 139
LapLink II, 87
LapLink Pro, 134, 136-38
LAP/M error-checking protocol, 45, 48-49
laptop computers. *See also specific brand and models*
  displays of, 29-37
  future of, 210
  programs for improving clarity of, 35-36
  resolution of, 30-31
  size and aspect ratio of, 31
  types of, 31-35
  early, 8-10
  manufacturers and vendors, 217-19
LCD (liquid crystal) displays, 31-34

long-distance modem dialing, 128-29
Lotus Express, 78
LU.EXE, 89
luggage computers, 5, 7
.LZH, 89

M

macro programs, 90-91
macros, online services and, 81-85
magazines, online, 168
  Prodigy, 184, 185
manufacturers and vendors
  FAX devices, 221
  laptop computers, 217-19
  modems, 219-20
  peripherals, 221-23
MCI Mail, 164, 175, 227, 237
  front-end programs for, 78-79
  overview and telephone numbers, 233
memory
  expanded, 29
  extended, 28-29
  RAM, 28
memory management programs, 27
memory-resident programs.

See TSRs
menus, xxvi, xxviii
messages, 13-16
   private, 15-16
   public, 14-15
Messenger, The, 75-76
Messenger for MCI Mail, 78
Microsoft Corporation, 228
MNP 4 protocol, 48-49
MNP 5 standard, 45
modems, 43-57. *See also*
   connections, making;
   FAX/modems
   acoustic. *See also* acoustic
     adaptors
     nonstandard telephones
     and, 113
   auto dial, 107-8
   cables and connectors for,
     55-57
   cellular, 121
   connectors for, 111-16
   cordless telephones and,
     113
   error checking by, 48
   features and options, 52-54
   future of, 210-11
   initialization string for, 98-99
   laptop computer battery
     life and, 41
   for laptops, 47-54
     external, 51-52
     internal, 49-51
   manual dial, 108
   manufacturers and
     vendors, 219-20
   setting parameters, 103-6
   standards for, 44-47
mouthpiece connectors, 120
MS-DOS, 25-26
MS-DOS computers, 25-26
multiplug, 201
multitasking operating
   environments, 80, 89-90

N

NEC AMerica, 218
NEWKEY, 91
newsletters, 166, 168
NewsNet, 18, 166, 237
   overview and telephone
     numbers, 234
newspapers, 166, 168
news services, 165-66, 168
   CompuServe, 174-75
   Prodigy, 184
Northgate Computer Sys
   tems, Inc., 218
Norton Commander, 78

No-Squint II, 35, 36
notebook computers, 10-11
   future of, 209-10
null-modem cables, 20, 133-34, 202, 249-57
   DB-9, 253-54
null-modeming, 85-87, 131, 257-58
   hardware for, 133-34
   software for, 134-38
      conventional communications software, 134-36
      null-modem programs, 136-38
numbers, entering, xxix
NUSQ.COM (?Q?), 89

O

OCR (Optical Character Recognition) software, 151
Odyssey, 67, 70, 226
online research. *See* Research, online
online services, 22-23, 161-89
   access speed, 194
   bulletin boards in, 15
   categories of, 161-62
   consumer services, 166-86.
      See also specific services
      offerings of, 166-69
   customer service numbers for, 200
   database and information-retrieval services, 165-66
   E-mail specialty services, 162-65
   FAXes via, 155-60
   foreign gateways, 206-7
   front-end programs for, 25-26, 71-72, 226-28
   future of, 212
   publishers of, 226-28
   future of, 213-14
   macros and, 81-85
   overview and telephone numbers, 231-35
   personal file-storage areas in, 132, 197-98
   planning ahead, 194-95
   real-time conferencing on, 16
   shortcuts and timesavers, 193-99
      file management, 197-98
      help system, 199
      learning about and exploring an online service, 198

menu/prompt levels, 196
online versus offline
   message creation and
     reading, 195-96
   profile settings, 196-97
   timing yourself, 194
   type-ahead, 198-99
   TSR programs and, 89-90
operating systems, 25-26, 228
operator-assisted telephone
   systems, 127-28
operators, 127
Osborne computer, 7

P

packet-switching networks,
   110-11
   customer service numbers,
     234-35
   getting online information
     from, 235-36
   international, 207-8
packing for a trip, 199-202
PAK.EXE, 89
palmtop computers, 11-12,
   188
PAN Network, 227
parameter files, 69-70
parity, 102
passwords, 108-9

communications pro
   grams, 139-40
pause command, in dialing
   string, 106
PBXs, digital, 129
PC-DOS, 26
PC FAXes, 147-53. *See also*
   FAX devices
PC-Link, 79
   overview and telephone
     numbers, 234
personal file area, 132, 197-98
PIF files, 80
pin adaptors, 55
pixels, 30
PKware, Inc., 229
PKZIP/PKUNZIP programs,
   88, 89
plug adapters, 204-5
Poqet Computer Corpora
   tion, 218
Poqet palmtop computer, 11
portable computers. *See also*
   laptop computers;
     notebook computers;
      palmtop computers
   categories of, 5
   definition of, 4-5
   early, 3-5
power adapter plugs, 204
power-down feature, for
   hard disks, 40,

Index 283

power-management features, 40-41
power supplies, 38-41
   for international connec tions, 204-5
preventing connection problems, 240
processors, 27-28
PROCOMM, 225
PROCOMM PLUS, 67, 70, 140, 141, 225
   Alt-key commands in, 83
Prodigy, 79, 181-86, 227
   overview and telephone numbers, 234
product support, online, 168-69
programs. *See* software Pro Master, 79
Promenade, 79
prompt, definition of, xxvii
PROPLUS, 79
protocols, file transfer, 17
"pseudofile compression," 45
public domain programs (freeware), 17
publishers, software, 225-29

Q

QEMM, 27

Quarterdeck Office Systems, 229

R

Radio Shack, 222
RAM, 28
RAM disks, 38
RAMdisk software, 90
real-time conferencing, 16
REDline, 35, 36
reference books on telecomputing, 229
reference services, 167. *See also* database and information-retrieval services; research, online
remote-access programs, 138-44
   communications pro grams in host mode as, 139-42
   specialized, 142-44
research, online, 18. *See also* database and information-retrieval services; news services
   CompuServe, 175
   GEnie, 180
resolution of displays, 30-31
response, definition of, xxvii

RJ-11 jacks and plugs, 57, 59,
   122-24, 205
RJ-12/RJ-14 jacks and plugs,
   114
RS-232 cables, 245-49, 255
RS-232C pin assignments, 255
RS-422 standard, 256

S

Samsonite Corporation, 222
screen blanking programs, 40
script files, 68
serial ports, 50-51
   connectors for, 55
setup files, 69
shareware programs, 17-18
Sharp Electronics Corporation, 218
shopping, online, 19, 167
Sidekick, 89
signing on, 108-10
SkiSoft Publishing Corporation, 36, 37, 229
Softklone, 143-44, 226
software. *See also* communications software;
   communications
   support software
   publishers of, 225-29
   required for telecomputing, xxvi
   to take with you, 201-3
speakers, modem, 53-54
special interest groups (SIGs; Forums), 167
   America Online, 170-71
   DELPHI, 177
   GEnie, 179-80
   for laptop computer users, 186-89
spelling checkers, memory-resident, 90
SprintMail (formerly Telemail), 164, 228
   overview and telephone numbers, 234
SprintNet, 110-11, 171, 178, 208
   customer service numbers, 235
   getting online information from, 235
S-registers, 105, 106
S-register settings, 54
   celullar telephone connections and, 120-21
stop bits, 102
Super VGA displays, 30
Support Group, Inc., 228
Symantec Corporation, 228
system, definition of, xxvi
System Enhancement Associ

Index   285

ates, 229
system power-down feature, 40

T

Takeover, 143-44
Tandy Corporation, 218, 221, 220
Tandy 140 HD laptop computer, 49
Tandy laptop computers, 187, 188
Tandy Model 100 computer, 8-10, 187
Tandy Model 102, 8, 9
TAPCIS, 75
Targus, 222
task-switching environments, 89-90
telecomputing, 12-13
  channels of, 19-23
    BBSs (bulletin board systems), 21-22
    dialing another computer direct, 21
    direct connect data transfer, 20-21
    local versus remote systems, 20

modems, 20
online services, 22-23
overview of activities and applications, 13-19
  file transfers, 17-18
  messaging, 13-16
  real-time conferencing, 16
  research, 18
  transactions, 19
Telecoupler, 117-18, 129, 130
Telenet, 110
telephone cable, wires in, 113
telephone jacks for modems, 53
telephone lines, 111-16, 129
  direct connections with, 122-26
  modem connections with, 56-57
telephones
  connectors for, 114
  cordless, 113
  future of, 211-12
  hardwired, 122-25
  nonstandard, acoustic modem cups for, 113, 117-18
Tele-Toolkit, 125-26
terminal emulation software. *See* comunications software
terms used in this book, xxvi-

xxix
Texas Instruments, Inc., 219
text-file converters, 91
386 computers, 27
Toshiba America Information
  Systems, 219
Toshiba laptop computers,
  49, 187
  internal cellular modems
    for, 121
Touchbase Systems, 220, 221
transactions, online, 19. *See
  also* banking, online;
  shopping, online transformers, 204
Traveling Software, 187, 222, 229
travel services, 167
  Prodigy, 185
Travel Tech, 223
"trickle charging" feature, 40-41
troubleshooting guide, 239-44
  online, 243-44
  sign-on, 240-41
TRS-80 Model I computers, 3
TSRs (terminate-and-stay-
  resident programs), 28, 89-90
Tymnet, 110, 111, 171, 173, 178, 185, 208
  customer service numbers, 235
  getting online information
    from, 236

U

Unlimited Systems, 119-20, 223
user ID, 108-9
USRobotics, 220
  HST modems, 46
utilities, publishers of, 228-29

V

V.32 and V.32 *bis* standards, 44, 45
V.42 and V42 *bis* standards, 45-46
VGA displays, 30
voice/data switch, 151

W

weather services, 166
  CompuServe, 175
Windows, 80
  cursor in, 36
Wizard palmtop computer, 11

word processors. *See also*
specific *wordprocessors*
for magnifying text,
36-37
Worldport 2496 FAX/
modem, 148-49

X

Xmodem protocol, 136
XMS (Extended Memory
Specification), 28-29
XWORD, 91

Y

Y-jack connectors, 114, 130

Z

Zenith Data Systems Corporation, 219
Zenith laptop computers, 187
ZEOS International, 219
Zmodem protocol, 136
ZOO.EXE, 89